RAGING
AGAINST THE
MACHINE

NEW INTERNATIONALIST
30 YEARS OF CAMPAIGNING FOR GLOBAL JUSTICE

edited by **Chris Brazier**

Raging Against the Machine
New Internationalist: 30 years of campaigning for global justice
First published in the UK by
New Internationalist™ Publications Ltd
Oxford OX4 1BW, UK
www.newint.org
New Internationalist is a registered trade mark.

Cover photo: Charles Dharapak/AP Photos

Book and cover design: Alan Hughes, New Internationalist Publications Ltd.

Printed by TJ International Ltd, Padstow, Cornwall, UK.

British Library Cataloguing-in-Publication Data.
A catalogue record for this book is available from the British Library.

ISBN 1-904456-02-2

Contents

Introduction

Chris Brazier

I REMEMBER my sharp intake of breath. It was 1996 and I was phoning around 'experts' on North Africa to canvass them about my idea of dedicating a whole issue of the *New Internationalist* to the cause of Western Sahara. The experts agreed that the Saharawis' cause was just, that they should have had their independence long ago. They were clear that Western Sahara had been well and truly shafted not only by the Moroccan invader but by the whole international community. The intake of breath came, though, the first time one of them pronounced that this was 'a lost cause'. 'You might give it a short feature,' he went on. 'But you would be crazy to devote a whole magazine to such a hopeless struggle.'

A red rag to a bull, that: how dare they dismiss a just cause so blithely, accept the cynicism of international power politics so readily? The New Internationalist Co-operative backed me to the hilt and the issue eventually appeared in December 1997, though copies of it are still being put to good use by campaigners today. This, it seems to me, is one of the best possible reasons for the *New Internationalist*'s existence: that it will readily champion the people and the politics, the countries and the causes, that are treated with disdain elsewhere.

But a good reason for existing and the financial ability to survive do not always go together, as the history of all too many 'alternative' publications readily testifies. The number of radical magazines that make it through to celebrate a 30th birthday – as the **NI** does in 2003 – is so small that they form their own very exclusive club. If you make it that far, you effectively become an institution in your own right.

The *New Internationalist* already showed some signs of institutional solidity by the time I joined it in 1984. Of course my perspective on what was institutionally solid might be thought to have been rather skewed by my own experience. I was fresh from the experience of working for another radical magazine which had just collapsed under the weight of its own debts. At *The Leveller* we shared all tasks collectively, which inevitably meant that there was huge, stay-up-all-night enthusiasm for the buzz tasks of writing and magazine production as well as an eternal appetite for thrashing out the latest politically correct line, but manifestly less enthusiasm for the rather drab business of getting on the phone to potential advertisers or keeping the accounts in some sort of order. Most of us worked for love and relied on unemployment benefit to put bread on the table.

At the *New Internationalist*, by contrast, people were not only paid something like a living wage but had defined areas of responsibility for marketing, accounts or design, even if they reported to a weekly co-operative meeting rather than a boss. Even more amazing to me at the time, they kept official minutes of meetings, recorded apologies for absence, went through 'matters arising' and finished with 'any other business'. So conventional, man...

By then the magazine had got itself on to a relatively firm financial footing. It was the brainchild of Peter and Lesley Adamson, who had been working since 1970 on a once-a-term magazine for the student organization Third World First. The *New Internationalist* was able to launch in March 1973 backed by the aid agencies Oxfam and Christian Aid, who were desperate to raise the profile of development issues with a distinctly uncaring public. The 1970s were a struggle against the odds and against all the assumptions of a publishing industry which was understandably sceptical that people would want to read about world hunger over their cornflakes.

The magazine survived to win its financial independence in 1978 partly through selling creative services on contract to UN agencies, whose ideas about how to make their reports about the developing world readable were themselves distinctly 'undeveloped' in those days. But its survival was also down to a series of inspired decisions: appointing people to deal with the accounts and with marketing from the outset (this might seem rather obvious but was distinctly novel in the field of Left publishing, in which there was a deep suspicion of anything that smacked too much of commerce); concentrating on subscriptions rather than news-stand sales (not so high-profile, but customers hand you their money in advance as a kind of people's bank loan); and launching the magazine in Canada, Australia and New Zealand as soon as possible (making the internationalism of the magazine a practical reality, not just an abstract aspiration).

The key to the success of the *New Internationalist* has been this determination to be as businesslike as it is co-operative. It survives in the cold, harsh world of the market and thereby earns its right to criticize that market from a thoroughly independent point of view, free not only from the tyranny of a proprietor but also from the necessity of kowtowing to grant-giving bodies. The magazine has always paid its way, paid its bills and – most extraordinary of all in the world of alternative publishing – paid its contributors. And much of the credit for this lies with the only two people who have been with the magazine from the very start: Dexter Tiranti and Troth Wells, who have been the creative impetus behind countless publications over the years, but who also embody this sense that there will be no campaigning for social justice if the business as a whole does not pay its keep.

The magazine, though, was originally Peter Adamson's, and no account of its history would be complete without a tribute to his unique vision and energy. He towered over the other editors and contributors in the 1970s, for the brilliance of his writing as much as for his intellectual appetite for grappling with the key issues in development. The pieces included here show the power and range of his work, from his superb account of what went wrong with the 1970s, *The art of development*, to his evocation of African village life in *The Rains*. By the time he left in 1981 to embark on a decade and a half of distinguished writing and campaigning for UNICEF he had established a template for the magazine's trademark campaigning.

The **NI** has always been passionate in its desire to change the world, to campaign for a 'new international economic order' based on justice for the peoples who live in what has variously been called 'the Third World', 'the poor world', 'the developing world', 'the South' and 'the Majority World' (none of the collective terms are entirely satisfactory but we have been forced to use each and all of them at least until a better notion comes along). If the magazine wanted to communicate just one thing to its readers it would be what it is like to live in poverty, whether that is in Mombasa or Manila, Manaus or Manchester – in the hope of stirring them first to anger and then to action.

All the same, the world has changed in ways the magazine's editors would not have wished, and they have had to cut their cloth accordingly. The difference between the journalism of the 1970s and that of the 1990s and beyond is remarkable, not so much because of the quality of the writing (though the general standard of that has certainly improved) as because of the assumptions that lay behind it. The editors of 1973 were operating in a world in which a fundamental shift in the direction of global justice seemed possible, even probable. Imbued with the radicalism and youthful energy of the 1960s, they excoriated the world for its refusal to change but somehow still exuded confidence that they would win in the end.

They were not alone in this. The world before the debt crisis took hold in the late 1970s was still one in which the newly independent governments of the Majority World were optimistic that their concerns on a range of fronts would be accommodated. Their sheer numbers in the one-country one-vote United Nations General Assembly seemed a promise of this. In the first big UN conferences, held in the early 1970s, they made their case on food, on population, on trade. There was a ferment of ideas abroad that made it the equivalent of the late 1960s in the rich world – and maybe the revolutionary momentum of 1968 in the West flowed naturally towards the Third World, where revolution seemed not just more possible but even inevitable. It was also a time when the genuine achievements of human development were starting to become apparent: people were living longer, levels of infant mortality were falling and more children were finding the door to the classroom.

There is an inescapable sense as you read the **NI** in its earliest years that its editors felt they were part of a vanguard and that it was only a matter of time before the ideas and moral principles of the movement for world development became mainstream. Certainly they were not yet afflicted with the doubts about the whole 'development' project that were later to afflict us (see the section *Guides to the ruins: whatever happened to development?* on page 213).

I was still at school when the first **NI** issues were published but I can still completely understand the sense of optimism, of apparent historical inevitability that permeated their pages. I remember reasoning that, since young people were inevitably more progressive in their thinking, it could only be a matter of time before such leftist ideas held sway. We would move onward and upward into a new age of equality, social justice and cultural liberation – a sad delusion, as we now know, looking back over the moral wasteland of the Thatcher/Reagan years.

This sense that world development was an idea whose time had well and truly come had a major influence on the presentation of the earliest magazines. Visual devices were few and far between. Readers were assumed to have an appetite for even the most abstruse aspects of development debate. Pages and pages were devoted to analyzing such subjects as the progress of the Yaoundé trade talks between the European Economic Community and developing countries. A front cover from 1974 trailed its wares with the unadorned lines: 'Conscientization: what's it all about?', as if conscientization – the Brazilian Paolo Freire's notion that education had itself to be a form of resistance to class oppression – was a word on everyone's lips, not just on those of the most committed activists.

By the late 1970s the penny had dropped that the transition to a fairer world was not going to be quite so smooth, and certainly not inevitable. By then the OPEC oil-price hikes had plunged the world into a recession which effectively put a full stop to the expansive atmosphere of the 1960s – and ultimately produced the debt crisis as bankers suddenly awash with petro-dollars started offering it by the barrowload to any old government they could find. Debt piled up and repayments turned into mountains to climb. By the 1980s, now routinely characterized as 'the lost decade' of development, all thought of transforming society to fulfil people's basic needs came to seem fantastic beside the grim reality of the bailiffs at the door demanding repayment.

Once it became clear that the **NI** was not going to be the house magazine of the New International Economic Order it set about the business which has occupied it ever since – of popularizing and explaining the key issues in this bewilderingly complex, savagely unequal world. Where other magazines simply collected together interesting articles that might catch the reader's eye, the **NI** tried to pull together a package containing everything you might need as an introduction to a particular subject. It started from first principles, never assuming that a reader had much prior knowledge. Realizing early on that it could not compete with the news coverage of the mainstream media, the magazine aimed instead to put the news in a comprehensible context.

Much of the energy over the years – most particularly in the 1980s – went into devising creative, visual ways of communicating the information rather than simply assuming that another academic treatise or journalistic report would do the trick. There were double-page spreads which offered the key statistics in a highly visual format that was much valued by teachers. There were games to play and quizzes to complete (early attempts at interactivity); there were posters aimed at that most educational of locations, the toilet door. Whole issues were given over to a comic book or a revolutionary new map of the world. No issue would have been complete without the complete history of the subject in question reduced to six or seven paragraphs, each with its accompanying illustration – often drawn by the inimitable pen of Clive Offley, who designed the magazine more or less single-handed for a decade.

But what kind of message lay behind all this? What ideological hoops did aspiring *New Internationalist* editors have to jump through in order to get the job?

Surprisingly few, actually. I almost did not bother to apply because I assumed the Co-operative would be looking for someone who had spent years living and working in Africa or had kept up to date with all the latest Marxist thinking about centre-periphery analysis – and I had done neither. Instead they wanted a writer who was burning with righteous anger at the injustice in the world – but who floated free of any particular party line.

This freedom from dogma was actually a rare thing in an 'alternative' publication of the 1970s and 1980s. Many of the progressive ideas abroad in the 'development' movement of the time were Marxist in origin – as were most of the anti-colonial movements still fighting for their freedom at the time. And the **NI**'s eternal concern with meaningful, structural change – rather than with the charity of aid or the vain hope that wealth might trickle down – naturally led it in a similar direction. There used to be a standing in-house joke about how the last paragraph of an **NI** 'keynote' editorial, whatever its subject, would always revert to a sweeping call for revolution.

Nevertheless, the **NI** editorial team would have been a sore disappointment to Marxist ideologues, whatever their sectarian stripe. They were even initially a slight disappointment to me – I might not have read *The Complete Works of Mao Zedong* but at least I had them there on my bookshelves. I seriously suspected my comrades of not owning a single work of revolutionary theory. A sign of this can be found in a *New Internationalist* from back in 1978 which aimed to serve as a primer to Marxism. It talked of the great revolutionary 'Nikolai Lenin' and compounded its error by captioning a photo of Lenin in the same way. No-one who had been through the standard mill of left activism at the time could have committed such a cardinal sin.

This independence from the more dyed-in-the-wool forms of 'struggle' (one of the words the magazine routinely eschewed in the interests of not deterring the faint-hearted) made it seem suspiciously 'liberal' to some. But it actually proved a fantastic strength, one that became all the more evident once the Berlin Wall came crashing down in 1989 and the old Marxist certainties started to fray round the edges. Relatively early on, for example, the magazine was able to identify environmental issues as absolutely central to its political agenda, at a time when politicos throughout the West tended to dismiss green activism as lacking in 'class analysis' – there was a special issue titled 'Trash and Grab: the Looting of a Small Planet' as early as 1976.

Something similar happened when feminism moved to centre stage in radical circles during the 1980s. The magazine began with alacrity to produce issues exploring the myriad ways in which 'the personal is political', carrying articles on sex or masculinity that many of its readers found shocking. Among those appalled readers were organizations that had backed the magazine from the start – including the leading Catholic aid agency in Australia. The eventual result was the emergence of a workers' co-operative in Australia (mirroring those in Britain and Canada) that has since taken the magazine from strength to strength – there are now more **NI** subscribers per head of population in Australia than in any other country.

There are, in fact, as many subscribers internationally now as there have ever been – around 75,000 – though the old expectation that subscriber numbers might grow every year *ad infinitum* is long gone. In the long term growth might come by another route, since we would like to develop continental bases in Africa, Asia and Latin America that would extend the magazine's commitment to reflecting the voices and concerns of people in the South – and an office in India, in particular, is a goal for the next decade.

I've been struck as I've looked back over the many millions of words in the *New Internationalist*'s 30 years of life by this increasing commitment to provide a platform for writers from the South. The willingness to do this was certainly there from the start – what other magazine in 1973 would have dedicated four pages to Lamin Sennah's remarkable memoir of experiencing famine (an excerpt from which appears on page 11)? But resources and the difficulties of international communication in the days before fax, e-mail and intelligible phone lines made it impractical to expect too much. By the early 1990s, however – certainly by the time of the special issue on the Earth Summit in 1992, *The South Speaks Out* – the necessity of going the extra mile to seek out writers from the Majority World had taken root. Some of the regular sections in the magazine of today bear this out: the *View from the South* column which rotates between Africa, Asia and Latin America, for example, and the *Southern Exposure* page which is dedicated to the work of photographers from beyond the rich world. Even the long-running *Letter from...* series, which started life as the meditations of white people on living and working in Zimbabwe or Bolivia, is currently in the hands of the excellent Lebanese journalist, Reem Haddad.

Running parallel with that has been a steadily increasing number of 'big names' in the pages of the **NI**. In the 1970s high-profile writers were generally notable for their absence – the biggest 'name' in retrospect was probably that of Graham Hancock, though readers at the time knew him as a humble hack with a strange fondness for the Somali dictator Siad Barré rather than as the controversial million-selling author of books like *The Message of the Sphinx*. When I arrived in the 1980s there was something of a culture of opposition to using big-name writers. They generally turned out to be more trouble than they seemed to be worth either by demanding more money than we could afford or by expecting special treatment that certainly did not entail having their precious copy roughed up by the callous(ed) hands of an **NI** editor. We invariably considered it was better to give the space to a good article by an unknown than a poor one by a celebrity.

If anything the standards we expect have been raised rather than lowered in the intervening years but the number of 'names' who have been prepared to put their shoulders to our particular wheel – and have produced some of their very best writing in the process – has certainly shown a marked increase over the last decade. Among them are the great Uruguayan writer Eduardo Galeano, the crusading Australian journalist John Pilger, the British thinker Jeremy Seabrook, the Americans Kirkpatrick Sale and Susan Griffin, all of whom are represented in this anthology.

Perhaps this marks the extent to which the **NI** has become more recognized over the years. For most of its life, despite rising circulation levels, the magazine's editors have felt eternally on the fringe of things, rather like voices in the wilderness raging against the machine.

So what's changed? After all, when George Bush and Tony Blair were considering their response to the 9/11 atrocities, they will certainly not have looked towards the **NI** editorial written by Wayne Ellwood which was very free with its advice to them at the time. The difference, I think, is that while the international powers-that-be continue to pursue their corporate, earth-destroying, militaristic agenda with alacrity, the main currents of resistance to that agenda have shifted in our direction. The core concerns of the magazine over the years – the ever-growing divide between rich and poor, the damage done to the earth by Western consumer culture, the dominance of transnational corporations and the IMF/World Bank/WTO axis that backs them up – have moved to centre stage. This is particularly the case since the high-profile resistance in Seattle in 1999 which gave radical activism back its good name and effectively handed on the torch to a whole new generation.

Faced with the depredations of globalization, there is no alternative but to defend our rights on an international basis, to share information and make resistance links right across our planet. The words 'new internationalist', about which I think at one stage we felt a touch apologetic (such a tongue-twister, couldn't we come up with something more snappy?), we now wear proudly as a necessary counterpoint to the globalizers' vision of an end to history.

When, in 1999, we made our own contribution to the welter of pronouncements on the meaning of the 20th century we chose to highlight the way in which ideas – from sexual equality to African independence – that were once considered marginal and wacky, advanced by crazed subversives, became the plainest, uncontested common sense. One day the relentless pursuit of economic growth – an emperor with no clothes which not one mainstream political party in the Western world has yet been courageous enough to expose – will be viewed in the same light. One day this phase of human history in which corporations are given licence to build a global trading structure in their own likeness will be put behind us. One day we will put the basic needs of malnourished children before the whims of rich-world consumers with more money than sense. One day, indeed, we will finally celebrate Western Sahara's freedom. Until then the **NI** will have to continue its crazed, subversive raging against the machine. ∎

Chris Brazier *has been a co-editor of* New Internationalist *magazine since 1984. Once a reporter for* Melody Maker, *he is currently principal writer for UNICEF's annual flagship report* The State of the World's Children. *He is the author of* Vietnam: The Price of Peace *(Oxfam 1992) and* The No-Nonsense Guide to World History *(NI/Verso 2001).*

1

Rich world, poor world, beggar, thief

EVERY three seconds a child under five dies in the Majority World; a child who would still be alive had the world taken the same responsibility for all its citizens as it takes for those born in Toronto, Edinburgh or Sydney.[1]

This is the kind of terrifying fact which brought the *New Internationalist* into being and Peter Adamson's editorial from the first magazine in March 1973 unfortunately still has resonance and relevance today. The magazine has always stared the divide between rich and poor in the face, has never allowed its readers to forget this central, inescapable injustice. Sometimes this has been by revealing what the world looks like from the ugly end of the North-South divide, as the great Latin American writer Eduardo Galeano does here. And sometimes it has been by exposing the profligacy of life in the rich world in all its madness.

Some of the **NI**'s very best writing, though, has tried to bridge the gap by connecting its readers with individual people and communities instead of talking about 'the poor' as an undifferentiated, abstracted mass. When Lamin Sennah remembers how his family coped with famine, when Nancy Scheper-Hughes, Mari Marcel Thekaekara or Jeremy Seabrook introduce us to women and men that they have known for many years, we understand that these are people with real bodies, real feelings – lives that have a beginning and a middle, not just some horribly painful end. Their loving and their laughing, their dancing and their dreaming, their pain and their joy, are not that different from our own. And this makes us care all the more about the material conditions in which they are forced to live their lives, which could hardly be more different from our own. ■

1 Calculated from figures in *The State of the World's Children 2003*, UNICEF.

March 1973
The second front
The first New Internationalist *editorial, by* **Peter Adamson.**

There are 1,500 million people on the planet without enough of the right kind of food to eat, or safe water to drink, or basic medical care.[1] And this situation is getting worse. There are now more malnourished, sick, uneducated and unemployed people in the world than there were ten years ago.

The front line in the war on this poverty is being manned[2] by the people of the poor countries themselves, and already they are financing over 80 per cent of their own development efforts from their own work and their own trade earnings.

But if the war is to be won, a second front must be opened – in the rich world. It is the rich world which lays down the rules of world trade within which the poor world must earn its living. It is the rich world which regulates the international monetary system within which the poor world must manage its finances. It is the rich world which commands 95 per cent of the world's technological know-how and 90 per cent of the world's income.

It is the rich world which can provide the kind of aid and investment which will help the poor world to develop its own resources for its own benefit; and it is the rich world which can and often does provide the kind of aid and investment which degrades and exploits the poor world for the benefit of the already rich.

Changes in the policies of the rich nations are therefore essential if the war on world poverty is ever to be won. But these changes can only be brought about through inter-governmental action at the highest level and on the largest scale. And this in turn demands a new political will and a new climate of public opinion in the developed world. For the ideal of world development will never be realized, as U Thant[3] said, *'unless it is rooted in the hearts and minds of millions of citizens everywhere... unless it can win their sustained support'*.

The campaign to win sustained support for a great new effort to bring justice and help to the world's poor is already gathering momentum in the developed countries. In Britain the World Development Movement, the Voluntary Committee on Overseas Aid and Development, Third World First, the Haslemere Group, the Standing Conference on the Second Development Decade, the educational wings of the major charities and churches, and many other local and national groups, are campaigning to create a growing body of people who know more and care more and do more about world development.

Similar groups now exist in almost every developed country and the strength of these groups and of the ties between them is increasing almost by the hour.

The *New Internationalist* arises from and in response to this growing movement. For the last two years it has been going out every term to the 33,000 students in British universities who are giving a percentage of their grants each year to overseas development projects through the Third World First bankers order scheme.

With this issue, the *New Internationalist* becomes a monthly magazine, backed jointly by Oxfam and Christian Aid, and aimed at a wider audience. It will report on the people, the ideas, and the action in the fight for world development; it will give a platform to the new social and political ideas from Africa, Asia, and Latin America; it will debate and campaign for the great changes which are necessary to bring justice and help to the world's poor.

The *New Internationalist* is only one part of this campaign. But in asking you to subscribe to it, read it, write to it, talk about it, publicize it, we are asking you to join this growing movement for action on the greatest issue of our times. ■

1 A similar broad-brushstroke figure from the first years of the 21st century comes from UN Secretary-General Kofi Annan: 'Half of humanity remains desperately impoverished, with 3,000 million people subsisting on less than $2 a day, and 1,200 million – half of them children – suffering absolute poverty, struggling to survive on less than $1 a day.' **2** Throughout this anthology we have not altered language such as 'manned' here, or 'man' to mean 'humankind' elsewhere, but retained it as being indicative of the climate of thinking at the time. **3** Former UN Secretary-General (1961-71).

October 1973
Come hell and high water
*On the news we see thousands, even millions, afflicted by drought and flood. But what is it really like for the individual people living through such disasters? In this excerpt **Lamin Sennah** recalls the hungriest months of his life, during his childhood in Gambia.*

Many days and weeks passed before we admitted that the dreaded famine was upon us. It was a difficult admission. We tried to pretend that worse could happen. In the meantime we picked every available leaf from the baobab tree in the back yard. After that we sat empty-handed. We had nowhere to go. We could, of course, pretend that there was something to cook: prepare the fire, fill the pot with water and fake business. It was a way of impressing our neighbours, but even here it was unsafe to overplay our hands.

Sometimes we were fortunate to have a meal in two days. There was a small quantity of cereals around the house. Mother boiled a few grains in a pool of water and added sugar to make it pleasant to gobble down. As the supply dwindled she herself went without food. She had a good store of kola-nuts which dulled her appetite and provided relief of sorts. At the beginning we all went far afield to hunt for scraps of food. But finally we gave up. The scraps were getting scarce and we were also getting weaker. Far better to remain home and crumple near the empty pots than stagger into a ditch away from home.

Minute by painful minute we grew weaker and weaker. We looked a ghastly family, with the thin slender arms of Mother hopelessly supported on her knees over us. We took a quick look at her empty eyes and rushed for cover behind her back. It was some time before we got used to those harrowing, haggard eyes. I think Mother knew how terrified we were of the prospects of waking up each morning and having to ask the same routine and awkward questions about food. She pawned her beautiful gold earrings one by one. After that she pawned other valuables around the house such as woven strips of cloth. Finally, in desperation, she picked up a small silver spoon and went out to pawn that too.

Mother attached a lot of sentimental value to that spoon. After she pawned it she behaved as if she had been fatally betrayed. An acute sense of bereavement pervaded the atmosphere of the house. Her eyes became more and more empty. As life ebbed out of those large eyes we began to prepare for the worst. It was the spiritual strength of Mother's face that had enabled us to survive for so long with a modicum of dignity. As the light in her eyes dimmed, our vision of a worthwhile status in life steadily faded.

The most difficult times to endure were the nights. We rehearsed to ourselves the frightful prospects of another day without a scrap of food to eat. In spite of that we tried to put on a brave front. We tried to be optimistic, stuck to old jokes but lacked the strength to laugh at them, tried to cheer Mother up but achieved a kind of collective defeat. We gazed into the open sky and remained entranced in that position of blank stare. A new source of anxiety replaced the pool of trust in which we previously sought and found solace with nature.

On a full stomach the passage from night to morning was direct and easy. On an empty stomach, however, the story was quite different. It was not easy to contemplate the loneliness of another day of food shortage. Hunger had a strange way of stimulating yawning, and we all yawned incessantly one after another. The yawns were seen by the adults as distress signals. 'Get the children out of the way,' they would say. Between the time we went to bed and the next morning when we woke up there were ten anxiety-free hours in which our constant and unabated clamouring for food ceased to pester the adults.

Sleep did not come naturally on an empty stomach. We tossed from side to side and kept moving our limbs, annoying each other. We fought hard sometimes, but our parents refused to intervene, knowing that the aggressive energy would be quickly dissipated and we would settle back into sleep. The discipline of hunger was a foolproof means of keeping us in line.

Next morning Mother would be sitting on the kitchen stool near the fire which no-one dared to light. We kept looking into each other's eyes without saying anything. Yet those silent minutes did not feel empty. Messages of the most fundamental nature were hurtling to and fro between us, primary communication about survival and the future, about life and present opportunities, was happening spontaneously. We kept contact with each other by the natural ties of mutual need and a common plight. Solitary and forsaken, we huddled together united by a search for the same goal, an end to hunger, and driven by the same brute instinct for survival. Audible words were unnecessary. We fixed our gaze on each other knowing that the distance to travel from a look to a meaning was short and all lit up in the blaze of our searing appetite for food.

Mother was afraid that someone might appear on the scene, stretch out a hand of relief, and in return demand a moral price such as descending from the family pedestal to make obeisance to one of inferior caste. She was extremely sensitive about this. The distance which separated her from members of low-caste groups must be maintained if the family honour was to survive. Grandmother had instilled into her daughter ideas of her noble ancestry, and although in this respect Grandmother was somewhat of an old-fashioned extremist, the spirit in which she inculcated her high-caste doctrines exercised a hold on Mother. The symbolic significance of the silver spoon proved this. With great concentration of effort Mother was determined that her children would not stuff themselves with unclean meat. 'We have never known slavery in our family,' she would say with emotion, her voice duplicating the shrill defiant tones of Grandmother. We felt reassured... ∎

*When he wrote this **Lamin Sennah** was studying for a doctorate at London University.*

January 1982

The ultimate experts

Peter Stalker explains why the poor need no lessons from distant academics.

Colonel Gustavo Alvarez of the Honduran Security Forces has definite views on the activities of civilian politicians.

'Their problem', he said recently, 'is that they promise people that things will improve. That is how revolutions get started. You have to say: "You are poor, and you are going to stay poor". Otherwise people get ideas.'

For a military man this is an understandable point of view. But it is based on a couple of false assumptions. The first is that people need to be told that they are poor. For most this is a reality that strikes them quite independently when they wake up in the morning. No great economic insight is required.

The second is that people believe what politicians tell them. To do so anywhere in the world requires a considerable act of faith. To do so in Honduras requires a frontal lobotomy.

Yet Hondurans flocked to the polls in November 1981 – and did so without surgery of any kind. They were taking advantage of the opportunity to vote in their first civilian government since 1963 – and to vote the military out. You have already read enough of Honduran military thinking to appreciate the sense in this.

This issue of the *New Internationalist* is based on the assumption that most people, rich or poor, can readily understand the position in which they find themselves and know the best course of action to take.

The world's greatest experts on the problem of campesinos in Honduras, for example, are Honduran campesinos. And that is why it is their voices that are heard in this magazine. We also have a leading authority on juvenile employment in Tanzania, a medical expert from South Yemen and distinguished spokespersons on the problems of women and family planning in Sri Lanka.

That is not to deny the value of a broader academic analysis but merely to point out that many people's problems are fairly straightforward and scarcely need pondering by the World Bank or Society for International Development.

Thick skin and raw courage are often more useful. The farmers of La Colorada in Honduras have identified their problem without any great mental activity: they do not have enough land. And the solution they opt for is direct action – a land invasion.

You would not find much in the international literature on agricultural development to support their conclusion. The United Nations conference on agrarian reform met in 1979 with all the usual pomp and circumstance. And the word 'invasion' never crossed the assembled lips.

This is understandable; governments in general have no great interest in internal disruption. Yet in this case it is clear that disruption is exactly what is required. True, it involves a disavowal of the Rule of Law. True, it is an act of violence against property – and sometimes against human beings. And true also there could be a degree of irresponsibility and selfishness. But in this case, at this time, it seems to be correct – according to the local experts.

Such acts of defiance tend to be viewed in a more sinister light from the outside. 'Communist-inspired' would be the considered judgement in

Washington and London. Yet ask the campesinos of La Colorada about communism and you get a slightly puzzled reaction. And as for Cuba and President Castro, they want nothing to do with them.

But US policy in Central America is based on the assumption that the citizens of countries like Honduras or El Salvador do not have minds of their own – that they are blank slates waiting to be written on by a foreign intelligence.

There are no blank slates. Indeed the problem for ideologues of any persuasion is that the slates are already packed to overflowing with all sorts of messages – important or trivial, clear or contradictory. This month's medical expert, Saleh Hamshal, from a village in South or 'Democratic' Yemen, has one indelible memory: the death of his third daughter from diarrhoea. Had she lived in Denmark or Australia she would still be alive today. For diarrhoea is a condition that is easily cured. And now the treatment is in Saleh's own hands. He has become one of Yemen's primary-healthcare workers – and wants to make sure that what happened to his daughter will never happen again in his village.

Saleh has the advantage that, in theory at any rate, the Government is on his side: government policies in Democratic Yemen are a world away from those in Honduras. But while Saleh's task may be less dangerous than that of the campesinos it is unlikely to be any less of a struggle. Because the world is strewn with similar systems of healthcare that, at best, limp along.

Socialist governments in the Third World do not have an unblemished record in such matters – ambitious rhetoric usually runs some way ahead of the delivery system.

Another of the local experts recruited for this magazine found himself on the receiving end of this kind of non-delivery in Tanzania. When we first met Tahona Silas he was in court accused of stealing. He could just as well have accused Tanzania of not offering him any other way of making a living.

Tanzania can – and regularly does – defend itself with the eloquence of President Nyerere. The country, he protests, is crippled by an international trade system that makes sure the poor stay poor. He has a strong case. The prices of Tanzania's exports are trailing far behind the prices we charge for the goods we sell them. The result is a foreign-exchange crisis that blocks the import of machinery and materials into the country, throws thousands of people out of work and slams shut the factory doors in Tahona's face. Barred from formal employment in a country with no social security, he has become an expert in keeping body and soul together in any way he can.

Simple survival is a skill widely practised in the Third World. Tahona's approach is to operate on the city streets on the edge of illegality – but there are many others. For the very poorest a traditional defence against poverty has been to have more children in the hope that they will bring the security that the state cannot provide.

As a result the population explosion has been a familiar theme over the past 20 years. Yet now it seems that things are changing. Some 83 nations held a census in the last twelve months and the results confirm some of the most cheering international news for a long time: that after hundreds of years of steady acceleration, the rate of world population growth has at last slowed down. To find out why, we turn to our experts in Sri Lanka – a country where the last 15 years have seen the birth rate fall by over a third.

But though population growth looks like steadying the rate of consumption of the earth's resources shows no sign of abating. And we should know. When it comes to swallowing hamburgers, burning oil or laying waste to the countryside, the expertise lies much closer to home – though many of us would be too modest to admit it.

One person with no such reservations is Berit Gronvold from Norway. It is with her story that this global report comes home to its logical conclusion. Berit's personal response to the gluttonous society goes way beyond guilt to a change in her own lifestyle; and from there to a confrontation in the snow with the armed defenders of economic growth. It is not a comfortable position to adopt. People object to objecters.

Our friend Colonel Alvarez of the Honduran Security Forces would certainly not approve. Presumably he would tell her to behave herself: 'You are rich, and you are going to stay rich'. But it is probably too late for that: Berit, and indeed all the other people you will meet in this magazine, have already got 'ideas' into their heads. ∎

Peter Stalker was a co-editor of the NI *from 1975 to 1990. He has since worked extensively for UN agencies, including editing the annual* Human Development Report *for UNDP between 1991 and 1997. Among his books are* The No-Nonsense Guide to International Migration *(NI/Verso 2001) and the* Oxford Handbook of the World *(OUP 2000).*

February 1983
The rains

*A brief excerpt from **Peter Adamson**'s groundbreaking report from Upper Volta[1], which used fictional techniques to portray the life of actual villagers he met in the province of Yatenga during the early rains of 1982.*

Under thatched eaves, a woman crouches in the doorway, watching the patterning earth. Dark blots appear on the terracotta jars stacked in the open by the dead fire. Across the small courtyard an old blackboard, long ingrained with chalk, is being spattered by drops of black rain. In a few minutes the earth's slow stain is complete but still Assita, second of the three wives of Hamade Ouedraogo, remains in the doorway.

Over the low earth wall which her own hands helped to shape many years ago, she sees the water running from the thatched roof of her husband's hut. The clouds have brought the evening early and already the loose door of woven rushes has been pulled into place across the entrance. Just beyond are the huts of the other wives. On one the thatch is grey and brittle, darkened by the rain. On the other water runs easily off the still supple straw, raw edged and palely yellow in the last of the day's light.

The rain, hesitant at first, is now beginning to insist. On the flat-roofed building, the only one in the compound, water is pouring from a clay pipe high on the wall. In the morning, when the first rains have washed the roof, a jar will be placed over the muddy depression where tonight loose water splatters heavily onto the earth. Somewhere nearby an infant cries a cry of hunger and is suddenly silenced at the breast.

Now the guttering pipe and the hard rhythm of the rain are the only sounds to be heard in the compound. And over the vanishing outline of the village, the first soft far-off lightning plays around the edges of the sky. Looking out as she reaches for the rush door, Assita wonders whether it is also raining in her own village and, for a moment, she imagines her own mother lying awake, listening to the same sounds under the same sky.

Inside in the darkness she slowly undresses. On the rumpled cloths her two-year-old son has been asleep since long before the rains began. Behind him, lying on their sides against the curved wall, her twin daughters are also now asleep. As she steps over their folded dresses, the thought crosses her mind that, from tomorrow, all their clothes will need much more washing.

Lying in the darkness listening to the deadened sound of the rain on the heavy thatch, Assita remembers how the rain sounded on the tin roof of the nutrition centre all those years ago, how impossible it had been to sleep under the loud drumming of its fingers. They had been the first rains in almost two years. And they had come too late.

At the end of the second dry August, the people had sat in the shade of the empty granaries or under the doorways and walls of the compound, almost everything around them turned to the same parched colour so that only the harsh light and dusty shade defined the familiar shapes of the village. The women still walked to buy cans of water when they could and the men came and went looking for work. But the elders scarcely moved from morning to night, and no children played.

'*Yel Ka-ye*,' people said when you asked how they were – 'no problems'. '*Tel Ka-be*', they smiled – 'no complaints'. '*Laafi Bala*', murmured the elders – 'I have peace and health'. And they were all starving. Every live leaf had been collected and even in the towns it was said there was no food. Finally, when even the red millet had gone and roots were being boiled, the time came when the infants began to be given back.

For Lassana, her first child, tonight would have been the twelfth rains. Tomorrow he would have been working in the fields by her side, his supple arms wielding his own 'daba' blade into the wet earth. His action would not have been as economical as her own, but she knew he would have refused to straighten his back before his mother paused. And then the sweat would have run down his tapered body between shining shoulders, and those with daughters to marry would have taken notice. At midday, he would have sat and talked with her in the shade of the neem tree, hands clasped round strong legs caked with dried splashes of the red earth. Nearby, his father would have watched and said nothing. But as the season wore on, the elders would have nodded their heads as her son passed by.

Then, in the darkness, her son came to her as he was in the last days. And she saw again the loose folds of the empty buttocks and the clustered sores on the perished skin; saw the veinless swellings on the tops of both his feet and the helpless wooden charm around his wrinkled neck; saw again the taut skin of the old man's head on the infant's body and the agitated look in his lovely eyes.

Then she saw Hamade. It was the first time she had ever seen her husband carrying the baby close to him, like a woman. And her mind had clung to how unusual it was to see a man carrying a child like that and she had almost laughed, suspending its meaning in the air, refusing to allow its truth to touch the ground. Dully, as Hamade walked away, she recognized the custom that only a man shall carry an infant to the grave and it sank into her soul that Lassana was cold against his chest.

Across the landscape groups of figures are already bent over their fields. Most of the village has been out since soon after dawn, for these are the valuable hours when the earth is still soft and the air is still cool. The rains will last only four months at the most; four months in which the land must be made to grow enough for the year.

Already the night's streams have disappeared and even the rivers will by now be beds of mud in which cattle are leaving deep oozy hoof-prints as they graze the pools. Only the Black Volta, more than a hundred kilometres away, flows all the year round. But here in Yatenga, the soil which yesterday would have answered the hoe only with a cloud of dust, can today be dug into, turned, planted. And as the morning sun climbs over the Sahel a million *dabas* rise and fall.

One of them is gripped by the hardened hands of Assita Ouedraogo, working together with her two co-wives, scraping hollows at regular intervals in the wet earth ready for the planting of grain. Within calling distance her husband, Hamade, works alone on a shoal of land between two footpaths, hoeing furrows of the broken heavy earth across the line of a scarcely perceptible slope.

Coming to the end of a row, Hamade straightens his back and stands for a moment, his sleeveless cotton shift, the colour of the earth, standing off his shoulders and making him look even broader than he is. As he rests, he contemplates what his neighbours are doing, which fields they have decided to work first, whose sons are working with them and whose are not. No hedged rectangles, no fences or ditches, tell him where one neighbour's land ends and another's begins. It is something he learnt while working these fields at his father's side, as now he works them with his own sons, gradually coming to know the shapes and peculiarities of the village fields in the same way as he came to recognize the faces and characters of village people. One field starts where the earth dips beyond the footpath and ends at the wide area of thin clay, like an unbroken skin on the surface of the earth, which is the field of the ancestors. Another field begins by the termite hill and ends at that invisible and meandering line between soil and shale, earth and sand, a dividing line of judgement between fertility and barrenness, marked by a fence of decisions that beyond it labour will be in vain. And as his educated eye recognizes the contours and boundaries of the land, so it also sees its virtues and vices: a depression in the earth probably means that soil has lodged there and that maize will do well; a darker patch has held its moisture well and can probably take sorghum again; a subtle change of colour means that the soil is too sandy and that millet had better be sown. Memory and the look and feel of the earth under the hoe tell him when a field should rest for another year, though even this morning Hamade has had to decide that fields which a farmer would leave fallow, a father must plant with food.

Normally the first day of the rains and the beginning of work brings with it a release of tension. For eight long months the level of the grain in the mud-built granaries has been steadily falling without anyone being able to do anything about it... until it rains. Now, at last, the work of restocking the granaries tight to their thatched roofs can at least begin. But for Hamade this morning, anxiety is not lessened as he swings the smooth-handled *daba*, feet slightly apart in the wet plastic sandals, and watches the soil breaking under the blows from his body.

An hour ago, as he reached into the sweet-smelling dimness of the granary to pull out the day's ration of grain, he had seen the granary floor. There are four more months to go to the harvest. Once again he has failed to make the *sesuka*, 'the welding', the joining of the last harvest to the next.

His family will not starve. Somehow the grain will be bought. It will be bought with the money buried in a tin under the floor of his hut, saved from the last time he left his home for the dry season and travelled a thousand miles by train to work for wages on the coffee plantations of the Ivory Coast. Or it will be bought by selling a few goats and sheep or by borrowing money from his relations or by going to the Naam warehouse in the town. The grain will be found. But he had hoped that the granaries would last a little longer, that he would only have to buy grain for two months, not four.

Hamade's forehead is glistening like the earth now as he strikes into the heavy soil and begins to break another ridge across the land. However unjustified the feeling may be, Hamade still feels the shame of having to go into town for grain. It is a feeling embedded in the centuries, rooted in the culture of necessity, a part of his sense of himself. Salt and spices can be bought with money, even *neere* or *karite* can be bought with money. But staple grains you grow with your own hands. And you grow enough to stretch across the seasons and make the *sesuka*, the joining. If you are known to be buying grain in the months before the harvest, then it is a matter of shame. You are lazy, you have not worked or you are not prudent, you are not a good manager. And you are not worthy of your family.

Circumstances have changed. And Hamade knows that there is not a man in Samitaba this morning who has enough grain to last until October. At the very least, shame should be diluted by the numbers of the shamed. But whatever the reason and no matter how many others are in the same position, Hamade is still disturbed, still feels the dishonour of seeing the granary floor on a morning in June. Not to be able to grow enough grain affects the way he feels as he works the land, subtly changes his sense of himself as he walks through the village and exchanges greetings with the elders or sits down in his compound to eat with his wives and his children.

Reaching the end of another row he straightens again and looks over his shoulder, roughly comparing what has been done with what is still to do. And as he looks around the family's lands, screwing up his eyes against the climbing sun, the feeling inside hardens into something close to anger as he sees again the evident truth that to fill only two granaries he and his family are working harder and more prudently than his ancestors ever did to fill three... ■

Peter Adamson was the founding editor of the New Internationalist. *From 1980 to 1995 he worked primarily for UNICEF, writing and editing their flagship annual reports* The State of the World's Children *and* The Progress of Nations. *His novel* Facing out to Sea *was published by Spectre in 1997.*

1 Upper Volta was renamed Burkina Faso in 1984.

July 1990
The madness of hunger

The people of Northeast Brazil are starving. But they put their own physical anguish down to 'nervous problems'. **Nancy Scheper-Hughes** *explains how drugs and politics have brought this about.*

I was going through the death-registry books in the *cartório civil* of Bom Jesus da Mata, a market town in the sugar-plantation region of Pernambuco in the Brazilian Northeast. I came across the following handwritten entry:

> **Died**: *18 September 1985, Luiza Alves da Conceição, female, brown eyes, aged 33, spinster.* **Cause of death**: *dehydration, starvation.* **Observations**: *The deceased left behind no children and no possessions. She was illiterate. She did not vote.*

That was the end of the entry but I was able to discover that Luiza had died in the municipal hospital of Bom Jesus and was buried in a pauper's coffin in an unmarked grave wrapped only in a hospital sheet.

I think about Luiza Alves from time to time. I imagine, from what I know of life in Bom Jesus, that she probably thought of herself as *fraca* (physically weak) or *fraca de juízo* (mentally weak) and prone to *ataque de nervos* (nervous attacks). She may have cried a good deal without understanding why. Perhaps sometimes she became angry. She may have lashed out, uncontrollably, at a ministering hand during her final *agonia* at the hospital.

I have seen deaths like these and they are not very pretty. The people of

Bom Jesus sometimes refer to them as *doença de cão* – literally dog's disease. They are referring to rabies, which in Portuguese is called *raiva* – literally rage, fury, madness. The madness of hunger is indeed very much like rabies and it is truly a dog's death.

References to the *delírio*, the madness of hunger, can be found as early as the 16th century in the writings of Portuguese navigators, and it is still a recurring theme in Brazilian literature now. It is the subjective voice, the primary experience of hunger.

The Northeast of Brazil is a land of many hungers, and of a formidable thirst. Infants who die of dehydration, their blackened tongues hanging from their mouths, compete for attention with equally brutal images of thirst-driven *sertanejos* who walk hundreds of kilometres to escape the drought of the *sertão* or hinterland.

So we must begin with the context, the million square kilometres of suffering that is the pock-marked face of the Northeast. Here cloying fields of sugar cane rot amidst hunger and disease; here authoritarian landlords compete for power with anarchistic bandits, and rural labourers are bound to a semi-feudal economy in a state of perpetual anxiety. The hunger of the coastal sugar-cane workers and their families is constant and chronic. The hunger of the *sertanejos* is periodic, acute and explosive.

Since 1964, when I first worked (and lived) in the region, I have been seeing starvation: a host of children of one and two years who cannot sit up unaided, who do not or cannot speak, whose skin is stretched so tightly over the chest and stomach that every curve of the breastbone and ribs stands out. The arms, legs and buttocks of these children are often stripped of flesh so that the skin hangs in folds. The buttocks are often discoloured. The bones of the face are fragile, the eyes prominent, the hair thin and wispy. The eyelashes can be extraordinarily long. Some children take on an unnatural, waxen appearance that their mothers sometimes see as a kind of death mask.

No other calamity has quite the shattering effects on personality and behaviour as the experience of acute hunger. The most obvious effect is a frenzied rage alternating with periods of euphoria, excitement and irritability, often subsiding into passive withdrawal and indifference.

At first in Bom Jesus one's ear is jarred by the way hunger and nervousness are interchangeable in the language of the poor residents of the hillside slum called Alto do Cruzeiro (Crucifix Hill). A mother will stop you on her way up the hill to say that things aren't good, that her children are nervous because they are hungry. Another woman returning from *feira* (market) tells you that she became dizzy, confused and 'nervous' at the price of meat. Dona Teresa tells you that her husband Manoel came home from work sick, his knees shaking, his body weak and so tired he could barely swallow a few mouthfuls of dinner. He is suffering from a *crise de nervos,* as is usual towards the end of the week, when everyone is anxious because there's nothing to eat.

I am sitting on the doorstep with several women of the Alto discussing *nervos* with them. Anger, discontent, anxiety, hunger and even parasitic infections (all related to their work as laundrywomen, rural labourers and domestic workers) are filtered through the metaphor of *nervos.*

Sebastiana: 'I'm always sick, I'm *fraca de nervos* (I have weak nerves).'

Me: 'What are your symptoms?'

Sebastiana: 'Trembling, a great chill in my bones. Sometimes I shake until I fall.'

Maria Teresa: 'There are many kinds of *nervos.*'

Me: 'What's "anger nerves" about?'

Rosa: 'That's if your *patroa* says something to you that really ticks you off, but because she's your boss you just go away without saying anything. But inside you're so angry you could kill her, you really wish she were dead. The next day you're likely to have anger nerves.'

Me: 'What about "fear nerves"?'

Maria Teresa: 'When her mother died, Black Irene gave out such a blood-curdling scream in the middle of the night that we all woke up with a jump. My son went running to Irene's house to see what was the matter. When he returned he fell down on the floor clutching his heart in an *agonia* of pain and trembling. Ever since that night he suffers from *nervos.*'

Sebastiana: 'I only suffer from overwork *nervos.* I've washed clothes all my life, for almost 60 years; and now my body is as worn out as Dona Carmen's sheets. [This is a slur against a notorious wealthy miser who is too mean to buy new sheets]. When I come home from the river with that heavy basin of wet laundry on my head, my knees begin to shake, and sometimes I lose my balance and fall right on my face. What humiliation!'

Me: 'Is there a 'cure' for overwork nerves?'

Sebastiana: 'I take tonics and Vitamin A.'

Rosa: 'Yes, lots of people take tonics, others take nerve pills, a lot take tranquillizers.'

Maria Teresa: 'Don't forget sleeping pills.'

Sebastiana: 'At night when everything is still, and the night is so dark, so strange, time passes slowly. The night is long. I almost go mad with *nervos* at times like that. I think of so many things, so many sad and bitter thoughts cross my mind. Memories of my childhood and how hard I was made to work, working like that in the fields on an empty stomach. Then the tremors begin, and I have to get out of bed. It's no use, I won't sleep any more that night. My illness is really just my life.'

What I wish to propose is that for this poor and hungry population many of the physiological symptoms of which they complain are also symptoms of chronic hunger. And during the past two decades of my involvement with these people I have seen a discourse on *nervos* and sickness replace a discourse on angry hunger.

I am not arguing that *nervos* can be reduced to hunger alone, or that *nervos* is an exclusively poor or working-class phenomenon. The 'beauty' of *nervos* as a folk illness syndrome is its flexibility. It is an all-purpose complaint, one that can be invoked by a frustrated middle class to express its dashed expectations in the wake of Brazil's decanonized 'economic miracle', by the urban working class to express their condition of powerlessness, *and* by an impoverished class of sugar-cane cutters and their families to express their hunger.

The question is, how did these people come to see themselves primarily as nervous and only secondarily as hungry, malnourished? How is it that mortally tired cane cutters come to define themselves as 'weak' rather than overworked and exploited? Worse, when resentment over exploitation is recognized, how did it ever get reinterpreted as illness? And, finally, how can it be that chronically hungry people will 'eat' medicines while going without their staple foods?

Nervos is a social illness. It allows hungry, irritable and angry *Nordestinos*, just now emerging from more than 20 years of militarism and political repression, a safe way to express their discontent. If it is dangerous to engage in political protest (and it is) and, as one of my informants Biu complained, if it is pointless to *reclamar,* to argue with God (and it would seem to be so), hungry and frustrated people can transform hunger into 'breakdown' and 'mental' problems. When people do so, the healthcare system and the political machinery of the community are fully prepared to back them up in their unhappy and anything-but-free choice of symptoms.

Because the people of Alto do Cruzeiro truly suffer from headaches, tremors, weakness, tiredness, irritability, angry weeping and other symptoms of what people call *nervos,* they look to the doctors, pharmacists and political bosses and patrons from Bom Jesus for a 'cure to the 'sickness'. They line up in clinics, in drug stores, in the municipal dispensary and they want powerful medicines to make them 'strong' and 'lively' (full of *animacao* – a kind of vitality and readiness for pleasure and enjoyment in the body and its senses that is so Brazilian). They do not leave without these magical, potent prescription drugs: *vitaminas, fortificantes, sôro,* but also antibiotics, painkillers and sleeping pills. And they get them, if they're lucky, even without paying for them.

Why medicine? If it is power that the leading families who supply them want, why not simply distribute food to hungry people? Medicalization mystifies. It isolates the experience of misery and it domesticates people's anger. There is power and domination to be extracted from the defining of a population as 'sick' or 'nervous'. To acknowledge hunger (which is not a disease but a social illness) would be tantamount to political suicide among leaders whose power comes from the same plantation economy that produced that hunger in the first place.

This 'bad faith' operates among the doctors and pharmacists who allow their knowledge and skill to be abused; among the politicians who wish to see themselves as community benefactors, while knowing full well that they are nothing of the sort; and even among the poor who are so often critical of the medical 'care' they receive yet continue to hold out for a medical solution to their economic problems.

The determination to see malnutrition and dehydration as something other than what they are, as a nervous condition to be treated with painkillers, tranquillizers, tonics and elixirs, represents the worst instance of collective bad faith in Bom Jesus de Mata. This, too, is the madness of hunger. ■

Nancy Scheper-Hughes is Professor of Anthropology at the University of California, Berkeley. Among her books is the classic Death Without Weeping *(University of California Press 1992).*

November 1990
The other wall
The view from the South. **Eduardo Galeano** *looks north, over the high wall of power, and finds contempt disguised as destiny at 'the end of history'.*

The end of history? That's nothing new for us. Five centuries ago Europe decreed that in America memory and dignity were crimes. The new owners of these lands banned the remembrance and the making of history. All we have been permitted to do since is to accept it.

Dark skins, white wigs, crowns of lights, cloaks of silk and jewels: at the Rio de Janeiro carnival the starving dream together and for a while are Kings and

Queens. For four days the most musical people in the world live out their collective delirium. And on Ash Wednesday, at midday, the party is over. The
police arrest anyone who stays in disguise. The poor take off their feathers
and paint, rip off the visible masks, the masks that unmask, the masks of fleeting freedom, and put on different, invisible masks, negating the human face:
the masks of routine, obedience and misery. Until the next carnival, the
Queens go back to washing dishes and the Princes to sweeping the streets.

They sell newspapers they cannot read, sew clothes they cannot wear, pol-
ish cars they will never own and construct buildings where they will never live.
With their cheap arms they present cheap products to the world market.

They made Brasilia, and from Brasilia they were thrown out. They make
Brazil, day after day, and Brazil is their land of exile.

They cannot make history. They are condemned to suffer it.

The end of history. Time has been pensioned off, the world has stopped turning. Tomorrow is another name for today. The places at the table are set, and
Western civilization denies no-one the right to beg for crumbs.

Ronald Reagan wakes up one day and says: 'The Cold War is over. We've
won'. Francis Fukuyama, a functionary in the US State Department, achieves
sudden fame and success by discovering that the end of the Cold War is also
the end of history. In the name of liberal democracy, capitalism becomes the
last port of call for all journeys, 'the final form of human government'.

Hours of glory. The class struggle no longer exists, and to the East there
are no longer enemies but allies. The free market and the consumer society
have won universal consensus, no more than delayed by the historical diver-
sion of the communist mirage. Just as the French Revolution wanted it we are
now all free, equal and fraternal. And property owners too. Kingdom of
greed, paradise on Earth.

Like God, capitalism has the highest opinion of itself and has no doubts
about its own immortality.

Welcome to the fall of the Berlin Wall! So says the Peruvian diplomat Carlos
Alzamora in a recent article; but the other wall, the wall that separates the poor
world from the opulent world, is higher than ever. A universal apartheid:
racism, intolerance and discrimination erupt increasingly in Europe, punish-
ing all intruders who scale the wall to reach the citadel of prosperity.

It's plain to see. The Berlin Wall has died a timely death. But it lived no more than 30 years. The other wall will soon be celebrating its fifth centenary. Unequal exchange, financial extortion, capital bleeding away, monopoly over technology and information, cultural alienation – these are the bricks that build up day by day, as wealth and sovereignty drain ever faster from the South to the North of the world.

Money works in the opposite way to people; the freer it gets, the worse it becomes. Economic neo-liberalism, imposed by the North on the South as 'the end of history', as the only and ultimate system, consecrates oppression under the banner of freedom. In the free market the victory of the strong is natural and the annihilation of the weak is legitimate. Racism rises to the status of economic doctrine. The North confirms divine justice: God rewards the chosen people and castigates the inferior races, condemned by their biological make-up to violence and inefficiency. In a single day, a worker from the North earns more than a worker from the South can in half a month.

Starvation wages, low costs, ruinous world market prices. Sugar is one of the Latin American products condemned to instability and decline. For many years there was just one exception: the Soviet Union paid (and still does) a reasonable price for Cuba's sugar. Now, in its euphoria, capitalism triumphant rubs its hands with glee. There are plenty of signs that this commercial pact will not last much longer. No-one thinks to say that this exemplary exception shows how to create a new, fairer international order, an alternative to the systematic plunder called 'deteriorating terms of trade' by the technicians. No: if the Soviets still pay a good price for Cuban sugar, that only goes to show the diabolical designs that guided Moscow's steps, poking its nose in where it did not belong, in the days when it sported horns, a trident and a tail.

The prevailing order is the only possible one: thieving commerce is the end of history.

Preoccupied by cholesterol, hunger long forgotten, the North nonetheless practises charity. Mother Theresa of Calcutta is more efficient than Karl

Marx. Aid given by the North to the South is much less than the alms solemnly pledged before the United Nations, but it allows the North to dump its war junk, its surplus goods and development projects that underdevelop the South and spread the haemorrhage to cure the anaemia.

Meanwhile, over the last five years, the South has donated to the North an infinitely larger sum, the equivalent of two Marshall Plans at constant prices, in the form of interest payments, profits, royalties and all kinds of colonial tribute. And meanwhile, the creditor banks of the North have gutted the debtor states of the South and ended up owning our public sector in exchange for nothing.

Just as well that imperialism does not exist. No-one mentions it any more, therefore it does not exist. That history, too, has ended.

But, if empires and their colonies have come to rest behind glass in the museum of antiquities, why are the dominant countries still armed to the teeth? Because of the Soviet threat? Not even the Soviets believe that alibi any more. If the Iron Curtain has melted away and the bad guys of yesterday are the good guys of today, why do the powerful continue to manufacture and sell weapons and fear?

The budget of the US Air Force exceeds the total of the budgets for the education of all children in the so-called Third World. A waste of resources? Or resources to defend waste? Could the unequal organization of the world, which pretends to be eternal, be sustained a single day longer if the countries and the social classes that have bought up the world disarmed?

This system, sick with consumerism and arrogance, which launched so voraciously into the destruction of land, sea, air and sky, now mounts guard at the foot of the high wall of power. It sleeps with one eye open, and with good reason.

The end of history is its message of death. The system that sanctifies a cannibalistic international order tells us: 'I am everything. After me, nothingness'.

From a computer screen, the fate of millions of human beings is being decided. In the era of super-enterprises and super-technology, some are merchants, others are merchandise. The magic of the market fixes the value of things and people. Latin American products are worth less every day. So are we, the Latin Americans.

The Pope in Rome forcefully condemned the brief blockade, or threatened blockade, of Lithuania. But the Holy Father has never uttered a word against the blockade of Cuba, now in its thirtieth year, or of Nicaragua, which lasted a decade. That's normal. And it's normal, too, that since we Latin Americans are worth so little while still alive, then the value placed on our dead should be a hundred times less than on the victims of the now disintegrated Evil Empire. Noam Chomsky and Edward Herman have taken the trouble to measure the space we merit in the leading North American media. Jerzy Popieluszko, the priest murdered by state terror in Poland in 1984, took up more space than the sum total of 100 priests murdered by state terror in Latin America in recent years.

They have imposed contempt on us as a custom. Now they sell us contempt as destiny.

The South learns its geography from world maps which reduce its actual size. Will future maps blot it out altogether?

Latin America was always the land of the future.

Cold comfort. But it was something.

Now we are told that the future is the present. ■

Eduardo Galeano, the eminent Uruguayan writer and historian, lives in Montevideo. Among his many books are The Open Veins of Latin America *and* Memories of Fire. *He is a regular columnist for the* **NI**.

September 1994

The new robber barons

Behind every fortune lies a crime. **David Ransom** *turns the spotlight on the richest of the rich.*

No rain ever falls on the starkly beautiful Atacama Desert of northern Chile. Here you will find the huge and fabulously rich Chuquicamata copper mine, one of the artificial wonders of the world, its terraces carved from the rock like a Greek amphitheatre for giants.

At the turn of the century only a few lonely prospectors wandering in the wilderness knew about its hidden wealth. But the Guggenheim family, who were making a relatively modest fortune from silver mining in Mexico at the time, were also sniffing around Chile and came across Chuquicamata more or less by accident. They snapped it up for a couple of hundred thousand dollars, figured out that it was the largest single deposit of copper in the world, and waited.

They did not have to wait for long. The richest of all the big US copper companies, Anaconda, had exhausted its old mines and wanted Chuquicamata badly. So badly that in 1902 they paid the Guggenheims $100 million – that's a billion (yes, 1,000 million) or so dollars at today's prices – for control of it. A nice little earner from a couple of years' work by the Guggenheims.

The Guggenheims eventually became great philanthropists and endowed one of the world's prettiest art museums in New York. Anaconda, on the other hand, had to set about the more mundane task of recovering its money. Chuquicamata would have to earn the most fabulous profits for the deal to pay off. It did, many times over, decade after decade.

The only people who made absolutely *nothing* from the deal were the Chilean miners who did the work. Their function was to toil away, forever digging what soon became the biggest artificial hole in the world, to pay Anaconda for a deal they had played no part whatever in making. They were, you might say, paying for the Guggenheim Museum in New York, when everyone thought it was the Guggenheims.[1]

Every fortune is made in this way, for personal wealth is no more than a badge of competence at getting someone else to pay your bills. What we are talking about here, however, is not just any old personal fortune or the nicer distinctions of wealth between most of us, whatever we may own or howsoever we may have earned it. There are individuals whose personal wealth is now measured not just in hundreds or thousands but in *thousands of millions* of dollars.

Their appetite for riches, for possessions and power knows no bounds. They are driven by obsessions akin to madness, by an evangelical belief in their own genius that, left to its own devices, would make monsters of us all. We only have to retrieve the evidence from our own history to see that this is so.

The turn of the century was a particularly good time for philanthropists. Not just the Guggenheims but the Rockefellers, the Carnegies and a raft of others were founding the super-rich dynasties whose names are better remembered today for the philanthropic institutions they named after themselves.

At the time, however, not everyone called these people philanthropic. In fact the preferred popular term for them was 'robber barons'. For this was the great age of private-monopoly industrial empires in the US. Extraordinary personal fiefdoms were built from oil, mining, railways, steel, newspapers, all the large-scale modern industries of the day. They were ruled as absolute dictatorships by a savage breed of ruthless megalomaniacs.

It was one of those moments in history when, as if by alchemy, fresh ways of making a personal fortune beyond anyone's wildest imaginings suddenly materialized. At first other people just looked on in stunned amazement. But eventually, after long and often violent conflicts with the people they employed, the robber barons were tamed. The dangers of unrestrained, monopolistic power wielded by individuals who frequently turned out to have been almost completely insane were recognized. 'Anti-trust' – anti-monopoly in the UK – and labour-rights legislation by governments with at least some democratic credentials moderated the excesses, or saved capitalism from self-destruction, depending on your point of view.

We are now, I think, living through a similar historical moment. At no time since then have the super-rich got richer and more powerful with quite such effortless ease. The fiefdoms of the new robber barons may look a bit different. Code names like 'deregulation' and 'structural adjustment' conceal their true identity. They are being built on new territory: retailing, information technology, mass communications, entertainment, financial speculation and 'kleptocracy' – government by thieves.

In the relatively fresh pastures of Japan and Southeast Asia the biggest bucks have so far been made from real estate, like the chunk of central Tokyo inherited by the Mori brothers that helps them to weigh in with a personal fortune of $13 billion. The shift from 'corporate' to personal wealth has only just begun in this part of the world. As elsewhere, it is happening because the restraints have been removed, the lessons apparently forgotten.

But in many essential respects the new fiefdoms of the robber barons are the same. They are, as ever, exclusively male. Apart from the odd monarch, widow or daughter of wealth, there are still very few women to be found among the world's richest people. This suggests that the quest for unlimited money and power is one of the nastier products of male fantasy. Unchanged too is the urge to found dynasties, the craving for monopoly power and the Napoleon-complexes of the individuals concerned.

Some of us were, I think, distracted by what we took for a brand-new world. We gazed with grudging respect at the glittering citadels of the global village, the flickering images, the limitless possibilities of new technology, the financial big bang. We talked in grand, abstract terms about everything that had gone: 'post-modernism', 'the post-industrial age', 'the post-Cold War era'. We were looking for something new in the New World Order.

Maybe when we'd read *Bonfire of the Vanities*, seen *Wall Street* or watched

Serious Money we imagined that after the stock-market crash of 1987, economic recession and the property slump, surely the nasty little 'Yuppies', the self-styled 'Lords of the Universe', must have gone bust. In fact, the number of dollar billionaires more than doubled between 1987 and 1992.[2] All that really happened was that the big fish ate the smaller fish and the concentration of wealth and power in the hands of super-rich individuals accelerated.

Multinational corporations had been made to look bloated and lumbering in a world of fast-buck footwork. They lost their aura of invulnerability to predatory raiders. 'Leveraged buyouts' by individuals wielding enormous quantities of borrowed cash enriched those who organized them and, more importantly, changed corporate culture. Short-term profits and share prices became the absolute arbiters of corporate policy.

To make themselves leaner and hungrier the corporations invited the predators into the boardroom. Quite extraordinary 'remuneration' packages, share options, performance bonuses, pension rights and other 'incentives' made corporate Chief Executive Officers and their boardroom buddies among the wealthiest people in the world. In terms of disposable income some of them became richer than the billionaires listed in *Fortune* magazine, the in-house journal of the super-rich.

Most striking is the case of Rupert Murdoch, who at one point owed his bankers $8 billion – yes, that's $8,000 million. Financial institutions and banks put an almost religious faith in the genius of individual 'entrepreneurs'.[3]

This attitude is now spreading to a wider public. The feeling seems to be that if you're a genius at making money, then you'll be a genius at running a country. The most celebrated example of this is the billionaire property speculator, football impresario, media monopolist and now Premier of Italy Silvio Berlusconi. Large sections of the Italian people, apparently exasperated by venal politicians and unabashed by the prospect of a return to fascism, decided that in the chaotic circumstances of Italian politics they might as well have the real thing and vote for Berlusconi himself.

He had a precursor in Ross Perot, the gadfly billionaire who financed his own campaign in the 1992 US presidential elections. And he will undoubtedly have his successors. There is just too neat a symbiosis, too tempting an investment here for the chance to be missed. Political ambition sits very comfortably with the megalomania of the robber baron. The coffers of the state offer rich pickings – 'privatization' has been a favourite in recent years – while there's no better way of taking out an insurance policy against your personal tax bills than running the government.

In the South we've become accustomed to seeing this sort of thing for some time. Kleptocratic rulers, hugely wealthy men sponsored by their Northern chums, steal taxes, land, loans, export earnings, anything that moves. At one time the 'fight against communism' was sufficient justification. Now we know this for the excuse it always was – at least in Zaire, Côte d'Ivoire, Indonesia, Haiti, Brunei, Saudi Arabia, Kuwait and a depressingly large number of other countries with openly kleptocratic rulers.

It is true that in Latin America military kleptocracy has become redundant. Very similar results can now be achieved by 'structural adjustment', which has enormously enriched élites through programmes of privatization, deregulation and cuts in social services. The 35 families in Mexico who 'earn' more than the 15 million poorest Mexicans; the five-billion-dollar swindles of former President Collor and his 'adviser' PC Farias in Brazil are just the most celebrated examples.

In the North, what JK Galbraith calls a 'culture of contentment' may have helped the super-rich to get away with the loot.[4] He reckons the relatively prosperous majority of the population in Europe and North America has not minded too much about the poor minority getting poorer or about a very rich minority getting very much richer, so long as it can stay contented in the middle.

We have also, I think, become bewitched by the rich and famous. We peer at their tedious, self-indulgent 'lifestyles' through banal 'keyhole' TV programmes and magazines with silly names like *Hello*! and *Voilà*! We read about revolting hereditary barons who stuff their heads into bags filled with cocaine; about the 'old' rich and the royals who seem to have been there always and therefore to represent some kind of inherent human condition. We muse about becoming rich ourselves, thinking it harmless. And, while we muse, tax and social welfare cuts in the UK, for example, transfer anything between $30 and $75 billion over our heads from the very poor to the very rich.

In Brazil you'd need to be quite mad not to see such things for what they really are. Here there has arisen in recent years a dystopian vision of strutting media barons feeding exotic soap operas to a society whose abandoned children prowl city streets in a state of glowering fury and tears. A couple of years ago, outside the city of Goiânia, I saw a few beef cattle owned by a very rich landowner strolling through lush fields behind high fences on both sides of a road. Packed onto a grimy, narrow strip along the verges, spilling into the road and clinging to the most tenuous form of life imaginable, were thousands of people. I could not help reflecting that it was they, more than the cattle, who were being farmed. This in a country, and among a people, that have waited in vain for an 'economic miracle' their resources and genius would otherwise quite easily permit. There is only one word for this: plunder.

It is one thing to diagnose the illness, quite another to cure it. Try thinking of the new robber barons as sufferers from a serious mental disorder of addiction. Therapists will tell you that the first step to recovery is for the patient to recognize that they are indeed disordered. The second – which also aids the first – is for everyone else to say so and refuse to collude in the patient's self-deception.

In more urgent and extreme circumstances we could do worse, I suppose, than follow the example of our friends in Chiapas, southern Mexico. They know all too well what their local barons look like and what they stand for. During the uprising there in January they decided to kidnap one of them (he was released unharmed).

The great advantage of keeping the new robber barons in our sights is that there are very few of them indeed and many more of us. It is not envy but contempt we should feel for them. Or are we to believe that profit is the only measure of value; that conspicuous consumption is virtuous; that 'the environment' is a golf course; that it is better to pay tax consultants than taxes; that everything done in the name of democracy and equity is wrong?

If so we should follow the new robber barons into the lunatic asylum and hope someone will be left on the outside to foot the bill. Midas, after all, turned everything he touched into gold, including his own daughter. Better, I say, to rename the Guggenheim Museum 'Chuquicamata'. ∎

*Formerly director of a charity for the homeless in the East End of London, **David Ransom** has been a co-editor of the **NI** since 1989. He is the author of* The No-Nonsense Guide to Fair Trade *(NI/Verso 2001).*

1 This story is based on my research in Chile while working at the London School of Economics between 1970 and 1974. **2** *Fortune International*, 28 June 1993. **3** William Shawcross, *Murdoch*, Pan Books, London, 1993. **4** JK Galbraith, *The Culture of Contentment*, Penguin, London, 1992.

June 1995
Across the great divide
Chris Brazier returns to a village in Burkina Faso ten years after making a film there. In this excerpt his wish to bridge the gulf between rich and poor is undermined.

'You whites – your skins are like those of new-born babies,' says Mariama one day, the day we walk seven kilometres through the bush in the midday heat to the neighbouring village of Sago. 'Ours are tough.' This emphasis on my difference becomes a recurring theme, which isn't exactly what I'd intended.

My main reason for returning to Sabtenga, after all, was to stress the human connection between people on either side of the Great Divide. And it's true that the cultural changes in the village over the last ten years – the impact of modernization, really – have, for good or ill, rendered people more comprehensible and closer to us.

Yet throughout my time in the village my most vivid feeling is one of pain and embarrassment at the vast economic chasm between us. I write about the interaction between rich world and poor world all the time – that's my job. But I have never before felt my nose so pressed up against the glass that separates us, been so acutely conscious of how much I have in material terms compared with all the people around me.

I have brought with me, for example, some photos showing my life in England – my partner and children, my house and car, my daughter's school, the **NI** office and team, a typical supermarket, a double-decker bus and so on. I knew people in the village would be fascinated by these and that they would help me to re-establish a connection with them. And I was right about that. But my primary purpose in showing people the photographs – to build a bridge of understanding between their world and ours – is consistently frustrated.

People are staggered by the sheer wealth of the world revealed by the snapshots. And for many of them it is as if they take the photos as a personal reflection upon their own poverty. Mariama's habitual sigh of '*c'est pas facile*' (it's not easy) becomes almost a mantra as she looks at them – and she tells me straight that this verbal reflex is a comment on the hardship of her own life. Another time she asks me if I think her house is as beautiful as she thinks mine is. What can I say? To say yes I find it beautiful (as I do in one sense) would be a condescending insult in this context. It would be more honest to talk about slavery, the colonial century and the foundation they have provided for my own comfort. I manage to escape without answering.

The place where the photos really do their job is in the lesson I give about life in England to the oldest class in the village school. This produces some lively interest – and some illuminating questions once the children overcome their inevitable reticence. How do you hunt? How do you keep animals? How do you eat? Do you fetch wood for your fire? Do you have wells? What do children wear to school? Are their teachers like ours? Do you have Peulh (nomadic pastoralists)? Do you have black people? Are black people accepted by white people? Do you carry babies on your backs like we do?

The school is a breeze-block building containing three classrooms. There should really be six classes here corresponding to the six years of primary education but in the absence of a second building the school can only take in new seven-year-old pupils once every two years. On the day of admission prospective pupils queue up and the first 64 are admitted for an education; the 50 or so others simply have to do without.

The Government has promised that it will provide three more teachers' salaries if the villagers can erect a second three-classroom building. So back in 1992 villagers got together to pay for and work on the foundations of this second school building – they knew they would have no chance of getting money from outside unless they showed this collective commitment. And despite lobbying of government and foreign aid agencies in Ouagadougou, there is still nothing but the foundations in place. Meanwhile every two years 50 of Sabtenga's children are left with no education. All for want of $22,000, little more than my partner and I just paid to convert the loft of our house into an extra bedroom.

The children sit at desks ranged in rows of three along both the long sides of the room, with blackboards at each end. Given the class size of more than 60 it's hardly surprising that the teaching methods have to be quite traditional. The teacher stands up front and runs the children through their paces. And the teacher I watch in action – Idrissa Ky, a tall and good-looking 34-year-old man from the Samo people on the other side of the country – seems pretty good to me. He is clearly in control, but his firmness is balanced by his careful and patient explanations.

The children range from 11 to 15 years and look an average enough cross-section of the village. They are doing mathematics, which is not my strong suit, but to me the standard seems surprisingly high, especially since they are coping with it in a foreign language (all education is in the former colonial language, French). Now I see the bridge those dusty, snotty kids running around outside cross over to become the sharp teenagers with whom I discuss things in the evenings.

The missing link personified is perhaps Zenabou's daughter Salamatu. She was just a toddler hanging on her mother's breast ten years ago – there was a magical scene in the film[1] when the two of them watched the first long-awaited raindrops falling. Now Salamatu has bright and lively eyes and radiates an enthusiasm for learning which is truly heartening – one day she proudly recites a poem to me on the way home from school. On another occasion she demonstrates her reading, using a grotesquely inappropriate textbook full of white children and Parisian landmarks. This must have dated from her parents' schooldays since now the texts are impeccably Africanized – though the exercise books the children use (from Côte d'Ivoire) are covered with pictures of black Americans like Michael Jordan and Whitney Houston. Salamatu's bears the words of rap artist Kris Kross: 'I'm the wrong brother for suckers to be messin with/ Cos when I put the mike in my hand I start wreckin it.' How appropriate...

I ask Salamatu's father Adama if he will be prepared to pay for her to attend secondary school in Garango if she is one of the 15 or so who pass the national exam at the end of six years' village schooling. He says he will, which is encouraging in itself since there are only 14 girls in a class of 64 in Garango at the moment. This is partly due to parents not placing high value on a daughter's education. But it is also because girls imbibe early on the idea that education is not for them. Salamatu's half-sister Rasmatu, for instance, used to leave home with her satchel simply to hide in the bush all day. Last year the teachers threw her out.

Education can be a route out of poverty in any society. And many parents are now aware that the sacrifices involved in paying for their children to be educated will pay dividends later on. Take Francois Moné, one of Sabtenga's most prominent sons, who passed a national exam to become an army pilot and now travels regularly in Africa and Europe for work. He maintains a very decent lifestyle in the capital and has enough left over to pay for new-style houses for some of his older relatives.

But the investment is harder for some than for others. Habibu is a widow who pays for her son Momini to go to secondary school. She lives just down the hill from me and early on in my stay I arrange for her to provide me with an evening meal in return for a decent daily sum. I feel this is the best way to cope with the economic divide between me and the village: to pay well over the market price for any services I receive, like Habibu's meals and Mariama's translation.

But otherwise I generally refrain from giving people money – rightly or wrongly I feel that once the dam of this rule bursts, I will find myself in serious trouble. The money backing me up effectively makes me a kind of god. So little in my own society's terms could make so much difference to people here. But I find myself utterly incapable of making godlike decisions. How can you give money to a boy to repair the bike he needs to get to school when an old woman elsewhere in the village is on the brink of starvation? How do you decide who should take priority?

I find it unbearable living alongside human beings who live so close to the edge, where people periodically die of hunger or disease born of plain and simple poverty. I have reluctantly got used to the idea that developing countries cannot afford to provide a safety net: you look after yourself or you die. But somehow ten years ago I – romantically – came to think of the *concession* (the compound of huts in which people here live) as the very embodiment of the extended family. I assumed that if a person fell on hard times someone else in the wider family would rescue them.

But it doesn't work like that. The sad and terrible fact is that people here live so close to the brink themselves that they can't afford to take responsibility for each other's misery – and this lesson of tough peasant stoicism must be etched on their bones. What right do we have to say it should be otherwise, given the hardship we gloss over in our own societies, let alone in these other quarters of the world?

Habibu is a classic case of someone truly on her own. Her husband Tasseré was poisoned in Abidjan – a mysterious case involving a curse and some of the old magic, by her account – and died back in the village after a year of her nursing him. Now she must simply grow enough for herself and her three children to eat all year from her own fields – and try to cook things for sale in the market to raise the cash needed for Momini's schooling. Life could not be harder and she has an air of weariness about her all the time. One night as the light from the kerosene lamp falls on her face, looking for all the world like she is in a painting by de La Tour, I ask about her hopes and dreams for the future.

'Just for us all to be healthy,' she says. 'And for Momini, who is my great hope, to find a job that will make us all secure.' It's a tough burden for a teenage boy to bear. And with the Government now going down the IMF/World Bank road of structural adjustment – while at the same time turning a blind eye to corruption and nepotism – the salvation of secure employment is unlikely. Educational qualifications simply do not lead to jobs even to the extent that they used to ten years ago. Politicians and businesspeople in the capital are now buying their relations the new posts.

I would be duping you and betraying the people of the village if, in my concern to look for hopeful stories, I did not tell you that the material gulf between our lives and theirs is obscene. Not all the world's people can live like we do – but we could still have a decent life while giving the people of this village, this country, this continent, this Majority World, the fairer deal that ought to be their birthright. As Thomas Sankara, Burkina's revolutionary martyr, said once: 'Whilst elsewhere people die from being too well-nourished, here we die from lack of nourishment. Between these two extremes there is a way of life to be discovered if each of us meets the other halfway.' ■

1 *Man-Made Famine*, a New Internationalist film screened on TV in many countries during 1986.

May 1997

The city our stepmother

Jeremy Seabrook introduces us to the poor community in Mumbai (formerly Bombay) that he has known for a decade.

Everywhere in the world dawn is grey, as the women who greet it know. The beginnings of day always reveal a landscape drained of colour.

Many women in Sanjay Gandhi Nagar are, in any case, up long before then – standing in line with their metal vessels and plastic pails to capture the trickle of water that comes through the municipal supply before it dries up by 5.30am.

Parvati sets out in the early morning, her sandals kicking up a small cloud of dust as her steps join the noiseless tread of servitude of the poor. The bus halts only briefly, as though reluctant to take on people: it is already over-crowded in its descent from Film City on the way to Goregao station. At the station, Parvati gets into the women's compartment in the chocolate-brown suburban train, already full if it is coming from the end of the line, still with space to sit on the hard wooden seats if it started at Borivali. Although free from harassment, there is no escaping the pushing and shoving. Every day she finds a bruise inflicted by someone's elbow, a scratch caused by a stranger's umbrella, a tear in her sari from a vendor's basket. Bodies are pressed so tightly together that there are even stories of people having sexual intercourse unperceived by those standing next to them.

Past the buffalo-sheds at Jogeshwari and the feral stench of the sleek black animals which provide milk to the privileged of the city; past the airport at Santa Cruz, where the planes come in from the Gulf with their cargo of labour, miraculously missing the high-tension cables above the slums; down to Bandra, where the old colonial bungalows are being sold off for the construction of ten-storey luxury flats and where the waters of the Arabian Sea glint, cobalt and silver, a mixture of clear morning light and industrial poisons.

Parvati holds her breath as the train rattles over Mahim Creek, trying not to inhale the stench of glassy black water and the mangroves that are being eaten by teak-fly. A red sun appears over the new bridge, innocent as yet of the intensity with which its glare will later fill the city. Next is Dadar, the heartland of Hindu fundamentalism, then the desolate area of Lower Parel, its mills fallen into ruin and monsoon creepers growing into the empty cavities of the broken windows. On to Bombay Central, where travellers and derelicts sleep on the stone floor of the station.

Grant Road follows, where prostitutes from all over South Asia stand in the doorways of the brothels in lime-green and scarlet saris, combing their long hair; where the Jain diamond-merchants make and lose fortunes each day; where the facade of the Opera House conceals no longer the plush seats for colonial exiles dressing up to see a third-rate touring company perform *The Barber of Seville,* but a poor, houseless humanity sleeping under rags.

Then the open vista of Marine Drive; the expanse of Chowpatti Beach, cleared in the morning of its hucksters, masseurs and tellers of fortunes; the burning grounds of Charni Road, where the acrid smoke of banyan wood from last night's cremations lingers; and finally into Churchgate station. There, the crowd moves like a single living thing.

All these things Parvati notices and does not notice. She has seen them every day for ten years. She climbs into the battered red-painted double-decker bus, which takes her past the Victorian architecture of the Raj, the Law Courts and University, past the posh Art Deco flats bordering the *maidan,* down to Colaba. The bus drops her outside the extensive apartment block of a Parsee housing society.

Her duties among the elderly Parsees she serves are repetitive. She can do them without thinking: cleaning floors, washing vessels, shopping for the old woman who can no longer go out. Her mind runs on her anxieties for the family and on the tasks that wait for her at home. She wonders whether she will get a seat in the train back to Goregao, or if she will fall asleep standing up, rocked by the movement of the tightly packed compartment.

Parvati works two hours a day in each of four houses, and earns 200 rupees a month at each house. The train fare costs 100 rupees a month and the bus half as much again. All of this has been added to her costs since she and the rest of Sanjay Gandhi Nagar were evicted from this area ten years ago. An hour and a half each way, sometimes two hours – time erased from life. Over a period of ten years, that represents several months in a train or bus, day and night.

After work, she may visit her husband. He is now living with his brother in Colaba, looked after by his brother's wife. He was an electrician, but can no longer work. One day, drilling a wall for some wiring, he fell from the ladder. He lost consciousness and it has never entirely returned to him.

Parvati came to Mumbai from Bidar in Karnataka to get married. She is a dignified woman, not crushed by adversity, but tired from a life of insecurity and servitude. Her employers are reasonable; sometimes they give her food and clothing; but no-one has ever wondered where she lives, or what her life is; nor has anyone observed the exhaustion with which she begins her daily work.

She is, after all, a servant. The rest is of no concern of those who pay her. P Sebastian, a human-rights lawyer who has been involved with Sanjay Gandhi

Nagar, points out: 'If you ask the rich where their servants stay, they will say they do not know. They know. They do know. But they won't say. They won't say, because it is the rich who create the slums they deplore. They employ human beings to do their work, but what they really want is machines. They will not pay enough for people to afford decent housing. What is intolerable is to say that they are criminals who have dirtied Bombay. I say to them: "Those criminals are in your houses, doing your work, looking after your children, cooking the food you eat." The rich are adept at rationalizing the injustice they do. To get servants at that salary, you must have slums.'

There are two common responses to the urban poor. The first is the belief that slums are concentrations of a dangerous and volatile population, who must be controlled and rigorously policed. This attitude echoes the revulsion of the middle classes at the slums in Britain in the early industrial era. It lives on, not only in the attitude of the rich in the South today, but also in the response of governments and administrators who are charged with running the cities.

The poor, goes this refrain, are criminals, prostitutes and thieves.

The second response holds that the city slums are communities of hard-working people, whose self-help, endurance and capacity for survival are a source of inspiration. This second view is far closer to the truth, as the interviews in this magazine show. Most people who live in slums may be exploited but they are resourceful and hard-working; their homes are emphatically not places of despair and demoralization. The word 'slum' tells us something of the living conditions, but nothing about the qualities of the people themselves.

Many governments in Asia, Africa and South America are currently implementing 'structural-adjustment programmes', economic reforms that follow the prescriptions of the IMF and World Bank. Global integration is the name of the game. This means embarking on programmes of liberalization and privatization. It also entails deep cuts in government expenditure; not on arms, because that would run counter to Western interests, but on social spending – nutrition programmes, education, health and welfare.

This has led to a change – from earlier repressive reactions to the urban poor to a policy of a benign neglect. If the people can help themselves, if they are self-reliant and generate their own employment, what need is there for government intervention? Their welfare can be turned over to private interests and they can be safely left to get on with seeking their own salvation. It is now clear that they are not going to rise up and dispossess the rich of their privilege. For generations, the urban poor have been regarded with a watchful and apprehensive eye by the authorities; but they have, for the most part, inserted themselves into the city economy and found a place, however precarious, in the existing order. In India, certainly, they have not risen up in revolt. The State can disengage and leave them to the mercy of market forces.

Most of the people who live in slums are in any case used to managing by themselves, through their own efforts. From the slums of Mumbai come some of the most beautiful artefacts imaginable – jewellery, pottery, glassware, carved woodwork, metal and precious stones, fabrics and clothing, although those who actually produce them rarely receive anything like the value of their work.

Parvati's only saleable commodity is her own domestic labour. Returning home in the evening, Parvati ponders how much has changed since the people of Sanjay Gandhi Nagar were forced to move here from the site in the centre of the city almost ten years ago. Then, she would not have had the long journey to work as employment was on her doorstep. But on the other hand, things were much less secure.

Sanjay Gandhi Nagar now has some assurance that its people will not be evicted. As a result the surroundings of the slum are different from a decade ago. The area around it is busier – permanent stores, shops, little restaurants have replaced the rough wooden stalls, though on the margin of the road fruit and vegetable sellers still provide daily necessities.

The quarry is now semi-solid with waste: plastic bags, old shoes, all the indestructible offal of industrial society simmers in a swamp covered with a bloom of vivid green algae. Separated from the built area by rusty barbed wire, people use it as a garbage dump.

The little streets are neat; the interior of most houses is clean. But there has been little improvement in the public spaces. Waste water still meanders in an indigo stream that empties into the former quarry. A second garbage dump on the other edge of the slum attracts swarms of flies, performing their black and silver dance above the vegetable waste. Mosquitoes are a constant nuisance: a recent outbreak of cerebral malaria in Thane, about 20 kilometres away, has frightened some people. The municipality has been using a pesticide, a liquid that turns the muddy water a milky grey.

The public latrines are close to the houses. There are few growing things – some medicinal herbs, a tulsi-plant in a thin strip of earth around the walls. But the houses are well spaced: a hectare for 300 families; an area open in the centre of the slum, where the coloured kites of children get entangled in the electricity wires that loop in sagging skeins from building to building. The electricity itself is unreliable; many connections have been illegally made, although the Residents' Association pays for what is used by collecting from

the people. Even after so many years it still has the air of an improvised settlement: rocky, barren, unbearably hot in its exposure to the sun. All around,
ominously, middle-class flats have been constructed.

But, like Parvati, most people feel that their lives have improved much in
the last decade. Her five children are grown up now and there is the prospect
of increased income from their work. Parvati's first son had to leave school at
the age of 11, to contribute to the family income. He worked at Sassoon Dock
in Colaba. His task was to empty the catch from the fishing-nets into machines
that would sort and grade the fish. One day, the net caught in the machinery
and his arm dragged with it. The arm was severed. He is now 19, getting the
schooling that was denied him as a child. Since he became disabled, he has
been painting with his good arm. A picture of his – some palm trees along the
shore and the sea – has been fixed to the wall of the house where they live.

Parvati's oldest daughter is married. Her second, Mahedevi, is a capable
and serious-minded 17-year-old. She is training as a diamond-polisher. After
six months, she has every chance of getting a secure, well-paid job. From
domestic labour to diamonds in one generation, thinks Parvati; and her heart
is filled with hope. ∎

The distinguished British writer and social commentator **Jeremy Seabrook** *is a regular
contributor to the* **NI**. *Among his many books are* The No-Nonsense Guide to
Caste, Class and Hierarchies *(NI/Verso 2002) and* Children of Other Worlds
(Pluto 2001).

March 1999
Calvin Klein and the tea pickers
What exactly is poverty? **Mari Marcel Thekaekara** *travels from south India to
Scotland and Germany in pursuit of an answer.*

'Are you rich or poor?' my 11-year-old daughter Tahira was asked by her
British cousin Leila. 'We're not exactly poor,' Tahira replied hesitantly. 'But
we're not rich either.'

'That's silly', Leila persisted, 'you must be one or the other.'

'Compared to the *adivasi* (tribal) kids at home we're rich,' Tahira
explained, 'but compared to our cousins in America we're poor.'

The conversation that followed was even more intriguing.

'Do you have a car?'

'No. But we can use the project jeep if we need it.'

'Do you have TV?'

'No. But my Gran does. We watch hers.'

'Do you have Calvin Klein jeans?'

Tahira didn't know much about jeans then. But she had fairly smart hand-me-downs from her American cousins.

To little Leila, the entire thing was bizarre. In her mind, the divide between rich and poor was absolutely clear. There was no middle path.

Throughout our visit to Britain, our concepts of wealth and poverty continued to be challenged, juxtaposed as the trip was with our experiences of ten years of working with *adivasis* [indigenous people] in the Nilgiri mountains of Tamil Nadu.

Years ago I heard a Frenchman say 'I'd rather be poor in India'. And I thought: 'What utter crap.' How typical. Romanticizing India, poverty and all.

Then, in 1994, as part of a North-South exchange, my husband Stan and I came to Britain, to visit housing estates in inner-city England and Scotland. The idea was to bring over ideas about social change in India and also to reverse the usual stereotypical image of a Northern aid worker coming to help the Third World.

We were told that Easterhouse housing estate in Glasgow is considered Europe's worst slum. We thought this was ludicrous. These people had assured housing, electricity, hot and cold water, refrigerators, gas or electric cooking ranges. By Indian standards this was middle-class luxury. At the back of my mind, I could see anaemic, emaciated adivasi women carrying water in pots from half a kilometre away. Huts without electricity. Women searching for firewood every day, thankful if they had a kilo of rice to feed their families every evening.

But then, suddenly, it hit us. Most of the men in Easterhouse hadn't had a job in 20 years. They were dispirited, depressed, often alcoholic. Their self-esteem had gone. Emotionally and mentally they were far worse off than the poor where we lived, even though the physical trappings of poverty were less stark.

We'd fallen into the trap of looking at poverty only from the point of view of material benefits. The Easterhouse people looked better off than the Asian poor. In reality they suffered as much social deprivation. The Easterhouse men who'd been jobless for 20 years felt far more hopeless than people in India who scrabbled in garbage heaps to sell scrap metal, paper and rags to feed their kids, though both groups were at the bottom of society. This was considered an absolutely outrageous suggestion by critics of our report.

We met young people who struggled to get a job knowing their addresses and accents were not exactly an asset. Women who couldn't fill in forms and were ashamed of the fact. In Dudley, social worker Viv Taylor helped a youngster get a decent jacket, the only really suitable outfit he possessed, to go off for an interview. He'd been ashamed to tell her this so his mother had secretly called Viv for help. It was heart-warming to hear about his jubilation when he actually got the job and set off for work. But the story reminded us of our teachers finding clothes for adivasi kids who had nothing to wear and so couldn't go to school.

We didn't encounter hostility or racism from the poor of Easterhouse or Dudley. Nor in Matson in Gloucester where Stan later spent a month as part of an Oxfam programme. But we did run into massive criticism, both hostile and racist, from the local press. 'Can Oxfam spot the difference?' ran one press clipping showing a skeletal, starving African child juxtaposed with a bunch of healthy British kids. Bob Holman, writer, social worker and our host in Easterhouse, had shown us underdeveloped Scottish children. A whole generation were growing up a head shorter, smaller than their parents and grandparents. But malnutrition in Britain! Even we were amazed. Lack of protein was a Third World problem, surely. Yet the examples were there. And to change these perceptions in people who were determined not to see them was incredibly difficult.

Interestingly, poor people themselves often spot the similarities immediately. They see beyond the physical differences and empathize with each other. Which brings them closer to each other than to the rich of their respective countries who at best can only sympathize with them.

It occurred to us then that even people working in development talked about wealth and poverty using a very narrow definition. We use cash as the sole measure. I've often read articles implying someone was destitute because they earned only a dollar a day. In India (and in other parts of the world, I imagine) a dollar a day would be a decent wage for a poor person. Whereas a North American or European would consider it shockingly little.

Most of us fall into the trap of working towards alleviating physical poverty thinking this is the solution to all ills. Economic prosperity, wealth, better incomes are put forward as ideals to aspire to. Yet paradoxically, at a totally different level, we attack the wave of consumerism which seems to engulf everyone, rich and poor.

In 1995, the adivasis took the challenge further. At a meeting to look critically at the last ten years, the adivasis were clear about their own notions of wealth: 'Our community, our children, our unity, our culture, the forest.' Money was not mentioned at all. We, the non-adivasis in the team, were stunned.

As we discussed concepts of poverty further, we realized that the adivasis didn't see themselves as poor. They saw themselves as people without money. It took a little bit of concentrated thinking for me to absorb that this was not necessarily the same thing.

Some other things happened to turn our stereotypical concepts on their heads. Community Aid Abroad approached us to invite a group of Aboriginal Australians to visit. Our people were shocked beyond words by the Australian stories, of children wrenched from their families, of the treatment meted out to them. Some of the visitors had personal experiences to recount. They themselves had been torn from their parents as kids and sent to white people's homes or institutions. For months afterwards, the adivasis talked about the visitors. 'Poor people, how they've suffered,' they said. 'Our problems are nothing compared to what they've been through.'

A poverty-stricken Indian saying 'poor thing' to an Australian might strike an outsider as slightly ironic, but the experience was even more surreal when we visited Germany. There had been a six-year ongoing link between a group of German students and our project. So in 1997, when six adivasis were invited to Germany, the visit generated excitement along with a great deal of trepidation. For the adivasis, this was a very big first. A pretty big plunge from their forest, mountain, village world into super-developed Germany. We wondered how they'd cope with the sudden exposure to great material wealth straight after stark poverty.

Their reactions amazed me. I realized later that what made their observations different was the fact that they did not look at the West as a kind of Mecca where you would find everything material you seek. This is in complete contrast to most other visitors who go there either as immigrants or tourists but always with shopping lists. The adivasis didn't hanker after German goodies. 'It's very nice to be here,' Chathi, one of the six, told me. 'But I couldn't live here. It's not my place. A man needs his family, his community, his own people around him. Just money can't give you a life. You'd shrivel up and die.'

They were speechless when they saw an old people's home. The concept was totally alien to them. 'How can children send their old parents to live alone?' they eventually asked in wonder. And later, in a meeting, Radhakrishnan, another of the six, solemnly resolved: 'We must ensure that such things never happen in our society, no matter how much we progress.'

Like Stan and me in Easterhouse, the adivasis were shocked at the spectre of unemployment which haunted some of our young German friends. They were particularly upset when Karl, whose commune home they lived in, came back stressed by the news that he might soon become redundant. Bomman worried all night about his friend. In the morning he announced: 'I have an idea. I can make bamboo flutes in Gudalur and Karl can sell them here till he finds a job.'

He did too. And though Karl did not lose his job after all, Bomman's concern was profoundly moving to everyone who saw it. That Bomman didn't feel at all poverty-stricken was evident to all of us, though by the standards of Karl's family, he definitely was.

German friends gave the group warm clothes and gifts for their families. They were happy to bring back presents for their children. But paradoxically, (because of our concern about the possible effect of a consumerist onslaught) the gift that Bomman and the adivasis valued most from Germany was that everyone treated them with respect and dignity. As equals. It was a terrible indictment of Indian society. And I was filled with shame at the realization that they'd experienced more respect and egalitarianism in a month in Germany than in their whole lives in India.

For us the whole visit was an exercise in humility which made us stop and think. It struck me forcibly that the only way to change stereotypes is to come face to face with people. In London, friends said 'Easterhouse! God, you've been going places! Wouldn't like my car to break down there.'

The Easterhouse people were lovely. We really enjoyed meeting them. This is not an attempt to romanticize the problem, but merely to state that stereotypes are equally ridiculous. I'm aware that meeting a neo-Nazi or a Chicago gangster on a dark, lonely night could have the effect of liberating you from all your earthly problems altogether; more instantaneously than you'd care to go.

The different visits also had unexpected spin-offs. Gudalur, in the Nilgiri mountains of south India, is tea country. In Gloucester, people drink tons of tea, paying three times the necessary price. The Gudalur adivasis produce tons of tea getting a third of the consumer price. Why not send our tea directly to Matson? And to friends in Germany and other parts of India...

In addition, the adivasis' visit to Germany gave them new confidence when it came to challenging the transnational companies who had evicted them from land they had owned for generations. Bomman, fresh from his overseas visit, stood in the village square and delivered an impassioned speech.

'This is a company controlling thousands of hectares. Yet they are not ashamed to evict poor adivasis who have under a quarter of a hectare of tea. Unilever is very powerful. But the days when adivasis were totally powerless are over. We now have friends in Germany and UK. We've met people working for Fair Trade. If we tell them what Unilever is doing here they will start a campaign to inform all the people of Europe to stop buying Unilever tea. They will fight on our side. We are no longer alone.'

Unilever backed off. The global links between people usually considered poor and therefore powerless had made a difference. To use Stan's favourite slogan, 'If there has to be globalization, let's create a world of our own choosing!' ∎

Mari Marcel Thekaekara has worked since 1982 on a project she and her husband started for adivasis in the south Indian state of Tamil Nadu.

2

Join the resistance: key campaigns

THE *New Internationalist*'s first campaign was also its most celebrated: the August 1973 issue highlighting corporations' marketing of artificial baby food to mothers in developing countries. Such marketing often persuades mothers to opt for milk powder instead of breastfeeding – yet mixing the powder with local water threatens their babies' lives. The **NI** has returned consistently to the topic and helped launch the boycott of Nestlé, one of the worst corporate offenders. Despite the establishment by the UN in 1981 of an International Code, the marketing of infant formula continues – and to this day many of the magazine's readers shun Nescafé and hundreds of other Nestlé products in protest.[1]

Another issue which had a major influence was the one from 1982 whose cover carried a poignant photo of a boy framed by the lines: 'Please do not sponsor this child: there are better ways to help.' Peter Stalker's thoughtful, coherent case caused a storm – but it also helped to change aid agencies' thinking. Some charities have since forsworn child sponsorship altogether while others are now much more careful about their practice of it – channeling funds into the whole community, for example, rather than giving all the benefits to one child. But other agencies have been impervious to criticism and many of the points made back in 1982 still need making today.

The **NI** has been like a dog with a bone in its challenge to the 'structural adjustment' policies imposed on poor countries by the World Bank and the IMF. The magazine is a small part of a worldwide campaign which has recently wrung from the World Bank at least a partial acknowledgment that its policies over two decades have been disastrous.

Two campaigns on particular countries stand out: East Timor, which has happily won its independence since John Pilger's powerful magazine; and Iraq, where we highlighted the damage done by UN sanctions, little knowing that three years later the US and Britain would be preparing for full-scale war. ■

1 Contact your local campaign via the International Baby Food Action Network, www.ibfan.org

August 1973
The baby food tragedy
Peter Adamson's editorial in an issue that helped launch a worldwide campaign.

On the cover of this issue is a photograph of grave number 19232. It is the grave of a Zambian baby. On it, the mother has placed a feeding bottle and an empty tin of milk powder. They are symbols of infant death and of the mother's attempt to do her best for her child during its short life. What the mother does not know is that the way in which she used that same milk powder and feeding bottle was also the main cause of her baby's death.

This mother is not to blame. The baby milk and feeding bottle were perhaps recommended or even given to her by a nurse in the maternity hospital. She was not to know that the nurse was employed by a baby food company. Or she may have seen one of the many large hoarding boards in the town showing a healthy robust baby sitting next to a tin of powdered baby milk and she may have gone out and spent a large fraction of her family's small income on buying this product in the belief that it would make her baby like the one in the advertisement. She was not to know that her own breast milk was better, cheaper and safer than anything she could buy in a tin. She may have mixed the milk powder with too much water to make it go further because she could not afford another tin that week. But she could not read the instructions on the back of the tin, nor work out the correct proportions. Or she may not have boiled the milk or sterilized the feeding bottle. But she did not fully understand that these processes are essential. And she probably did not have cold running water to cool the bottle even if she had been able to boil it.

She did what she thought best and could little afford. But her baby drank over-diluted feed and so became malnourished. Malnourishment lowered the baby's resistance to disease – which was always threatening from the unsterile bottle. Disease prevented the baby from benefiting even from the diluted milk powder. And so a vicious circle set in. Gradually the baby lost weight, shrivelled up like a little old man, and died.

Had that dead child survived, he or she would now be one of 200 million children growing up physically and mentally stunted by malnutrition. For the wrong food in the wrong quantities in the vital early months of life can and does inflict irreparable damage on both body and brain.

Anything which can lead to further malnutrition in young babies is a tragedy – for the children themselves, for their families, for their nation, and for the whole process of development which they can neither fully benefit from nor contribute to.

In this issue, two leading child nutrition experts give evidence that the inappropriate promotion and consequent misuse of artificial baby milk in poor and often illiterate communities is leading directly to an increase in infant malnutrition. They tell of techniques of baby-milk selling, including the use of irresponsible advertising and the employment of nurses as sales-girls, which in the context of poverty are disastrous and dishonest.

We must accept that research into the effects of artificial feeding in the poor world is recent and incomplete. We must accept that it takes time for companies to respond to new findings with new policies. We must accept that in many situations baby-milk companies can and do play a vital humanitarian role. But we must not accept the creation of more malnutrition for the sake of commercial gain by the selling of artificial baby milk to mothers who do not need it, cannot afford it, and are not able to safely use it.

The International Organization of Consumer Unions has prepared a draft code of practice for the promotion of infant foods in developing countries. It stipulates that no food should be advertised as suitable for a baby of three months or less; that no claim shall be made which will in any way encourage the mother not to breastfeed her baby; that instructions for the use of artificial milk should be both clear and feasible in the context of the community to which it is sold; that photographs of babies must not be used in advertisements in a way which might mislead a mother as to the likely benefits of the food; and that all persons selling baby food direct to mothers should be licensed to do so by the national health authorities.

There is no time for fiddling while children starve. There is urgent need for:
1 The ratification of such a code of practice by a consensus of expert opinion.
2 The strict observation of the new code by all baby-food companies and its strict enforcement by all governments of developing countries.
3 A stepping up of research into the effects of artificial baby foods in poor communities.
4 A new international campaign to encourage mothers to breastfeed their babies wherever possible.

The initiative for such action could come from a number of different sources. As it concerns food it is the responsibility of the Food and Agriculture Organization; as it concerns health it is the responsibility of the World Health Organization; as it concerns children it is the responsibility of UNICEF; as it concerns their products and exports it is the responsibility of the baby-food companies and their governments; as it concerns their future generations it is the responsibility of Third World governments.

But neither is there time for buck-passing. The *New Internationalist* will therefore be submitting evidence to all these bodies and reporting back on their reactions. ■

May 1982

Please do not sponsor this child

There are better ways to help.

Sponsorship of Third World children has now become a major fundraising tool for voluntary agencies; it is a sure-fire way to attract money. But it is not such a good way to spend it. **Peter Stalker** *argues that there are better ways to help.*

One million 'foster parents' in the West are now sponsoring children in the Third World – each giving around $20 a month – in what has become an extraordinary international exchange.

This is a very 'personal' form of giving – and from the outset the needs of the individual donor are taken into account. Advertisements for Save the Children in the US offer the prospective parent a long series of multiple choices. You check one box to choose the sex of your child and then another for their location or race. After this, as with most of the organizations, you get a child 'on approval' – with a photograph and a case history. If you accept, the process starts; you send your monthly aid and get letters from the child of your choice.

The appeal of all this is almost irresistible, and it is hardly surprising that this is one of the fastest-growing sources of money for voluntary agencies. The organizations concerned – like Foster Parents Plan[1] and World Vision – are expanding rapidly.

There can be no doubt about the good intentions of most of the donors. They wish to help identifiable individuals and hope to learn more about the places where their money is being used. It is a more attractive proposition than working through a conventional aid agency, which might fund a thousand projects from a central fund and appears much more impersonal.

Offering sponsorship is certainly an easier way to raise money. But is it a good way to spend it?

The most obvious disadvantage of such programmes is that they are expensive to run. The photographs, the monitoring of each family's progress and the translation of an endless flow of letters – all cost money. And that means the people that you want to help will get less.

But most donors will be aware of this and probably accept it as the price of the service they are receiving. What they may not realize is that in almost every other way in which the donor is better off through a sponsorship scheme, the sponsored child or family is correspondingly worse off.

Take the instant appeal of helping one person. The children do of course exist as individuals. But they are also part of a family, a village or a school. My first contact with the sponsorship phenomenon was in a children's home in Colombia. Ten-year-old Jose wanted me to organize a foster parent for him. Most of his friends had sponsors and he hadn't. In the fiercely competitive world of childhood he was dependent on the charity of the more fortunate children – which meant that he only got the teddy bears when the ears had been pulled off.

Helping an individual is divisive – and is particularly damaging in societies which are already sharply divided in all sorts of ways: rich and poor, black and white, high caste or low caste, literate or illiterate.

Nor is trying to help an individual likely to succeed. Catapulting even one person out of poverty is a daunting task – especially on $20 a month. And while there will be some successes they will be few and far between. Most of the poor (*harijan* children in India for example) have the odds stacked against them. And unless you do something about changing the odds they will not stand much of a chance,

Another disadvantage of being in contact with just one person is that they are also in intimate contact with you. Manuel, the little boy on the front cover of this magazine, lives in a squalid slum on the edge of a Latin American city. The regular letters he gets from his sponsoring family give accounts of their interesting lives – of ski-ing holidays in Austria, for example. For the European family this correspondence might offer an interesting educational experience for their own children. What Manuel gets from it, apart from a vague feeling of inferiority, is much less clear.

Many donors would try to avoid being so insensitive in their letters. But, no matter how much care you take, things can be read into the letters, even when they are not the writer's mind. One of my most depressing experiences in Peru recently was talking to a 16-year-old girl who was living in the most appalling conditions of poverty and overcrowding. She honestly believed that some day her sponsor, who lived in Toronto, was going to invite her to go and live there. When I asked her for more details she was a lot less sure. One of the younger children in the house had run off with all the letters and lost them. Now she could not quite remember what had been said.

Creating this kind of empty aspiration is the other side of the 'educational' coin. The donor may gain but the foster child loses.

Not that the donor gains all that much. Few of the letters that they are likely to receive are going to be strong on information. Manuel's response to the ski-ing family was:

Dear foster parent,
I write to let you know that I am well. I'm getting ahead in my classes and hope
to be a professional in the future to visit your country. My parents are very grate-
ful for your nice aid. Warm greetings from my dear brother Segundo. He likes to
play marbles. I say goodbye with much love…

Most of the letters come from small children so their limited content is not too surprising. But the letters are also censored as they pass through translation so that controversial items, such as criticisms of the aid agency or political comment are edited out.

Also edited out are appeals for more money. Giving to one person means that the sponsored children are correspondingly receiving from just one person who is clearly much richer than they are, Not surprisingly many of the recipients feel that they could put up a good case for more money.

Indeed sponsorship in general plays up the 'aid' side of development. Using outside aid to promote self-reliance is something of a contradiction, but one which many of the Western donor agencies manage to live with by keeping a low profile. The recipients can be so bound up with their own lives and the work of the project that they may not even be aware that there is much outside funding, let alone where it is coming from. Placing the weight of sponsorship on any project is bound to restrain the enthusiasm: there's nothing like writing a regular thank-you letter to keep you in your place.

But ironically the sponsors are giving money in this way precisely because they think it is more useful: there seems less likelihood that the money will go astray. And it is true that the sponsorship agencies maintain a small army of social workers who travel round keeping tabs on the families and looking at how the money is used.

But is this more reliable than simply making a grant say, to a Gandhian organization in India? This is doubtful. Having so many supervisory staff is in itself a potential source of misuse. Favouritism between the social workers – who usually come from the local community – and certain families is not unknown, and nor is dishonesty. Sponsorship agencies are no more open to abuse than other organizations, but there is no reason to suppose that they are any less so.

There is, however, a more significant consequence of building up a supervisory system. The agency becomes a local 'institution'. In sensitive situations – and that means almost everywhere in the Third World – this is no small disadvantage.

In fact, one of the greatest advantages that voluntary aid usually has over government aid is that it is lighter on its feet. Small groups can be funded here and there as the opportunities crop up. But the sponsorship agencies in many ways forego this advantage. They are rooted in one place and need to be on good terms with the local authorities if their system is to work. And this restricts the kinds of project that can be funded.

El Salvador is an extreme example. Most organizations feel that they can no longer carry out effective development work there – indeed many of the people involved in their projects have now been slaughtered by the military. Foster Parents Plan, however, has had no such problems and is proud of the fact that its programme is still running.

But if you need to be inoffensive to the powers-that-be, the chances of promoting constructive change are not high. And for any donor worried about getting value for money that should be a matter of some concern,

We quote the case of Chimbote in Peru later in this magazine. The families sponsored were often workers in the local fish-canning factories and the exploitation there was a significant contribution to their children's poverty. More relevant than the welfare programmes that the sponsored families were getting might have been legal support to press for better working conditions. But that would have made them unpopular in certain quarters. Alleviating the problems of the poor is one thing. But solving them involves much more difficult choices.

Yet solutions are more and more what the sponsorship agencies claim to be offering. 'Community development' is the cover-all catch phrase. Housing programmes, irrigation schemes, health services or making handicrafts – these have now been moved to the centre of the publicity platform. And all, of course, are activities that any agency could become involved with. Yet like the word 'aid' itself, community development is an umbrella that can cover a multitude of intentions and effects. An irrigation ditch dug in one place can help a whole community grow more food. Dug in another it can so increase the value of the land that the poor can no longer afford to farm it – and have to join the ranks of the landless.

Everything depends on how the programme is designed and on the political consequence that it has; to say that you are involved in community development is not enough. The intended impact has to be carefully chosen – and the sponsorship agencies are not in a position to make the best choice.

Some sponsorship agencies would even claim that they are 'non-political', though in this context that would only mean that they have very little impact at all. But that might be better than nothing. And it is argued that there are people who give to sponsorship agencies who would give on no other terms. So no matter how defective the aid might be it could have some role to play. Sometimes there could be enough benefits to set against the negative impact of sponsorship but there are too many cases where the best thing that the sponsor could do is keep their $20.

What is certain is that there are better ways to help. The organizations without the sponsorship burdens have much sharper and more cost-effective operations. And they have no shortage of programmes that help children: in nutrition, in education or in health.

You may get a less direct satisfaction – no letters, no thank-yous. But the people who do get the satisfaction are the people who matter. ∎

1 Now known as Plan International.

March 1994
East Timor: a land of crosses
A great silence has accompanied the Indonesian occupation of East Timor.
John Pilger reports on the betrayal of a courageous people.

Crosses are almost everywhere in East Timor: great black crosses etched against the sky, crosses on peaks, crosses in tiers on hillsides, crosses at almost every bend of the road. They litter the earth and crowd the eye.

I had with me a hand-drawn map of where to find a mass grave where some of the murdered of the 1991 massacre in the Santa Cruz cemetery had been buried; I had no idea that so much of the country was a mass grave, marked by paths that end abruptly and fields inexplicably bulldozed, and earth inexplicably covered with tarmac; and by the legions of crosses that march all the way from Tata Mai Lau, the highest peak, 10,000 feet above sea level, down to Lake Tacitolu on its Calvary line of crosses that looks across to where the Pope said mass in 1989 in full view of a crescent of hard, salt sand beneath which lie countless human remains.

All the time film director David Munro and I were in East Timor we felt we were on borrowed time. We had only an aeronautical map, with blank spaces. The Indonesian military knew the roads and we didn't. At first, as our four-wheel-drive vehicle edged along perilous roads, people seemed absent; but they were there. At the end of a long ravine was a village, from which people emerged slowly and with unsmiling, diffident expressions.

The village straddled the road, laid out like a military barracks with a parade ground and a police post at either end; and the inevitable crosses. It was a 'resettlement centre'. To the Timorese, these are little better than concentration camps. 'It is difficult to describe the darkness over us,' said Antonio (a pseudonym). 'Since the invasion, of fifteen in my immediate family, only three are left: myself, my mother and a brother who was shot. My village was the last Fretilin base to fall in 1979. The estimate is that our clan has been reduced from 5,000 to 500.

'Up until 1985 or 1986 most of the people were concentrated in what they called the "central control areas", in concentration camps. Only in the last three years have some of us been allowed to return home, but we can be moved again at any time. The Indonesians use spies everywhere; and certain things are not to be said, even within the family. People have to pretend that everything is okay. That is part of finding a way to survive. But a human body and mind have limitations. Once it boils over, people just come out and protest and say things which means they'll wake up dead the next day. I suppose you can compare us to animals. When animals are put in a cage they always try to escape. In human beings it's much worse. You must understand that for us who live here, it's hell.'

A silence has enveloped East Timor since the Indonesian invasion in December 1975. The basic facts ought to be well known, but they are not. As a direct result of the invasion some 200,000 people, or a third of the population, have died. This estimate was made in 1983 by the head of the Roman Catholic Church in East Timor. What in other countries would be condemned as a crime against humanity has, it seems, been quietly deemed acceptable.

Proportionately, not even Pol Pot in Cambodia killed as many people; yet Western intelligence has documented the unfolding of the genocide since the first Indonesian paratroopers landed in the capital, Dili, on 7 November 1975 – less than two months after two Australian television crews were murdered by Indonesian troops, leaving just one foreign reporter, Roger East, to witness the invasion. He became the sixth journalist to die, shot through the head with his hands tied behind his back and his body thrown into the sea. Thus, in the age of television, hardly a single image or a reported word reached the outside world. There was just one radio voice, picked up in Darwin, 300 miles to the south, rising and falling in the static. 'The soldiers are killing indiscriminately,' it said. 'Women and children are being shot in the streets. We are all going to be killed... This is an appeal for international help. This is an SOS. We appeal to the Australian people. Please help us...'

No help came. Tens of thousands of people died just resisting the invasion. 'I was the CIA desk officer in Jakarta at that time,' Philip Liechty told me, 'I saw the intelligence that came from firm sources. There were people being herded into school buildings by Indonesian soldiers and the buildings set on fire; anyone trying to get out was shot. There were people herded into fields and machine-gunned. We knew the place was a free-fire zone. None of that got out.'

There was little verifiable news for two years. In 1977 two nuns in Lisbon received a letter from a priest in hiding in East Timor. 'The invaders,' he wrote, 'have intensified their attacks. The bombers do not stop all day. Hundreds die every day. The bodies of the victims become food for carnivorous birds. Villages have been completely destroyed. The barbarities, understandable in the Middle Ages, justifiable in the Stone Age, all the organized evil, have spread deep roots in Timor. The terror of arbitrary imprisonment is our daily bread. I am on the *persona non grata* list and any day I could disappear. Genocide will come soon...'

On 12 November 1991 a brave British cameraman, Max Stahl (a pseudonym) videotaped Indonesian troops murdering a crowd of young people in the Santa Cruz cemetery in Dili. This broke the silence. Some, like Australian Foreign Affairs Minister Gareth Evans, one of the Indonesian regime's most reliable friends, sought to explain away the massacre – which had left 528 people dead and 'disappeared' – as an 'aberration'. But such apologetics were undermined by the reaction of Indonesia's senior military officer who said he wished to 'wipe out' more 'delinquents', and by international revulsion at the visual evidence of wounded, helpless people dying among the gravestones.

The history of East Timor is very different from that of the other islands that make up the volcanic stepping stones, rising from clear deep seas, east of Bali. The Suharto regime has tried to justify its illegal occupation on the grounds of what it calls 'deeply felt and long-standing ties... of common brotherhood'. In fact, the East Timorese have little in common with Indonesia and especially the Javanese who rule it. Whereas most Indonesians are Muslims, Hindu or Buddhist, the East Timorese are animist or Catholic. Even their colonial experience was different, with the Portuguese 'Latinizing' the eastern half of the island and insulating it from the upheavals of the Dutch colonies, including West Timor, that became Indonesia in 1949.

Portuguese rule was benign, neglectful and, as in other Portuguese colonies, multi-racial. Not even the Catholic Church, it seems, resorted to forced conversion, which perhaps explains why Christian and animist beliefs and prejudices coexist with harmony. However, the Church, as elsewhere, ran the schools and created an élite indebted to its liturgy of power. This changed dramatically with the Indonesian invasion. An East Timorese church emerged which represented a direct challenge to the Indonesian occupation. Thus, the Church became, as the historian Peter Carey has written, 'the only institution capable of communicating independently with the outside world and of articulating the pain of the East Timorese people'. In 1989 Bishop Carlos Felipe Ximenes Belo, the head of the Catholic Church in East Timor, appealed directly to the world in a letter to the United Nations Secretary-General. 'We are dying as a people and as a Nation,' he wrote. He received no reply.

In April 1974 Portugal's old fascist order was swept aside by the *Revoluçao dos Cravos*, the 'Carnation Revolution'. Events in Lisbon moved quickly and chaotically. The tiny 'overseas province' of East Timor, 'asleep at the end of the earth', as one Portuguese commentator later wrote, 'was on no-one's list of priorities'. However, within a month of the revolution in Lisbon two main political groups had formed in East Timor. The Timorese Democratic Union (UDT), led by members of the colonial administrative élite and coffee-plantation owners, called for federation with Portugal and eventually independence. The Timorese Social Democratic Association (ASDT), which later became the Revolutionary Front for an Independent East Timor, or Fretilin, comprised most of the younger nationalist opposition who wanted genuine economic reforms.

The Indonesian military dictatorship claimed that Fretilin would turn East Timor into a base for communist insurgency, which was absurd. Most of Fretilin's leaders were Catholic socialists who looked to the Cape Verde philosopher Amilcar Cabral and the Brazilian priest and educator Paulo Freire. Above all, they were nationalists who wanted their people to control their own destiny, trade and resources.

Many of Fretilin's leaders were the sons of Timorese who had saved the lives of Australian soldiers fighting the Japanese in Timor during the Second World War and were confident that their former allies would discharge their moral debt, especially now that the inspiring anti-colonialist Gough Whitlam was prime minister. His Labor Government would surely support the rights of the people of East Timor. Australia had been among the first to recognize the former Portuguese colony of Guinea-Bissau; and Whitlam's personal relationship with Suharto suggested that his views would be taken seriously in Jakarta.

What the Fretilin leaders could not possibly measure was the depth and complexity of post-war Australia's obsession with Indonesia. In September 1974 Gough Whitlam met Suharto in Java. According to journalists briefed by Australian officials, Whitlam and Suharto 'agreed that the best and most realistic future for Timor was association with Indonesia', and that Whitlam had made clear that 'an independent Timor would be an unviable state and a potential threat to the area'.

In October of that year a clutch of generals close to Suharto launched a secret intelligence operation, code-named *Operasi Komodo*, aimed at destroying the burgeoning independence movement. A coalition formed by Fretilin and the UDT was undermined by Indonesian provocateurs and collaborators, leading to a civil war that claimed some 1,500 lives. By September 1975 Indonesian special forces had infiltrated the country; and their discovery by two Australian television crews, near the town of Balibo, resulted in the murder of the six newsmen.

The official Australian attitude to Indonesia was expressed by the ambassador in Jakarta, Richard Woolcott, who in July of that year cabled Canberra: '[We should] leave events to take their course... and act in a way which would be designed to minimize the public impact in Australia and show private understanding to Indonesia of their problems... I know I am recommending a pragmatic rather than a principled stand but that is what national interest and foreign policy is all about.'

On 28 November 1975 Fretilin – which had won the civil war and a majority in local elections – declared unilateral independence before a cheering crowd in Dili. One week later President Gerald Ford and his Secretary of State, Henry Kissinger, arrived in Jakarta on a visit described by a State Department official as 'the big wink'. The invasion had been set down for 5 December; but the Americans demanded that the Indonesians wait until after the President had left; and on 7 December, as Air Force One climbed out of Indonesian airspace, the bloodbath began.

The inhabitants of Dili were subjected to what the historian John Taylor has described as 'systematic killing, gratuitous violence and primitive plunder'. At 2pm on 9 December, 59 men were brought on to the wharf at Dili harbour and shot one by one, with the crowd ordered to count. The victims were ordered to stand on the edge of the pier facing the sea, so that when they were shot their bodies fell into the water. Earlier in the day, women and children were executed in a similar way. An eyewitness reported: 'The Indonesians tore the crying children from their mothers and passed them back to the crowd. The women were shot one by one.'

As in Pol Pot's Cambodia, the first to die were often the educated – public officials, nurses, teachers – and minorities. The Chinese population was singled out. Five hundred were reportedly killed on the first day of the attack. An eyewitness described how he and others were ordered to 'tie the bodies to iron poles, attach bricks and throw the bodies in the sea'. The killing of whole families and children appeared to be systematic. An officer explained: 'When you clean the field, don't you kill all the snakes, the small and large alike?'

The UN General Assembly and Security Council passed a total of 10 resolutions calling on Indonesia to withdraw its troops 'without delay'. Unlike the UN's resolve against Iraq's invasion of Kuwait in 1990, nothing happened. In a secret cable to Henry Kissinger, the US ambassador to the UN, Daniel Patrick Moynihan, boasted about the 'considerable progress' he had made in blocking UN action on East Timor. This, he explained, was part of 'a basic foreign-policy goal, that of breaking up the massive blocs of nations, mostly new nations, which for so long had been arrayed against us in international forums'.

Australian Prime Minister Malcolm Fraser, who had succeeded Whitlam, flew to Jakarta in October 1976 and gave the first public recognition of the Indonesian occupation. He said his Government 'acknowledged the merger' but 'only for purely humanitarian reasons'. Fraser was accompanied by the head of BHP, Australia's largest company. BHP had recently acquired a controlling share in the Woodside-Burmah company, which had been drilling for oil in the seabed off East Timor, said to contain one of the richest oil and gas fields in the world.

Western governments vied with each other to sympathize with 'Indonesia's problems' – and to sell Jakarta arms. In 1978, at the height of the massacres, British Foreign Secretary David Owen approved the sale of British Hawk ground-attack aircraft. He said estimates of the killings in East Timor had been 'exaggerated'. Britain is today the biggest arms supplier to the Indonesian military; in 1993 British Aerospace agreed a $1,200 million deal for more Hawk aircraft. A succession of ministers has misinformed Parliament that the Hawks would not and could not be used in East Timor. There is plenty of eyewitness testimony to the contrary. Max Stahl, David Munro and I have interviewed people who have seen the distinctive Hawk's devastating effect on the civilian population.

We also have evidence that the Indonesians conducted a second massacre following the killings in the Santa Cruz cemetery in 1991. In our film, *Death of a Nation: The Timor Conspiracy*, witnesses tell how Indonesian soldiers systematically murdered the wounded.

In 1989 Gareth Evans, Australian Foreign Minister, and the Indonesian Foreign Minister, Ali Alatas, toasted each other in champagne flying above the Timor Gap, having just signed a treaty that allowed Australian companies to drill for oil and gas. Professor Roger Clark, the world authority on international law at Rutgers University in the US, told me: 'It is acquiring stuff from a thief. If you acquire property from someone who stole it, you're a receiver.' Evans described the Indonesian enquiry into the Santa Cruz killings as 'positive and helpful' and 'very encouraging', adding that the victims unaccounted for 'might simply have gone bush'. Amnesty International dismissed the enquiry as lacking all credibility. On the day of Amnesty's condemnation further Timor Gap contracts were issued.

There have been some hopeful developments in the last year. An amendment to a Foreign Aid Bill before the US Congress calls on the President to 'consider' the human-rights situation in East Timor before approving arms sales to Indonesia. Meanwhile, the UN Human Rights Commission has voted to condemn Jakarta over East Timor; Portugal is taking action at the World Court in The Hague over the legality of the Timor Gap Treaty; a similar action is before the Australian High Court.

Jose Ramos Horta, the special representative of the National Council of Maubere Resistance – East Timor's foreign minister in exile – has put forward an imaginative three-phased peace plan which would lead to a referendum on the country's future. 'Indonesia,' he said, 'should seize the olive branch we are offering.' Peter Carey says Portugal could play a key role just as Britain did in the decolonization of Zimbabwe in 1979 and 1980. 'The first step,' he said, 'should be the withdrawal of all Indonesian troops... For the Government of Indonesia, it must be made clear that international respectability will elude them until after the East Timor issue is resolved.'

By all accounts the Timorese resistance should have been wiped out years ago; but it lives on, as I found, in the hearts and eyes of almost everyone: eyes that reflect a defiance and courage of a kind I have not experienced anywhere else. Recent opposition has come vociferously from the young generation, raised during Indonesian rule. It is they who have kept alive a nationalism that combines a political entity with a spiritual love of country and language that Indonesian terror and bans have only strengthened. And they have been able to endure, it must be said, by the lifeline provided by an extraordinary network of solidarity groups and exiled Timorese around the world.

In 1989 a courageous Australian woman called Shirley Shackleton managed to get to Balibo, the Timorese town where the Indonesians murdered her husband, Greg, with the other television news reporters. She had wanted to plant a tree in Greg's memory. A priest offered the yard behind his church; and Shirley planted the sapling with Indonesian troops surrounding her.

'They had not allowed any Timorese to be there,' she said. 'But as I knelt, saying a few words to Greg, the most wonderful singing washed over me. On the other side of the road, a young people's choir had timed its practice to my being there. I shall never forget those beautiful voices. They came through the barrier the Indonesians had set between us, and they comforted me. They will never be defeated.' ■

The campaigning Australian print and TV journalist **John Pilger** *has guest-edited three* New Internationalist *issues, on Cambodia, East Timor and Burma. Based in London, his most recent book is* The New Rulers of the World *(Verso 2002).*

July 1994
Squeezing the South: 50 years is enough
Activists from all around the world are challenging the economic gospel according to Bretton Woods institutions like the World Bank and the IMF. **Richard Swift** *tests the winds of change.*

Montserrat's not going to get a toxic-waste dump. At least not yet. You might well ask why this tiny Caribbean island, the Emerald Isle of the Leewards, would even consider letting a US toxic-waste dumping company set up shop in the first place. Montserrat, one of the last British colonies, is just 21 kilometres long by a couple of kilometres wide. Except where the goats have played havoc with the vegetation it is a lustrous green most of the year. Tourism of a quiet and mostly unobtrusive sort is the main foreign-exchange earner. Not a good mix with toxic waste, one would have thought.

That's exactly what most Montserratians felt when they heard that local politicians had been in intense negotiations for over a year with a US multinational named, with typical euphemistic panache, Energy Processing and Supply. Opposition quickly mounted. A local doctor wrote a scathing critique in the island paper where he drew a vivid picture of cruise ships emptying passengers among the toxic-waste drums on the docks of the island's capital, Plymouth.[1]

This is a small story about a small place but it illustrates the inexorable pull and push that draws the countries of the South into the global economy – no matter what the costs to their people and ecosystems. The pull is obvious enough: the American Dream bounced off TV satellites into the most modest of homes in surprisingly remote corners of the Third World. The push is more complicated: a subtle combination of budget and trade deficits, and debt obligations. But together this lends a seemingly unstoppable momentum to the race to get as big a slice as possible of the illusive global economic pie.

This momentum is exactly what the Bretton Woods Conference held 50 years ago this month was all about. When the world leaders gathered in that fashionable old resort hotel deep in the hill country of New Hampshire their agenda was clear: they aimed to bury forever the nationalistic protectionism they saw as the main culprit in creating the Great Depression of the 1930s. To do this they put in place the pillars of a global economy where borders were to be as porous as possible to goods and capital from anywhere in the world. As part of the design they set up two key institutions, the International Monetary Fund (IMF) and the World Bank, to deal with problems that might lead governments to inward-looking economic policies. This was followed shortly by another organization, the General Agreement on Tariffs and Trade (GATT), which set the rules and pressures for open economies and free trade. Together with the regional development banks these are collectively known as the IFIs, an acronym for international financial institutions.

These were not neutral economic mechanisms set up to co-ordinate the world economy: they contained a powerful bias in favour of global competition and corporate enterprise. There were warnings of problems ahead from a few discordant voices, the most prominent of which was the eminent British economist John Maynard Keynes. He advocated a balanced world trade system in which surpluses and deficits would not be allowed to accumulate and there would be strict controls on the movement of capital across borders. He held that the free movement of all goods and capital, advocated most powerfully by the US delegation, would inevitably lead to inequalities and instabilities.

From the standpoint of 1994 these warnings seem all too prescient. Today budget and trade deficits plague most countries in the world. The debt load on all governments, but particularly those of the Third World, has crippled their fiscal capacity to look after their citizens. Capital moves so freely that it is often impossible for governments to find, let alone tax. Corporations treat the world like a global chessboard bidding down wages and taxes, avoiding environmental regulation and pillaging natural resources. Their right to do this is no longer even considered controversial. They are courted by politicians of all political stripes. The stability of communities from rural Zambia to Bangladesh and even the decaying rustbelts of the US heartland or the British Midlands are casually undermined by processes that appear 'natural' but were in fact carefully constructed at Bretton Woods.

Abandoned factories and children who make a living on the street seem light years away from that magnificent temple to money, the IMF building on 19th Street in downtown Washington. At the IMF it isn't easy to get past security. It seems like 5 per cent of black Washingtonians are employed to keep the other 95 per cent out of such white inner sanctums. If you are curious about the IMF you will be directed to the well-appointed Vistors' Centre complete with art gallery just next door. There, if you are interested enough (few were the rainy December afternoon I showed up) you will be shown a video tellingly entitled *One World, One Economy.* It's a choice piece of propaganda for a globalist worldview that doesn't really seem to need propagandizing any more, becoming as it has the common sense of our age for most economists and politicians. In the video a parade of besuited, mostly white men lecture on the merits of IMF medicine for ailing economies. It has some real classics of understatement such as 'While the Fund cannot force its members, the Fund's suggestions are taken seriously.' A parade of faces of colour speak gratefully about the wisdom of IMF policies in their countries.

The debt crisis of the 1980s which really gave the IMF and the World Bank (the huge hulk on the other side of 19th Street) leverage over desperate Third World economies is referred to mildly: 'A workable solution was required to avoid defaults that would severely damage debtor countries, as well as financial institutions'. The solution, structural-adjustment programs or SAPs, proved a lot more 'workable' for the big international banks who got their interest payments than it did for the laid-off public-sector workers of Latin America or for the African families who can no longer send their kids to school because of SAP-related 'user fees'. These ordinary people were the ones who had to do the 'adjusting'.

When the dust had settled, the 'short-term pain' of the SAPs had not got rid of the debt: total Third World debt actually shot up from $751 billion in 1981 to $1,355 billion in 1990. What it had done was to pry open Southern economies to the world market. The formula was deceptively simple: international competition would result in growth that would be good for everyone. And this glittering promise of the global economy remains for most policymakers, North and South, the only game in town.

But growth has proved elusive. There has been significant economic growth in some adjusting Latin American and Asian countries and new élites have profited handsomely from the privatizing of public industries. But for every South Korean success story there are dozens of unmitigated failures such as Côte d'Ivoire and Venezuela where absolute destitution has skyrocketed. A recent World Bank study, *Adjustment in Africa*, which makes great claims about the success of SAPs on the continent, is so full of holes that the usually restrained British agency Oxfam UK was forced to characterize it as 'a blend of half-truths, over-simplifications and institutional propaganda'.

But if the grand architects of Bretton Woods have through their design managed to defeat 1930s-style protectionism they have been less successful with that other scourge of the Depression, unemployment. While total world output has doubled since 1975, employment has actually declined.[2] The global economy, with its emphasis on reducing labour costs and on currency or property speculation, does not put a high priority on providing sustainable livelihoods. An underlying assumption of the growth economy is that Northern-style overconsumption can be achieved by every society on the globe. Only recently has attention started to be paid to the ecological impact of such a design.

Those who speak for the IFIs are genuinely puzzled when the Bretton Woods institutions are blamed for such problems. They are simply messengers pointing out the obvious: dispensing the advice necessary to survive the rigours of the global economy. They point to their limited budgets, a few billion dollars and a few thousand personnel, when an estimated trillion dollars crosses borders every day in response to the slightest change in currency and interest rates. They point to their minimal influence over the industrial North and even the larger Third World governments like those of China and India.

But the role of these institutions cannot be reduced to their budgets. They help create and maintain the rules for the global economy. They sustain its momentum and make sure that any alternative vision proves impractical and unworkable. The lack of their 'stamp of approval' makes it virtually certain that freethinkers like Sandinista Nicaragua will be starved of capital and subjected to rigorous external pressure. If problems occur such as the 1980s debt crisis, the IFIs guarantee that any resolution will respect the interests of Northern fund managers and banks first. The price will be paid in the shantytowns of Lima and on the family farms of Uganda. In Africa the IFIs have taken over the bulk of public debt and now directly wring payments out of enfeebled African economies. As a result both the World Bank and the IMF now take more out of the Third World in repayments (even from the poorest countries) than they provide in new finance.

Nobody talks about a debt crisis any more, but while it no longer endangers world financial institutions it is still very much a crisis for those who have to pay. Along with the opening up of Third World economies, this transfer of the debt burden from the rich to the poor has been the IFIs' greatest triumph. Their greatest failure has been in delivering the orderly world financial system that Bretton Woods promised. Narrow technocratic thinking and cynical power politics have put short-term gain ahead of stability. Public finance the world over is in a mess. Private wealth and public squalor are the order of the day. It is written right into the World Bank's constitution that it cannot fund projects that compete with private enterprise. The IFIs have exerted consistent pressure to minimize state involvement in economic life from Bogotá to Bangkok. This despite the clear evidence that the development success stories of Asia (Taiwan, South Korea, Malaysia and Thailand) have all involved strong government intervention to order society, protect the domestic economy and promote growth.

The irony is that in many ways the IFIs show the same weaknesses they criticize in government bureaucracies. Their bloated and privileged staffs resemble more the command economies of old-style Communism than the lean mean private sector they celebrate. While they lionize risk-takers there are no risks attached to an IFI loan: a government (or rather its benighted citizens) has to pay it back no matter how wasteful or ill-considered it was in the first place. The distance between an IFI head of mission who lives in a comfortable Virginia suburb and a hard-pressed Argentinian pensioner or a mother in Benin struggling to keep her family alive is just too great. Staffers are too well insulated from the effects of their own advice.

The IFIs' single-minded insistence on an export-driven growth formula also shows the weakness of centralized economic decision-making. Whether we are talking about huge transnational corporations, over-ambitious state planning or the global economic management ambitions of the IFIs, wasteful diseconomies of scale are inevitable. The IFI loan portfolio is a prime example. It leans towards big loans for big projects such as dams or port facilities that will 'aid international competitiveness'. It is a lot easier to manage one big loan than a lot of little ones. Unfortunately experiences like those of the Grameen Bank in Bangladesh and its support for micro-enterprises shows that it is many small loans that work best in spreading economic benefits.

The research and on-the-ground experience which shows this is conveniently ignored. Small loans usually don't build up a country's capacity to earn foreign exchange and therefore don't help pay off debt. But more exports don't necessarily help either. Producing more of a cash crop tends simultaneously to lower its price on the world market. This has cancelled out any significant gains for five of Africa's main exports.[3]

The message echoing down the decades from those heady days in New Hampshire is always the same: 'there is no choice'. GATT has set the rules for the global economy and the IFIs must enforce them. The slash-and-burn economic policies adopted both South and North are the only way forward. Economies have to compete on the world market no matter what the human costs. There is simply no alternative.

This is of course the big lie. State socialism has collapsed, but that was never the only and certainly not the best alternative to global capitalism. There is a rich vein of alternative economic initiatives and ideas: co-operatives, self-managed enterprises, various mixes of private and public sector, eco-development, ideas for a diversified regional and community-based economics, innovations in planning the economies of cities, fresh approaches to taxation, and blueprints for converting military production to basic needs. In each of these alternatives the people affected would have more power over decisions and the health of the environment would weigh heavier in economic calculations.

Small may be both beautiful and possible but the decisions taken at Bretton Woods make it unlikely. After all why waste time and resources trying to do things differently when you can earn good foreign exchange from toxic-waste dumps, exporting weapons, depleting your natural resources and letting transnationals exploit your workers?

There is another less discussed cost of a global economy directed by those who control international capital. Gradually democracy itself is slipping through our fingers. Today it hardly matters if a finance minister comes from the Left or the Right if their main concern when preparing a budget is how the IMF and the money markets are going to react. Voters may support anti-SAP politicians as they have in Venezuela, Argentina and Brazil, but those who buy and sell government bonds and hold the national debt will see to it that SAPs get implemented anyway. But people and politics have proved a lot less malleable than economics to the IFIs' designs for global management. In Eastern Europe structural adjustment has produced results inconceivable a couple of years ago: the political rehabilitation of the Left. In Hungary, Lithuania and Poland the Socialists have become the most popular political party.

A much more disturbing by-product of adjustment has been the stoking of anti-immigrant feeling and lifeboat ethics across the industrial world. The economic dislocations accompanying the IMF-encouraged market reforms in Russia and eastern Germany have helped set in motion a vicious nationalism based on race and violence; the fascist Right have been revived in both Rome and Berlin. These are just the kind of political developments Bretton Woods was intended to forestall.

It is in the Third World, however, that the breaking of glass and the explosion of teargas canisters have formed a recurrent soundtrack of protest. Enraged citizens from Cairo to Caracas are taking their insecurities about the global economy to the streets. At its worst this has led to authoritarian politics (the dictatorship of Alberto Fujimori in Peru) or political pathologies such as Islamic fundamentalism that reject not only the superficialities of Western materialism but most recognizable forms of democracy as well.

More promising is the emergence of 'internationalism from below' as networks of activists from North and South come together to expose the impact on livelihoods and environment behind the globalist cant. Organizations have sprung up on every continent and in any country that allows them the political space to operate. So far the main activity of these networks has been to challenge the priorities of the export-driven growth model of development. They have been in the forefront of opposing the structural-adjustment policies of the IFIs. It is this 'internationalism from below' which has put the reconsideration of the decisions and institutions of Bretton Woods on the agenda. For them, 50 years is enough!

To have real effect, however, this citizens' movement needs to move beyond opposition to proposition. Grassroots organizations the world over are seeking an economics driven by community need rather than export opportunities. Strategies will vary, but the emerging common thread is the rejection of the grand designs and globalist illusions of Bretton Woods as undemocratic and anti-ecological. Bretton Woods stands as a cement block in the path of rethinking what a peaceful and sustainable world might look like. The words of singer Jackson Browne could be directly addressed to the men in suits who dominate the IFIs: 'Boys, boys, this world is not your toy. This world is long on hunger. This world is short on joy.' ■

Formerly a radio journalist, **Richard Swift** *has been an* **NI** *co-editor based in the magazine's Toronto office since 1984. He is the author of* The No-Nonsense Guide to Democracy *(NI/Verso 2002).*

1 *The Montserrat Reporter,* 14/1/94. **2** Mahbub ul-Haq, *Bretton Woods Institutions: The Vision and the Reality,* North-South Roundtable, Bretton Woods, New Hampshire. **3** Salim Lone, 'Troubled Adjustment Efforts', *African Recovery,* UN, Vol 7 no 3/4.

November 1994
Lethal lies

The murky world of the arms trade escapes public scrutiny most of the time. **Vanessa Baird** *visits Somalia, where its bloody consequences are all too apparent, and asks what can be done in a world awash with weapons.*

'I don't know anything about it,' says Mariam with a big, knowing smile. 'I want to live a long life,' she adds, with an even bigger smile.

We are in Hodur, a dusty little Somali town close to the Ethiopian border. A camel ambles past the open door. Beyond the camel stand shelled husks of buildings set against a vast flat landscape of shrub and sand.

I've heard that this is a gunrunning town, with a good market for AK-47s and the like. There is supposed to be an embargo on arms to Somalia but the weapons are pouring in all the same – from Ethiopia, from Sudan, from Egypt, from Kenya, from Italy.

Virtually every household has a gun. Civil society has disintegrated into clan warfare. Government infrastructure has collapsed and the United Nations is trying – and mainly failing – to keep order. Fighting can flare up at any place, at any time. The guns come out of the houses and all hell is let loose.

But Mariam does not want to talk about this. She wants to talk about nutrition. She is here running a UNICEF mother-and-child health post. People in this region suffered greatly during the height of the civil-war-created famine that claimed 300,000 lives two years ago. The skeletal images from Baidoa that haunted our television screens in 1992 would have come from Hodur had the TV crews got as far as this place.

There is still malnutrition today – about 20 per cent of children are affected – and a feeding centre continues to operate. But the situation is vastly improved. The problem now is trying to find ways of generating income apart from gun-trading. What do the women who come to the health centre have to say about the fighting?

'They don't talk about it,' says Mariam firmly. 'They are concerned with the health of the children. With making sure they get enough to eat.'

Mariam's attitude is altogether understandable. She is firmly focused on her immediate objective. Besides, too much talk can cost you your life in this place.

But she is not the only person unwilling to discuss the trade in weapons. Before coming to Somalia I had conversations with some high-ranking UN officials in Nairobi. They were quite happy to talk about the conflict in Somalia, to condemn militarism and the damage done by the 'men with guns'. But on the subject of how and from whom those men with guns got those arms, they shut up or went off the record.

Why? There are many complex reasons – and one very simple one. The countries that are the most powerful in the UN are those which have permanent seats on the Security Council. These are the US, Russia, the UK, France and China – the Big Five. They also happen to be the world's biggest suppliers of arms – accounting for 86 per cent of sales to the developing world. During his 21-year rule – which ended in 1991 – Somali dictator Siad Barre built up a huge arsenal of arms, supplied first by the former USSR, then by the US. From 1980 to 1990 nearly three-quarters of his arms came from the US. During this time Somalia was spending five times as much on the military as on health and education put together – the highest ratio in the world.[1]

I'm thinking about this deadly legacy while standing on the tarmac of Mogadishu airport, having flown to the capital city of Somalia from Hodur a few hours earlier. The runway is surrounded by barbed wire and UN armoured vehicles. Fighting between the clans of the two main opposing warlords in Mogadishu – General Aideed and Ali Mahdi – has got so bad during the past few days that I can't get security clearance to enter the city. Most of the development agencies still here have moved their operations onto the airport tarmac.

I'm watching an aircraft being loaded up with UN emergency relief supplies. Unused in Somalia, they are being redirected to Rwandan refugees in Goma, Zaire. The news coverage of that crisis has so far focused on 'tribal' conflict – with the connotations of the 'primitive' and 'uncivilized' that accompany that word.

Little has been said about the fact that while the former Hutu government of Rwanda was conducting its genocidal campaign against Tutsis and other political opponents, 'civilized' countries like France and South Africa were busy supplying the murdering regime with military equipment.[2]

The arms trade has never been ethical. But the pressures on suppliers to sell are greater today than ever. There are too many of them chasing a shrinking post-Cold War market in a world that may seem conflict-ridden to the normal person, but is not nearly conflict-rich enough for the trade. Embargoes are vigorously circumvented whenever and wherever possible.

There are two main reasons for this state of affairs. One is the cascade of surplus arms that NATO and the Warsaw Pact countries have unleashed on the world as a result of the scaling-down of their own militaries at the end of the Cold War.

The other reason is that military spending cuts in the North have caused a fall in domestic demand. The most usual response to this from arms manufacturers has not been to diversify and make something else, but a frantic export drive – the targets being the world's trouble spots.

The arms trade cannot be blamed for starting the conflicts in Bosnia or Angola or Sudan or Burma or Turkey. But it is certainly playing a major role in prolonging these conflicts, in shattering hopes of democracy and replacing them with the rule of the gun and armed madness.

Nowhere is this more in evidence than in Somalia. From Mogadishu I fly down to the southern port of Kismayo. It's only 14 kilometres from the airport to the town but the stretch of road that links the two is reckoned to be too dangerous to travel. The only way in is to get a helicopter from the airport to the seaport and from there take a military escort into town.

The military escort is incredible. It consists of a convoy of three 'technicals' – jeeps fitted with machine guns, an army truck and about 15 jittery Indian soldiers. They have reason to be nervous – two of their colleagues were killed recently by a Somali militia.

At the UNICEF residence, Baba, the Nigerian aid worker in charge, explains that he and his colleagues have to be accompanied by the convoy whenever they set foot out of their compound. Aid workers are targets in Somalia – UNICEF has lost 11 staff so far. Agencies hire vehicles which come complete with armed militiamen for protection.

It's hard to see how any development work can be done under conditions where visiting a project becomes a major military exercise. Aid workers feel frustrated. The temptation to ignore the security procedures is great.

On 2 January 1992, one of Baba's predecessors, Sean Devereux, did not take the convoy. He set out to walk the 20 minutes home from the office. He was shot and killed by a local militiaman. The outspoken British aid worker had recently gone on Radio Mogadishu and talked about clan control, about militias and about the part played by the arms trade.

Devereux had worked in Liberia prior to coming to Somalia and had come to the conclusion that the single biggest obstacle to development was the arms trade. He also became aware of the secrecy, silence and hypocrisy that surrounds the trade and was determined not to keep quiet about it.

His anger and frustration – though not necessarily his courage – are shared by many. And yet those governments most heavily implicated in the buying and selling of arms can carry on doing so with precious little scrutiny or criticism.

The governments and military élites of poor countries that spend outrageous sums on weapons tell their populations that the weapons are necessary for security reasons. In most cases, though, the security they are providing is for themselves, for their own power base, at the expense of their people.

Take Pakistan. In 1992 the Government ordered 40 Mirage 2000E fighters and three Tripartite aircraft from France. The cost of that one deal could have provided safe water for two years for all the 55 million people who lack it, family-planning services for the 20 million couples who want them, essential medicines for the nearly 13 million people without access to health care and basic education for the 12 million children not in primary school.[1]

People in many Third World countries have no idea just how profligate their governments and military élites have been. But the truth may yet emerge. For the past three years the IMF has started collecting data on the military debts of developing countries, some of which look set to exceed their developmental debts.

The governments of countries that are major suppliers of arms also tell their people that the arms trade is good for them. During the Cold War the argument was that we needed ever more sophisticated weapons to protect us from the 'enemy'. The military-industrial complex was cast in the West as the profitable 'booster rocket' of capitalism. For this reason industrializing countries like Brazil, South Korea and Indonesia were keen to get in on the act.

But today the most powerful argument for maintaining a defence industry in the North is employment – or rather the prospect of massive unemployment if it goes. It is estimated that of the 14 million defence-industry jobs in the world today, 4 million will have been lost by 1998.[1]

It may seem paradoxical but evidence is mounting that the arms trade actually *creates* unemployment. To see how this works you need to look at the larger picture and the longer term. The arms trade does not make economic sense – it is not and never has been genuinely profitable. It is capital-intensive – and its products often sell for less than they actually cost to produce. Defence manufacture is not even particularly labour-intensive. But during the Cold War it was hugely subsidized by the public via overpriced defence-ministry contracts. If the public money that was sunk into the arms industry had gone into a host of smaller, more flexible high-tech enterprises it would have created more wealth and more employment.[3]

Today it is no longer possible to justify such huge public spending on defence. Instead all sorts of hidden subsidies are used to keep defence manufacturers afloat. In the UK an entire government department – The Defence Export Services Organization – is geared solely to promoting arms sales. Western governments have also been keen to underwrite loans and 'export credits' to potential buyers of weapons with the effect that taxpayers in the selling country are actually footing the bill for up to a third of all weapons sold.[4]

You are not likely to know about this – because the arms trade is shrouded in government secrecy. No other business is so officially protected from public scrutiny. The excuse is 'national-security interests'. This calls to mind the child abuser who invokes family unity to establish the abuse as 'our secret' and obtain collusion.

We have all been abused by the arms trade, in one way or another. From the unemployed worker in Detroit to the skinny, withdrawn child in Baidoa taking part in a programme for war–traumatized children.

So what can be done in this world battered into a military mould? What can we do to disarm our societies both physically and psychologically? In Somalia the opportunity for literally taking the guns away from the militias has passed. But there is another, perhaps more durable way. The seemingly insatiable demand for arms can only be lessened by creating a civil society based on peaceful, democratic forms of organization. Somalia has local teachers, health workers and others committed to this. Fatima Jibrell, for example, has returned from exile in the US and is trying to set up women's projects with this in mind. She shows me a text that Somali women took to a conference in Addis Ababa in March 1993. It begins:

'We Somali women have followed behind our men in the wake of the devastation and destruction of our homeland. Now it is time we leave our role as followers and become leaders of our people into peace.'

Transforming a military culture and economy into a civil one is a task for all of us in this post-Cold War era. There was a golden opportunity to do so. Cuts in military spending from 1987 to 1994 produced a global peace dividend of $935 billion – $810 billion of this in industrial nations. Where has it gone? The simple shocking answer is: it disappeared, no-one knows exactly where. According to a UN Development Programme report: 'Most savings appear to have been spent on reducing budget deficits, rather than on development or on environmental improvements.'[1]

The text goes on to say: 'It is frustrating that – just as social and human agendas were pushed aside at a time of rising military budgets, they continue to be neglected even when military budgets are being reduced.' Not just 'frustrating', it's outrageous that governments have used this money to conceal their own economic incompetence.

A future peace dividend of $460 billion is anticipated for 1995-2000. Is the UN going to sit back and let governments squander this too? Or is it going to agree systems to keep track of this money so that it becomes an accountable item in national budgets? The UN could do much in this area. It could take up the proposal of Nobel Peace Prize winner Oscar Arias to set up a global demilitarization fund, large chunks of which would be spent on converting from military to non-military production and retraining demobilized soldiers.

Today the UN finds itself with the role of peacekeeper in many areas of conflict around the world. It is reaping the harvest of decades of military build-up and arms trading. Would it not make sense to tackle the problem at an earlier stage? Some tentative steps are being taken. UN Secretary-General Boutros Boutros Ghali has introduced a voluntary Conventional Arms Control Register which could lead to greater openness and accountability. But it is only voluntary and several countries have refused to comply. The UN also seems poised to ban the trade in certain arms, such as landmines. And there is talk of taxing arms transfers.

But while arms sales are the norm it is easy for traders to get round obstacles, such as bans on particular weapons or embargoes against certain countries. What if, however, there were a global ban on all arms sales which was lifted only in exceptional cases? People facing genocide at the hands of well-armed aggressors – the Kurds for example, or the Bosnian Muslims – might constitute 'an exceptional case'.

The main pressure the UN will have to exert in the next few years will be on its most powerful members: the main arms-selling countries, the Big Five. 'Bloody warlords,' said one angry Somali health worker referring to those men whose struggle for power has brought the country to its knees. 'Nobody wants them.' Indeed. But 'warlords' come in all shapes, sizes and guises. Those people in the corridors of political or corporate power who are easing the bloodiest trade in the world could be described as 'warlords' of a kind. And we don't want them either. The lies, secrets and silences that surround and protect their activities are not only immoral, abusive and undemocratic. They are lethal. ■

Formerly a reporter based in Lima, Peru, **Vanessa Baird** *has been a co-editor of the* **NI** *based in Oxford since 1987. She is the author of* The No-Nonsense Guide to Sexual Minorities *(NI/Verso 2001).*

1 United Nations Development Programme, Human Development Report 1994. 2 Human Rights Watch, US 1994. 3 Trust for Research and Education on the Arms Trade, London 1994. See also the work of Mary Kaldor and Seymour Elman. 4 World Development Movement, London 1994.

September 1999
Iraq: the pride and the pain

Nikki van der Gaag finds that human rights have a different meaning when viewed from Baghdad.

'Don't talk to me about human rights.' Nasra al-Sa'adoun's voice is firm. 'Your analysis is too simplistic. You see the West as good and Iraq as bad. You think you have the right to interfere in our affairs because you have always done so.'

Nasra is a neat, grey-haired woman with a degree from the Sorbonne in Paris and a knowledge of British history which far exceeds my own. She can quote chapter and verse of the deals, the betrayals; the whole complex web of Anglo-Iraqi relationships so redolent of colonial and neo-colonial relationships around the world. In a word, she blames the British. It is hardly surprising. Her grandfather, who was Iraq's Prime Minister, committed suicide rather than surrender to the British. His statue now stands in one of

Baghdad's main streets, which is named after him, a small, Gandhi-like fig-ure in bronze. He was 40 years old.

On 17 January this year, the ninth anniversary of the Gulf War, Mustapha, Nasra's husband, friend and partner died suddenly at the age of 52. A heart attack, they said.

No-one knows why fit and healthy people like Mustapha just collapse, leav-ing their families deep in grief. Iraq is festooned with the black banners that announce a new death. Perhaps you can die of a broken heart after all.

Nasra feels that she is facing yet another bereavement: the death of her country. 'Where are our human rights here in Iraq? We have no electricity, no clean water, no trains, no safe cars, an environment which is being destroyed, and you are bombing us every day. I tell you, we would rather have a real war than this slow death. This is genocide.'

The sanctions on Iraq are the most draconian ever imposed by the United Nations. The UN is caught in the ambiguous position as both the cause of suf-fering and the body responsible for alleviating it. These are the only sanctions this century imposed as a complete embargo on all trade (with a few excep-tions) rather than just an embargo on particular goods or areas. In this sense, says Sabah Al-Mukhtar, an Iraqi living in London who is President of the League of Arab Lawyers, 'the whole country is being kept prisoner and denied the basic requirements for survival.' Denis Halliday, who resigned from his post as Humanitarian Co-ordinator in Iraq rather than administer the sanctions regime, puts it even more strongly: 'We are in the process of destroying an entire nation. It is as simple and as terrifying as that. It is illegal and immoral.'[1]

The figures speak for themselves. UNICEF believes that between 5,000 and 6,000 children die each month as a direct result of sanctions. The mortality rate for children under five has risen from 48 per 1,000 in 1990 to 122 per 1,000 in 1997.[2] One in four children is malnourished; a rise of 73 per cent since 1991.

And yet the country is sitting on probably the second-largest oil reserves in the world. In May 1996 Iraq was allowed to sell a limited amount of oil in return for food, but this improved the situation only marginally. The infra-structure does not exist to pump the allocated oil, and oil prices in any case remain very low. With a large amount siphoned off for other purposes Iraq ultimately gets around $1.5 billion worth of humanitarian goods over a six-month period. It costs $600 million to give each person one kilo of sugar over the same period.

But deprivation is not only physical, but emotional as well. Many parents of the young people growing up today were well educated, well fed and well travelled, but the new generation is angry, hungry and isolated from the world. New young cadres in the ruling Ba'ath Party believe that President Saddam Hussein and the current Government have compromised too much with the West, and take a much harder line. Other children simply see the US as the enemy. This was encapsulated for me when I met Dina, aged 7, whose mother and father are both civil engineers. Dina is keen to show me her drawings, which are detailed and imaginative. Many are the princesses and mermaids, mummies, daddies and school friends that you would expect from someone her age.

But then I come across one of a soldier. He is standing on the right of the page and seems to be shooting something on the left. 'What is this?' I ask her. She whispers something shyly. Her parents are clearly embarrassed. 'She says this is an American soldier and he is shooting the flowers.'

'But why?'

'She says Americans don't like flowers'.

It is not surprising. Dina, like all children in Iraq, has known only an aggressive, punitive West. The flowers in her family's garden bloom, but up to half the palm trees – in a country which exported 80 per cent of the world's dates – have died. This is due to not only a lack of agriculture equipment and chemicals but also the fallout from the Gulf War which has so polluted Iraq's environment. Radioactivity from depleted uranium (from Western bombs and shells) leaves a terrible mark on the faces of those Iraqi children who suffer from cancers and leukaemias.

In addition, in the north and south, people face almost daily bombings,[3] which began when the US and the UK launched Operation Desert Fox in December last year. The death toll then was over 10,000. And the bombing has never stopped.

I myself witnessed the aftermath of just one of these everyday tragedies. A family of six shepherds (the youngest six years old), their herd of 100 sheep and their sheepdog have been wiped out. The animals are still there; their stench fills the air. You can see a ripped tire, a blasted shoe, and fragments of metal, testaments to more unnecessary deaths. The local cemetery holds only two graves; there were simply not enough pieces left to bury.

The US and Britain justify the bombing of the 'no-fly zones' (which they unilaterally imposed) with the claim that they are protecting the citizens by bombing the military. Yet in the place where the shepherds died there were no camps or soldiers to be seen, just the village of Basheka, known for its vineyards, some three kilometres distant. Otherwise it was just bare earth with mountains on the horizon. But somehow a military directive calls this a 'target-rich' zone.[4] It was Gandhi who pointed out 'what does it matter to the widows, the orphans, the homeless, whether the mad destruction is wrought in the name of totalitarianism or the holy name of liberty and democracy?'

Jawdat al Kazzi is a priest from southern Lebanon who has lived in northern Iraq for 13 years. He is grey-haired, with a quiet manner which somehow makes his fury palpable: 'If Clinton and Blair were really Christians they wouldn't do this to us.' His voice is clear, determined.

'But then, you see, a capitalist society cannot be truly Christian because it puts money before everything else. Dollars before people. Here in Iraq, we have no money any more. Iraqis have lost everything. But they still have their morality; they are a very moral people.'

We sit in the flickering light of an oil lamp in a Dominican church whose French connections go back to the wife of Napoleon III who donated the church bell. The priest points out the inconsistency of the American stand: 'There is one rule for Iraq, another for America's friends, like Israel. America allows Israel to break all the rules, to ignore 37 UN resolutions, to invade and occupy Palestine, Lebanon and Syria; to have a nuclear bomb and chemical weapons... and what happens? Nothing. Yet Iraq has nearly honoured all the Security Council resolutions but the US will not permit the lifting of the embargo. This is hypocrisy of the highest order.'

'Sanctions' said US Secretary of State Madeleine Albright, 'are the most powerful weapons in our armoury.'

Yet the other irony in all this is that the sanctions and bombing regime has achieved the opposite of what was intended. It has consolidated rather than weakened the Government's power; Saddam Hussein has become for many in Iraq – and indeed in the Middle East – a symbol of Iraqi resistance and determination never to bow to Western pressure. Opposition within the country is simply not tolerated, and the Iraqi opposition in exile has been rendered ineffective by the multiplicity of parties (as least 85 according to a US State Department list). Acrimonious exchanges between the various groups suggest they hate each other almost as much as they hate the regime.[5]

In the West, the public are led to believe that everything that is happening – or at least everything that is allowed to reach their ears – is the fault of the Iraqi regime; or more specifically, of President Saddam Hussein, who since the Gulf War has become the man the world most loves to hate. He is portrayed as a ruthless monster, a dictator who murders his own people by the thousands, and stockpiles food and medicines rather than feed his starving people.

It is clear that the regime – and it is the regime, not just the President –

brooks no dissent and punishes those who speak out with imprisonment or execution. This has been presented as a targeting of minorities. It is not. The Government in general allows its minorities – including the Kurds – more freedom to practise their religion and culture than any other Middle Eastern government, so long as they are not seen as a threat because of their national aspirations. Those who are seen as a threat are simply not tolerated. Amnesty International in its 1999 Annual Report finds the regime guilty of 'torture and ill-treatment of prisoners and detainees'; hundreds of executions and thousands 'disappeared'; a record that echoes that of many other dictatorial governments in other parts of the world.

Yet prior to the Gulf War Saddam Hussein was seen as a good guy, armed and supported by the West in the Iran-Iraq war. Even after the chemical bombardment of Kurds in the town of Halabja in 1988, the US Commerce Department continued to export military equipment to Iraq – including chemicals necessary for the manufacture of nerve gas.[6] Military regimes such as Iraq's are in many ways a product of the West, born of the Cold War when proxy battles were fought throughout the Majority World. Dictators were spawned with the firepower to keep a tight and often repressive hold on their own people and to freely implement their masters' desires. The West also fears Islam. After the Iranian Revolution, it supported Iraq as one way of keeping the Shi'a regime there in check.

But Western alliances have a habit of changing when it suits other strategic objectives, as Tariq Aziz, Iraq's Deputy Prime Minister, points out: 'You know, 12 years ago, when I was received in Washington at the White House; Yasser Arafat was a terrorist. Former terrorists in Northern Ireland are now received in Washington and London. But now our specification as an ally has changed, and Iraq is the monster, the terrorist.'[7]

Inside the country many people point to the undoubted development that took place under Saddam Hussein's regime in the 1980s when Iraq was a prosperous country despite the crippling Iran-Iraq war.

Between 1984 and 1989 Iraqis were on average eating about 3,372 calories a day (compared with a minimum requirement of 2,100). Adult literacy had risen to 95 per cent (Iraq won the UNESCO prize for literacy three years in a row); 92 per cent of the population had access to safe water and 93 per cent access to a clinic or hospital. Both education and health were free and Iraq's welfare system was 'one of the most comprehensive and generous in the Arab world'.[8]

So was its aid programme. Iraq prided itself on the support it gave to countries in need and the important role it played in the power balance of the Middle East. Economic rights were a priority, civil liberties were not. Now the Iraqi people have neither.

Sanctions were originally imposed by the UN in on 6 August 1990 – before the Gulf War and the anniversary of Hiroshima Day – to get the Iraqis out of Kuwait. So why weren't they lifted after this was achieved militarily?

The regime refuses to comply with UN resolutions, says the West. But the US has at various points tied the sanctions to the continued rule of Saddam Hussein – not the UN-endorsed disarmament requirements. It seems that they are simply making conditions so difficult to comply with that sanctions will remain indefinitely. Not surprisingly people in Iraq are pessimistic, and see US motives as having more to do with tying Iraq's hands as a political force in the region and keeping its oil off a volatile market.

In 1996 American journalist Lesley Stahl pointed out to Madeleine Albright, then US Ambassador to the UN and now US Secretary of State, that half a million children were reputed to have died: 'that's more children than died in Hiroshima. Is the price worth it?' Albright did not question the figures but replied 'I think this is a very hard choice, but the price – we think the price is worth it.'[9]

When I thank Nasra before leaving, she replies bluntly; 'I don't talk to you for your sake, but for the sake of my country.' Her grandfather's pride and passion for Iraq is never far beneath the surface. 'You know,' she smiles quietly to herself, 'I was asked the other day by another foreigner: "What should I tell people when they ask me why the Iraqi people haven't risen up against Saddam Hussein?" I told him to tell them that the Iraqi people are perfectly capable of sorting out our own affairs. "Tell them," I said. "Tell them to mind their own business. Lift sanctions and let us rebuild our country."' ∎

Formerly with Minority Rights Group and Oxfam, **Nikki van der Gaag** *was an* **NI** *co-editor based in Oxford from 1993 to 2000. She has since been working for Panos in London.*

1 *The Independent* 15 October 1998 **2** *State of the World's Children 1999*, UNICEF. **3** Except for two weeks in March and a few days in May. **4** Language reminiscent of the Gulf War and more recently of the war against Serbia. Death and destruction become 'collateral damage'; the war a 'just war'. **5** Material on the opposition supplied by Karen Dabrowska. In December 1998 the US Congress passed the Iraq Liberation Act, making $97 million available to the opposition. But many parties refused to have any part in this, fearing that the opposition could become no more than a mouthpiece in the service of American foreign policy. **6** *The Gulf Between Us: the Gulf War and beyond* edited by Victoria Brittain (Virago 1991). Among the items prohibited under the sanctions regime are: ambulances; baking soda; books, magazines, envelopes, paper; cassettes, CDs and videos; cloth (including shroud cloth); coffins; hearing aids; light bulbs; paints; shampoo; shoes and shoe polish; spark plugs; toys; washing machines; watches; wheelbarrows. **7** In *Middle East International,* May 21 1999. **8** Food and Agriculture Organisation and the World Food Program, quoted in *Starving Iraq* (Campaign Against Sanctions on Iraq, 1999). **9** Interview on CBS's *60 Minutes,* 12 May 1996.

3

Pushing the boat out: the idea frontier

SOME time in the late 1980s the editorial team at the **NI** made a conscious decision to start seeking out at least one article per issue that would be significantly more challenging than the rest. The magazine had always been prepared to grapple with difficult ideas but usually on the basis that it would try to explain the current thinking on a topic in clear and simple terms – 'an instant briefing', 'quicker to read than a book', as our marketing promised at the time. We still wanted to start from first principles but felt we should be offering more to those readers who had already grasped these and would relish a deeper exploration of the territory.

It is no surprise to me that most of the 'idea frontier' pieces I have ended up selecting were written by North Americans – and commissioned by our long-standing Toronto editors, Wayne Ellwood and Richard Swift – since there has long been a tradition of elegant, thoughtful writing on the North American Left into which we have been fortunate to be able to tap. That said, the Latin American, European and Australian pieces included are no less stylish and thought-provoking.

The articles that follow are united by nothing but their willingness to push the boat out. They range from an imaginary session with Columbus on the psychoanalyst's couch to an evocation of the poetry of the sea, from a gauntlet thrown down before the work ethic and its postmodern ghost to a meditation on the ethics of compassion. They begin, though, with Jeremiah Creedon's piece from 1989 about the architecture of the modern age which takes as its prescient starting-point the twin towers of the World Trade Center in New York. ■

December 1989
Towers of the new gods

*Ever since the pyramids in ancient Egypt humankind has built structures that soar to the heavens. Today our impulse to build upwards threatens to block out the sun with reinforced concrete. **Jeremiah Creedon** wonders what it is we are trying to rise above.*

I once fled the American Midwest for New York City, thinking life in the big town would be more suited to my sophisticated character. I survived this illusion; my exalted self-image did not. A few months later I returned home in defeat, having spent all I owned on pizza-by-the-slice, with the unpleasant truth that my role on earth was a minor one.

My conversion to realism happened in the course of a single night, just before Manhattan spat me out into the heartland. I was living in a room on the Lower East Side which had nothing going for it except a decent view. The sudden awareness that I had been living in the clouds all my life made it hard to sleep, and after cursing myself for several hours I got up and went to the window. A few miles away the twin towers of the World Trade Center were materializing through the grey light before dawn.

As I stared, their tops began to shimmer with a blue-pink iridescence, lit by a new sun that for the rest of the city had yet to rise. The beauty of these towers struck me. They lorded with an ethereal purity over the grime and tensions of the jumbled cityscape below. Now, I can see the irony of a penniless, distraught young man finding a moment's peace in the sight of those upended silver ingots, the ultimate monuments to global commerce. Then, it was all I could do to break my gaze and rejoin what I had come to dread as the ferocious ecology of capital in the streets below.

The World Trade Center, completed in 1977, has been faulted by some architecture critics for its 'contrived elegance'. Others are more blunt, deriding the 110-storey towers for pushing modernity's most prominent emblem – the skyscraper – to 'banal' heights. As one who has stood at their bases and felt dwarfed by their inhuman scale, I can appreciate this learned disdain; but I also recall my pleasure in looking on those massive objects from a distance – an idealized view similar to the architect's when admiring the model of a new design.

These conflicting responses make the Trade Center a good place to begin looking at the psychological ties between human culture and inhumanly big buildings. It is a bond that harks back to the earliest civilization. The twin towers are also an eloquent comment on *present* civilization, whose two most salient traits – technological hubris and spiritual insecurity – yearn upward, equally desperate, toward a now godless firmament.

'Architecture,' wrote Ludwig Mies van der Rohe, 'is the will of the age conceived in spatial terms.' Mies, one of this century's most influential architects, was stating an ancient truth: what a society chooses to build is often a consciously designed model of what it thinks. Mies intended his steel-framed, glass-curtained office buildings and apartment high-rises to be symbols of a 'new social order'. For him, the will of the age implied a particular ideology – the left-wing European collectivism he took to the US after leaving Nazi Germany in 1937.

In the past, the manifestoes that could be read from architecture were just as specific. The Egyptian pyramids, the Babylonian ziggurats, the Parthenon, the Gothic cathedrals and the Eiffel Tower are also statements, inseparable from the social and geographic circumstances that gave rise to them. Even the materials used to build them and their alignment to the surrounding landscape reflect different visions of the world – and different ideas about the realms and power beyond it.

All these examples share one thing, however: the American geographer Yi-Fu Tuan calls it 'the vertical aspiration'. The urge to defy gravity is only one aspect of a wider human tendency to overlay nature with abstracted, often religious ideas of order. 'At the world's primary centers of urbanism,' Tuan writes, 'cities arose not only in response to economic and commercial forces but also to the call for the establishment of sacred space, modelled after the cosmos.' Cities in ancient China thus tended to be square, while those in the Islamic lands were often circular. Both embodied the effort to impose 'sacred' geometry on the apparent chaos of the 'profane' wilderness.

In Tuan's view, Washington DC is a modern example of the 'ideal city'. So is Brasilia, the capital of Brazil, which planners and architects set about building from scratch in the 1950s. Its cruciform shape is said to suggest a bird or a plane, poised for takeoff on what otherwise is an empty expanse far from Brazil's populated coast. Tuan sees the futuristic Brasilia as a symbol both of modern Brazil's collective ego and of an enduring primal desire to bridge the distance between the human earth and the superhuman sky.[1]

The art historian Robert Hughes looks more harshly on Brasilia as a 'vast' example of what happens when people design for an imagined future, rather than for a real world. He calls it 'an expensive and ugly testimony' to what gets built 'when men think in terms of abstract space rather than real space, of single rather than multiple meanings, and of political aspirations instead of human needs'. He traces this failure back through Brasilia's principal architects, Lucio Costa and Oscar Niemeyer, to their mentor Le Corbusier, who is perhaps the only figure to surpass Mies van der Rohe in his influence on 20th-century architecture. Both were prominent in the so-called International Style, which gave the world the now ubiquitous glass 'box' sky-scraper and Le Corbusier's dubious ideals for urban planning, known as 'The Functional City'.

Hughes argues that modernist architecture, like much of modernist art in general, was 'value-free and could serve almost any ideological interest'. The same could be said of the age-old desire to build up and to build big. Thus the Russian constructivist Vladimir Tatlin could design, in 1920, a giant revolving monument taller than the Eiffel Tower to honor the socialist utopia that supposedly began with the Russian Revolution. It was never built. Nazi architect Albert Speer envisioned a mammoth dome in Berlin to honor Hitler's Thousand Year Reich. It was never built either. Whenever such plans are realized – as in Brasilia – the results tend to be the same. Hughes calls it 'an architecture of coercion' that physically reiterates the individual's symbolic nothingness compared to the looming power of the state.[2]

Brasilia marks the end of an era. What lies beyond Brasilia – some call it post-modernism – is a transitional period in which the builder-heroes like Mies, Walter Gropius and Le Corbusier no longer dominate the architectural imagination. Meanwhile, the architects, like artists in many other fields, wait for the new paradigms and manifestoes that will energize them.

The World Trade Center, designed by Minoru Yamasaki (with help from Emery Roth and Sons), belongs to this interim. While obviously related to the modernist 'box', the towers also recall earlier technical and aesthetic strategies. Their weight, for one thing, is carried by their outer walls rather than 'hung' in Miesian fashion from a steel skeleton. In appearance, these high-tech surfaces echo the tracery that adorns the Gothic cathedrals – a conscious borrowing from the past that a high modernist would no doubt have resisted.

What do these changes in architecture reveal about changes in society? What can they say about an age whose 'will' is otherwise still a mystery to itself? A clue can be found *inside* the Trade Center by riding its innovative elevator system to the observation deck.

An exhibit on display there illustrates the history of trade by arranging various artefacts – ancient coins, wampum beads, old paper bills, whatever – along a time line. Turning to the windows, one can see beyond the Verrazano Narrows Bridge to the Atlantic Ocean, the maritime highway that first gave New York access to the world's markets. Looking up the length of Manhattan, high above the great metropolis, one can also envision the Trade

Center itself as an artefact: a giant symbolic antenna in the electronic global economy, sending and receiving great sums of money the new-fangled way – at the speed of light.

Another clue to the role of big buildings in social change can be found in a catalogue of the world's paper money. Such bills offer a glimpse into a country's self-image, which makes it curious that only a few nations decorate their money with the symbol of the modern skyscraper. Other buildings are well-represented: Pharaonic monuments, Buddhist temples, Himalayan monasteries, government complexes, national banks. The preference for state architecture or for ancient sites of national glory is clear.

The dozen or so bills (out of 9,600) that do feature modern high-rises tell particular stories: Kenya's 100-shilling note, for example, displays the 28-storey Kenyatta Conference Center in Nairobi, an object of national pride because it was financed entirely from domestic sources.

Hong Kong and Singapore also feature high-rises on their currency, but to different effect. In these cases, the buildings become symbols of a global order beyond the modern, in which nationalism as a force of social cohesion is equalled or surpassed by corporate allegiances. These are the post-modern city-states. Their geographic and political circumstances have allowed the new order to emerge more fully, unconstrained by the social forces and the burdens of history that still partly shackle a city like New York to the old ways. Singapore, especially, appears to identify with tall modern buildings taken together as a single entity – the so-called 'skycity'. Singapore may also be the only place in the world to decorate its currency with the image of high-rise housing.[3]

The traditional powers seem universally wary of adopting this skyscraper imagery, let alone the apartment complex, as a national symbol. This stands to reason: they've got too much invested in the old notion of statehood as a function of military and geographic might. The very name 'International Style' justifies this wariness. The allegiance of the modernist architect was to the client who had hired him. That might be the Indian state of Punjab for whom Le Corbusier designed a new capital complex. Or a whisky manufacturer like Seagram's, for whom Mies built a corporate headquarters in Manhattan that most critics consider the modern era's 'impeccable image of power and prestige'.

The only other allegiance these architects knew was to themselves. That is why their giant creations are also often monumental paradoxes, at once glorifying the cult of the individual and dehumanizing the real individuals who must live and work in their shadows. Since the waning of modernism, architects may

no longer be the cultural heroes they once were, but the paradox endures –
under new ownership. Thus financier Donald Trump has a glittering tower
soaring over midtown Manhattan that any bygone potentate would envy.
Meanwhile, on the streets below, thousands sleep under newspapers and in
cardboard boxes.

My own experience in New York proved to be more about falling than rising. Never again would I view the city and its tall buildings as a projection of
my character and destiny. And so I will end with a descent, a search for whatever it is that human beings with their 'vertical aspiration' are so desperate
to climb above.

The entry to the tenement where I lived formed a sort of cave in which
homeless men would gather at night. In the morning some would be lying in
heaps on the urinous tile, while others sat propped against the wall looking
dumbstruck, as if astonished beyond words by a shocking vision that had
come to them while the others slept. A few had swollen feet that had burst
their shoes, revealing toes that had gone necrotic and black. One man with
a shrunken head was forever mumbling angrily and swatting at bugs that
were not really there. Invariably someone would extend a hand for money.

In the ancient world a single tall structure might have dominated an
entire city. It drew all eyes to a common point, symbolizing a political order
whose authority was just as concentrated. Our own age, in contrast, has no
center. The tall buildings in New York spring upward like so many giant
trees, each vying for a share of the available resources. Together, they form
the equivalent of the jungle's canopy, whose pure energy is transformed into
capital. They may thrive; but the system is a selfish one that dooms the low-
est realms to perpetual dusk. There, the most abject beings wait with open
palms to catch whatever sustenance filters through, in beggarly denomina-
tions.

The metaphor of the urban jungle portrays what is least flattering in the
contemporary age. It also points to a strange reversal in the way people view
the world now that human hands have largely redesigned it. The ancient city
with its monumental pinnacle was that rare place where human beings
found haven from the profane wilderness. Today the wilderness is all but
gone, which can only increase the impulse to build upward, beyond the new
profanities of our own creation. ∎

Jeremiah Creedon *is currently editor of the* Utne Reader *and is based in Minneapolis.*

1 Yi-Fu Tuan, *Topophilia: A Study of Environmental Perceptions, Attitudes, and Values*, (Prentice-Hall, 1974). 2 Robert
Hughes, *Shock of the New*, (Alfred A Knopf, 1981). 3 Albert Pick, *Standard Catalogue of World Paper Money – General
Issues*, (Krause Publications).

December 1991
Columbus on the couch

Rummaging through dusty archives, historian **Kirkpatrick Sale** *unearthed the following rare document: a psychiatric case study of Christopher Columbus by 15th-century doctor Sigmundo Feliz, based on clinical observations and the famous mariner's own writings.*

Case: 1492
Patient: Cristobal C
Occupation: Admiral of the Ocean Sea, one-time colonial governor
Date: May 1506

This represents one of my most regrettable cases, for despite my best endeavours I was too late to be of any substantial benefit to this patient, and he died shortly after our last visit, a bitter, sorrowful man, still a victim of the paranoia and melancholia that seems to have afflicted him most of his adult life. He was a victim too, in a more physical sense, of a congeries of ailments I diagnose as Reiter's Syndrome – that is arthritis, uveitis, and urethritis, serious inflammation of the joints, the eyes and the urinary tract, leading most often to incapacitating stiffness, retinal bleeding and dysmicturition, sometimes as well to mental instabilities of a general sort.

I was fortunate to have in addition to several lengthy visits with this patient in recent months, full access to his most intimate papers, including logs of his major voyages to the Indies, letters written by him to the court over some ten years, notebooks he assembled for King Fernando and our late Queen Isabel, and marginalia in the numerous books in his library. From these I have been able to arrive at a reasonably sound judgment as to his basic character traits, his obsessions and his general psychological makeup. Of these I have isolated four as the most determinant and the ones I believe most useful for later researchers.

1 *Aradixia*

To be without roots, without a sense of home and place, is one of the most serious, though one of the least emphasized, psychological disorders. This patient suffered from this to an unusual degree. From what I have been able to discover, he had so little of that feeling we Spaniards call *querencia* – a love of home and a sense of inner well-being – that he could truly be called a man who never lived anywhere, who simply never had a home.

Late in his life, in a will, Cristobal C made one reference to having been born in Genoa, but nowhere else in all his voluminous writings does he refer to this as his home town, nor does he mention growing up there, or his parents or family, or any of its sights or sounds. (When he wishes to make comparisons between New World phenomena and elsewhere, he always picks Castile: 'very high mountains, all resembling Castile', 'fish like those in Castile', etc). Nor does he ever write a word in Genoese, or Italian, nor refer to a single Italian scholar or artist, past or present. It is as if, supposing this indeed to be his place of birth, he has chosen to eradicate it – and significantly, his parents – from his mind, a psychosis the effects of which are well recorded in the literature.

After his place of birth, the patient never once seems to have found a fixed abode for any length of time. His only real home, from his accounts, was on the deck of a ship, any ship, though one could hardly call the inconstant and ever-changing sea a psychologically fit 'home'. His only real wish, even then, was to go sailing to a different part of it, always somewhere else beyond the horizon.

As to family ties, those were similarly negligible. His only reference ever to his parents was a phrase in one will about praying 'to the souls of my father and mother'. His wife in Portugal is never mentioned in his writings and we do not know the date of his marriage or of its issue, his son Diego. His mistress in Cordova, by whom he had a second son, Fernando, is mentioned but once, in his last will, and nowhere are there any love letters or poems or memorabilia of this deep attachment, though from other writings we see he was a passionate man. I have encountered this stubborn resistance to acknowledging family in other patients, and though it ranges in degrees from a simple kind of forgetfulness to a full-blown blacking-out of a painful past, it is never healthy.

Lastly, I might mention the partiality that the patient seems to have had to several different names over the years – Colombo, Colomo, Colom, Colon – and yet he refers to himself by name only once in all his writings, and when it comes to signing his name he never uses the last name at all, choosing to use only his first name (as a lord or king might), or his title.

2 *Pseudologia*

Bending truth to suit unusual circumstances is a normal enough trait, but a persistent habit of equivocation and misrepresentation, while not necessarily pathological, is certainly dysfunctional – in some cases indicative of full-fledged disorders. This patient appears from all my evidence to be someone who found it difficult, even in non-threatening circumstances, to tell the truth, a habit of delusion that at times developed into self-delusion.

For example, it seems that he chose to keep what some have called a 'false log' on the first voyage of discovery, to record for the crew different distances made at sea from the true ones. If it was a written log it would have been entirely useless, a real sign of self-delusion since the crew could certainly not read, and if it was rather some oral presentation it would have been entirely counterproductive, since it gave the mileage each day as less than the real distance when of course the crew would want to be reassured that they were going faster to their destination. Why the deception? It seems simply to have been in the man's character, something he had to do, its utility aside.

For another example – among many, I am constrained to say – there is the curious incident in 1494 in which the patient made his entire crew swear, to a notary public in an official document and with a punishment of 'the cutting out of the tongue' if anyone should deny it, that the island along which they had been sailing, Cuba, was actually part of some unspecified mainland. True, the man seems to have been in a predicament, since he had declared to the Sovereigns that he would find a mainland on this second voyage to the Indies and so far he had only found islands, and impoverished ones at that. But still – he might have had the men agree informally to that tale, and anyway should have known that the King and Queen wouldn't take the word of a million sea-men without some further proof of there being a mainland there.

The deceptions and self-deceptions are so recurrent in the man's career that we must reckon duplicity is a central part of his character. It is almost as if he had an imperfect understanding of truth and falsehood, or didn't care so long as one or the other served his purposes – but more, as if the one were as real, as true as the other. That way, as we know from our work, madness lies.

> '*I saw two or three villages and their people came down to the beach calling to us and offering thanks to God. Some brought us water, others food... but should your majesties command it, all inhabitants could be taken away to Castile, or made slaves on the island; with 50 men we could subjugate them all and make them do what we want.*'
> Columbus in his report to the Spanish Crown after his first voyage to the Americas.

3 *Monomania*

Although the obsessive drives that characterized the patient's life were tri-partite in nature – we might traditionally put them as God, gold and glory – cynically we may regard them as exhibiting this singular psychosis.

If any further proof of Cristobal C's preoccupation with God were necessary other than his fulsome letters, I have seen his *Book of Prophecies* and it is
one of the strangest, most unsettling documents in patient lore that I have
come across. Not only is it a jumble of Biblical and canonical quotations
designed to prove that the patient had a holy mission to proselytize the world
and reconquer Jerusalem – 'He made me the messenger thereof and showed
me where to go' – but it is shot through with a wild millenarianism of such
uncanny precision that it figures the end of the world exactly 155 years into
the future. The book reveals a conviction of divine purpose ('In this voyage
to the Indies the Lord wished to perform a very evident miracle') that suggests all-out dementia.

As to gold, one has only to read the log of the first voyage, where the
search – or permit me to call it the lust – for treasure is patent on every page.
I troubled myself to count: there are 16 references to gold, some quite
lengthy, during the first two weeks in the islands, another 13 in the next
month, and then finally 46 references in the next five weeks. (The Spanish
word *oro* is used 140 times in all – though he brought back only a few small
nuggets and pieces of jewellery in the end). Later on he is even more revealing: 'Gold is most excellent,' he said on his final voyage, and 'whoever has it
may do what he wishes in the world.'

And glory, this mania of an entirely personal kind: the patient, though
in failing health, managed to compile 44 lengthy documents into a book
for the Sovereigns in which he presented evidence for his claims to titles,
rewards, benefits and revenues from the Crown far in excess of anything
they were prepared to offer. The fact of such a notebook, which might be
presumed a true effrontery to Catholic royalty, is amazing enough evidence
to compulsion. But the tone of martyrdom and victimization ('Had I
despoiled the Indies... and given it to the Moors, I could have been shown
no greater enmity in Spain.') bespeaks an almost total misunderstanding
of the patient's true relationship in the royal schema, indeed in the world
at large.

4 *Phrenitis*
Finally, I must draw attention to a psychotic trait that can only be described
as phrenitis – repeated delusions that occur with such intensity that they
raise serious questions about how we are to regard his general sanity in the
rest of his life. Moreover, the fact that he himself recorded these with perfect
straightforwardness, and without shame – and indeed presented them in
writing to the notoriously cold-blooded Sovereigns – suggests that he must

have regarded such episodes as 'normal'. That is to say, he must have fairly well lost that ability to distinguish the normal from the abnormal that is one of the hallmarks of *compos mentis*.

Take, for example, the discovery of 'Earthly Paradise' reported on his third voyage – no, I am not making this up – and presented in a straight, sober letter to their majesties: 'I am completely persuaded in my own mind that the Terrestrial Paradise is in the place I have said,' where the earth 'has the shape of a pear, which is all very round, except at the stem, where it is very prominent, or that it is as if one had a very round ball, and on one part of it was placed something like a woman's nipple, and that this part with the stem is the highest and nearest to the sky, below the equinoctal line and in this Ocean Sea at the end of the East.' And 'all men say that Paradise is at the end of the East, and that it is.'

Angels and Paradise on a nipple: the patient truly seems to believe in these things, truly seems to see himself as a prime agent in them. It cannot be called incoherence, for the writing is too firm and deliberate for that, but it must be regarded clinically as some form of phrenitis, or paraphrenitis, and at rather an advanced stage.

Luckily, perhaps, the death of the patient has saved me from having to make a full diagnosis of his ailment and from having to prescribe some sort of therapeutic regimen that might enable him to settle comfortably into ordinary quotidian society. I certainly would find it most challenging to do either.

But I am moved to reflect upon the character of this patient, for it strikes me as very significant that this is a man who has braved many great dangers, travelled great distances, faced up to great challenges, and achieved great discoveries, and none can take that away from him. What are we to make of the fact that it seems to take a person with the abnormal character traits of Cristobal C to accomplish all that? What does it mean that the most momentous achievement of our age was rendered by a person distorted by several afflictions, any one of which might be regarded as a functionally disabling mental illness? What does it say about the nature of such achievements, about 'discovery' itself or even the desire of individuals and societies to strive for them? What is it about our culture, our cherished European civilization, that it needs to breed and put forth such people in order to find its salvation in the new, the far-off, the other, the elsewhere? Could madness be the hallmark of our achievers, our progress, our very civilization?

This much at least we can conclude. It has been said that the world owes all its outward impulses, its conquering of space and species, to men ill at ease, while the happy man inevitably confines himself within ancient limits and possibilities. Whatever else, Cristobal C was not a happy man – indeed, more ill at ease in a dark psychotic way than most around – and it might be argued that he represented supremely what was not a happy culture. ■

[signature]

Sigmundo Feliz
Valladolid, Spain

Kirkpatrick Sale is a leading American environmentalist. Among his books are The Conquest of Paradise (1990) *and* Rebels against the Future (1995).

August 1992
Sleepwaves and dream tides
The sea is all around us, but there is also a sea within us. **Sharon Doubiago** *explores the mythology and meaning of the oceans.*

9th SUMMER – Being dragged back by the undertow, being hit then from behind by an eight-footer, being thrown down, smashed down, ground face down into the gravel, crushed by the ton of water, ripped by the centrifugal force of flying stone, sucking shell, dark deafening crushing suffocating roar of water pulling you back to deep ocean, so wanting to breathe, to rise to the air, to see your parents' tent in the sand dune, to hear Mama's cries yes, yes, please yes coming now in the same rhythm and roar of the ocean, the full moon full tide sea that is rising over Pacific Coast Highway, over her body bringing your father's body over onto her.

11th SUMMER – Paddling way out in the inner tube, eyes to the backs of the rolling glistening steel-green breakers folding over the land, exploding all the way up to the line of tents and trailers where Mama is telling Daddy yes and the ocean is the rocking of their bed, my brother and sister and I 'asleep' in the front of the 15-footer, this summer the blood is coming and Mama is instructing this is love, this is joy, this is pleasure, this is the miracle of life. I keep paddling out, further out than the sea-bleached surfer who takes my breath away, to see around Richard Dana's Point, north to LA, the whole coastline, the hidden beach, the secret: Laguna Beach on which Gae and I were violated by her cop-diver father, smell of his semen, sea iodine.

But then the sky turns, the air suddenly colder, the water darkening to short chops. Marine is the colour of fear: I've gone too far. But, Lifeguard within me, shell of balance, the castrated genital Scales of Love tread me back, exhausted, to the boys and men on the beach everywhere their taunts of rape, torture, murder, oblivion. But promise of love too, of pleasure and meaning, Mama and Daddy, yes. Sucking lifesavers to that surfer seaboy on the sand, my suntan.

I was conceived on Redondo Beach, in Southern California. I was born in Seaside Hospital in Long Beach. But my parents were Southerners. They pronounced 'buoy' boy. I've had the sense that *el niño* in the Pacific, or the Pacific himself, called them to its shore even before my conception.

They told me the sound was a boy out there telling boats how to come in through the fog. I listened to the waves slapping him around. I heard his crying, his lonely orphanage in the sea. When we fished, I cast my line to him, I was coming to the sea when I was born, the buoy I heard through water and storm was a boy calling me.[1]

The coming in, the going out, the longing for the sea, the longing for the land, the yearning for the Other, the pull both ways. The water is pulled away from the earth on one side of the globe and the earth is pulled away from the water on the opposite. 'There is a gravitational attraction between every drop of water and even the outermost star of the universe.'[2] Tidal, meaning time. Knowing time as this, that the water will return.

The sea is like the self – does it think? Psyche in her ebb and flow, the least graspable of our existence. Which is the Miracle: we don't know who we are. Being under the sea, living or dead, is our condition in the universe. (What *is* the Gaia hypothesis?) In each wave washing in, so abundant with life, then drawing back, are Laws unknown, and unknowable, liberating. On the beach one's community (any time, any place), is put into perspective that is, proven less. The sea is not, will never be the unjust law of men – not cruel or stupid. It can't be tamed, controlled, or 'known.' Hallelujah! I shout to every wave washing out the possibility of getting stuck. I'm freest when a storm's big ones are hitting.

Where the two worlds meet in an ever-changing pattern of exchange I know the primal: relationship. I'm happy, I'm psychic, I'm turned on, I have hope because I know the Other, which is God. Which is Birth, endless threshold. Seaweed of laminaria dilating the cervix, 'Mother-letter M (Ma): an ideogram for waves of water,'[3] mare nostrum, the moment when the water washes back: the newborn on her belly, cord not cut, before breath. Do we not feel the Moon itself as our child, a part of our missing body, torn from Earth's side by the oscillating solar tides, the massive hole filled with our human tears, milk, blood, urine, albumin, jellyfish of uterus, abalone prostate? Water doesn't 'evolve.' It's the same water since the beginning, water of every human, animal, plant, creature who's ever lived. You never know, to paraphrase James Joyce, who you're drinking.

Living on the coast causes you to know the planets' relationships to us, *Earth*, her rotation as the stars set, her loneliness in space, the pull of sun and moon on her, oscillation of her ovulations, her deaths and rebirths. You can't be linear at the beach! Knowledge of the tidal cycle is essential to your survival. You tread the shore 'line' exactly as Neruda says the ancients trod it: 'that they might recognize that touch come night, come death.' To die to the sea, to die in it, is preferable, oh, *huaca, temenos* holy! to the hands of the mob. To the traffic at intersections. Or iatrogenic, at the hands of physicians. This is why, during the Inquisition, all the women of one German town marched singing into the sea the night before the men's schedule to burn them. When the Coast Guard searches for the drowned I'm on land praying they're never found. Let me be where all the Universe bent to bring me. Let me be fish, seaweed, salt, sea.

Neap tide, ebb tide, high tide, slack water, there is more oxygen where ocean hits land than at any other place on earth. Perhaps this explains the common experience of people who first move to the coast to suddenly 'remember' their repressed pasts, their dreams. And why I fall into their sleepwaves and dreamtides. Poets notoriously need a watery atmosphere, fog and rain, rivers and seas. Perhaps water, especially salt water, is a current, maybe electrical, like radio waves, (I don't know) that carries images, words, stories, the kind of deep thinking that motivates poetry. Souls come back in raindrops, some cultures believe, and rain comes from the ocean, which comes from our bodies. Or perhaps the rhythm of that enormous body beats at the deep muscle tissue, the deep organs, setting off the rhythm of the human body in the way stutterers do not stutter when singing.

Like Isadora Duncan who learned her dance on the Pacific shore, I learn my craft, my poetics from studying wave formations.

In *Thalassa, A Theory of Genitality*, the Freudian psychobiologist Sandor Ferenczi believes that with the drying up of the seas we were thrown up on the land, of neutral gender. The stronger of the species, in its longing to get back to the ocean, developed a penis by which to penetrate the weaker, thus simulating in coitus a return to the ocean – i.e. the womb.

Freudian, yes, because the desire to be the ocean is not the 'weaker position'.

But the sea origin theory – we, Thalassians, taking the seas' place – asks a more essential question: what does it mean that in our present evolution we seem to be relying almost exclusively on technology, and, concomitantly, are destroying nature, maybe even our bodies?

SUNDAY MORNING, 20 SEPTEMBER 1987: We are walking through the Oregon dunes, wading across the mouth of the Siuslaw to North Jetty Beach three days after Daddy has finally died. And Mama is telling a story I have never heard before.

'On the Sunday before you were born we were at the beach at Point Fermin. We were in the rocks – there's a picture of this day. Two guys were out in a small boat, cutting up, just having a good time. I was getting a kick out of them, but I said something awful. "Serve them right if one of them drowned." Then it happened, maybe a wave turned them over. They were calling for help. Your father ran for help and I stood on the rocks, calling to them to hold on, help is coming. It went on all afternoon, it was terrible, terrifying. Then one let go. The other kept going under after him, kept trying to pull the drowned body out. I was depressed for days. You were born six days later, on Saturday.'

Déjà vu, my life with its ever theme of drowning and near drownings shifts slightly, a missing piece falling into place like a grain of sand from the dune we're walking. I had 'already seen' him.

Many of these drownings – in dream, writing, the psychic realm, and 'reality' – are explainable by my lifelong proximity to water, but if I listed here, with minimal description, the 'coincidental,' intertwined, life-changing, some inland, stories, most likely I would not be believed. *Déjà vu*, I pull up to a beach and become part of a drowning. *Déjà vu*, I camped on a beach near Chappaquiddick the night of the infamous drowning, was tormented all night by a waking nightmare of a young woman trapped in a leaking air container out under the ocean, calling me to rescue her.[4]

At a loss for an explanation that will fit our masculine/masculinist logic we label my experiences psychic, extra-sensory perception. I am at least communicating, however judged. But extra-sensory? My experiences always lean into the sensory – into the body itself. How do the grunion know the highest wave? The salmon their natal creek mouth? Are we not one body? Does not science know this? We begin to grasp that, strangely, we re-enact our childhood dramas as adults; inexplicably, I've re-enacted my prenatal experience all my life.

Was 'something' born in me that opens me to the calling from water? How many others heard and saw and felt or otherwise knew Mary Jo in 'dream' that night?[5] Was not the water itself sending her message? Could we not have saved her if we respected this world as much as we respected the men in their spaceship on the way to the moon that same night? Would not such crimes be less? Our over-reliance on technology reduces and diminishes our naturally evolving psychic-biological evolution; we are retarded, made immoral, by our fear and hatred of Earth.

But what we could do if we turned around and embraced ourselves, Okeanus-held! From behind the wave we always swim back for the human, for our varying skin colours, tribes, cultures, geographies. For the taste of sweat, saliva, skin, semen, blood. We want tears and urine, the menstrual cycle, faeces, old-age, even death, that seed of life, the Joy of my parents' cries in our beach camps, on vacation.

OLDEST, STILL RECURRING NIGHTMARE (*mare*: the sea; *Mary*: female goddess; *mer*: to seize): We come to the bridge, the wide white modern one that goes over the ocean, my father driving, all my family in the car. Amazing! Men have actually managed to build a bridge across the Pacific Ocean!

But halfway over to Japan the bridge gives out. Too fast, too late to stop, to turn back, the deep, deepest marine rollicking careless happy sea oblivious to our fear, our folly, infinite miles from any life saver. ∎

Sharon Doubiago is an American poet and writer. She considers the Pacific coast, from San Diego to Seattle, her home.

1 From 'I Was Born Coming To The Sea,' from *Hard Country*, Sharon Doubiago, West End Press, 1982. 2 *The Sea Around Us*, Rachel L Carson, Mentor Books, 1957. 3 *The Woman's Encyclopedia of Myths and Secrets*, Barbara G Walker, Harper & Row, 1983. 4 See 'Chappaquiddick', in *The Book Of Seeing With One's Own Eyes*. Sharon Doubiago, Graywolf Press, 1988. 5 Mary Jo Kopechne, drowned at Chappaquiddick.

September 1993

Can memory survive the storm?

The Chinese emperors, Stalin, Hitler: throughout the ages those in power have tried to reshape human memory. **David Watson** *fears that TV and consumer culture are succeeding where others failed.*

Most of my life has been spent in the inner city of Detroit, a place both like and unlike many others in the industrialized world. I still live in the neighborhood where I did my growing up, attended school, met and married my wife. Despite the urban desolation, I'm tied to the place; even after long sojourns abroad, I always return to the same few square blocks. Our house looks out on land that was gradually cleared of buildings after the 1967 black rebellion and the city's economic decline in the 1970s. In the Sixties it had been a thriving community of poor whites and blacks, students and young radicals. I found the local anti-war committee, a friendly poor people's diner, communes, poor churches, and a sense of community there.

Like so many of the decade's dreams, the neighborhood was demolished. It left a fascinating miniature urban wilderness of great old trees, wildflowers mixed with perennials where once there had been gardens and a rich bird habitat. Eventually this green place was also flattened and a typically ugly housing development constructed in its place. Recently the builders returned to the section directly across from us. In a few days it was fenced and all the trees were smashed. Expensive condominiums, almost completed, are being leased at rents well beyond the means of most locals. Our view of a park and the sunset is blocked. Someone is getting elegant, sterile housing and someone else is getting rich, but our lives seem incrementally poorer.

Such things happen all the time, happen everywhere. One might wonder what they have to do with history and its abuses. I think that in a small, perhaps obscure way, our experience is like that which many people have had walking down a familiar street and realizing some landmark is missing but not quite remembering what. It is for me emblematic of the disappearance of memory which is occurring relentlessly around the globe. The process may seem anonymous because it is inertial, or because nearly everyone assumes it to be perfectly natural. But history, big and small, is not just disappearing; it is being disappeared just as surely as human beings are 'disappeared' by dictatorships.

Of course, history has always been an ambiguous affair – a (consciously and unconsciously) constructed official story employed by powerful men to legitimize their rule ever since the armed Mesopotamian god-kings conquered the wilderness to build their city-states. Since then, history has been a long series of cataclysms. In the 1930s, Walter Benjamin described the 'angel of history' being thrown backwards by a storm out of Paradise. At his feet lies 'one single catastrophe which keeps piling wreckage upon wreckage'. While the angel would like to 'make whole what has been smashed', the storm 'irresistibly propels him into a future to which his back is turned, while the pile of debris before him grows ever skyward. The storm is what we call progress.'

Despite its many disasters, there have always been counter-stories to imperial myth, and history has remained contested ground. Individual memory is a knot in the web of collective memory, and this shared history is an immense, diverse psychic commons sustaining our sense of human community, a reservoir where glimpses of freedom, and the remembrance of atrocities and triumphs are all preserved. We need this common historical space to replenish our inner capacity to remain human in the same way that forests and wild places are needed to nourish and renew the land. But just as the world's forests are being destroyed, so too is memory's commons.

Empires have always worked to undermine authentic memory – for example, the book burnings by the Ch'in emperors of ancient China, a method still employed in our time. (This strategy was updated in 1970s China under the Maoist regime, when photographs of a line-up of party leaders were retouched to turn purged bureaucrats into shrubs.) Monumentalism is another age-old form of control. One grotesque recent monument was the construction by the Balaguer government in the Dominican Republic of an enormous lighthouse, far from the sea, to honour Columbus and his 'discovery' – a project which levelled poor *barrios* of Santo Domingo and now causes frequent electrical 'brown-outs' throughout the city.

Despite their destructiveness, such methods have limited results, to which the patent shabbiness of the Columbus story and the toppling monuments of the Soviet bloc dramatically testify. There are now greater threats to memory, greater weapons in power's arsenal. The modern transformations in consciousness brought about during the last century by mass communications and consumer society seem to be changing the *form* memory takes. And history's form shapes content as surely as it takes particular words or kinds of words to make a certain kind of statement.

This change evokes the legend of the Chinese emperor who decreed for himself the exclusive use of the pronoun 'I'. The modern media have now donned these imperial robes, speaking while everyone else listens. One can no longer even make a revolution without making sure to seize the television stations (as apparently was the case in Romania), since instead of directly making history, people watch the screen to see what is happening. The contemporary erosion of people's capacity to think for themselves, and the monopolization of meaning by media, seem to be succeeding at what the legendary emperor could only have imagined.

A new society emerged in Western Europe and North America during the last century as the organic structures of life began to unravel. In the United States, where this development seems most pernicious, the colonization and control of culture was an explicit strategy to obtain labour discipline and mass consumption. As historian Stuart Ewen has pointed out, by the early 20th century business leaders, coming out of a period of mass labor unrest, recognized the need to manage not only production but consumption as well. A new kind of citizen had to be shaped to respond appropriately to the plethora of industrial products offered by the emergent corporate market system. As one entrepreneur wrote in the 1920s, education must teach 'the masses not what to think but how to think, and thus... how to behave like human beings in the machine age'.

By the 1950s industrial expansion and economic growth provided the twin pillars of a universal secular religion, and consumerism an unquestioned cultural norm. This consumer ethos (if not necessarily its material benefits) is spreading rapidly to the countries of the post-colonial world and the former Soviet empire. Today the question culture critic Vance Packard asked back in 1950s is increasingly relevant: 'What is the impact on the human spirit of all these pressures to consume?'

Since then, the impact of television – which has become the key instrument for consumer culture worldwide – has confirmed Packard's fears. Television flattens, disconnects and renders incoherent experiences and history. Its seemingly meaningful pastiche of images works best to sell commodities – objects devoid of any history. But more importantly, it also affirms the whole universe of commodity consumption as the only life worth living. Wherever the set is turned on, local culture implodes.

Though sold as a tool that could preserve memory, television utterly fragments and colonizes it. What remains is a cult of the perpetual present, in continual giddying motion. The jumbled, packaged events of recent and remote history come to share the relative weightlessness of soap operas and dish detergent. Perspective evaporates. Power no longer needs to shout since, as Mark Crispin Miller once remarked, 'Big Brother isn't watching you so much as Big Brother is you, watching'. Historical memory is now becoming what was televised, while that commons of the mind, domesticated and simulated by the media, is receding.

A striking case in point is the way people (especially North Americans) were manipulated into supporting the Gulf War. Someone who has already seen tens of thousands of people 'killed' on TV has a difficult time understanding the human suffering caused by the TV-filtered special effects of techno-war. Yet even the war hysteria, which one journalist described as a 'nightly electronic Nuremberg Rally', faded with time, as the images crystallized into scraps of last year's mini-series. When Iraq was more recently attacked and several civilians killed, many passive patriots who had been glued to their sets during the War were now barely aware of it. It was all, as is often said, 'history' – which is to say, it no longer existed. Their indifference today is as disturbing as their spasm of enthusiasm was yesterday.

The media-driven market system is doing something to human meaning far more serious than government propaganda or censorship ever could. Just when the peoples of the former colonies (as well as women and other formerly invisible groups) are rediscovering their own stories, long suppressed by official history, modern technique is poised to shape everyone's story, making them all a fragment in one long photomontage. How will so many different peoples be able to tell their own unique stories when TV itself has become the dominant mode of communication and recall? How will memory express diverse modes of being when work, buying and selling are the core of what is rapidly becoming a global monoculture? Will those cultures that aren't compatible with televised sensibility just disappear altogether, like the trees that once stood across from my window?

The disappearance of languages and cultures is as terrifying a prospect as the current mass extinction of species. At current rates, some 90 per cent of the world's languages will be moribund in the next century. And without language there can be no memories. Ironically, the greatest threat is to those scattered cultures whose memory precedes official history – the primal and indigenous peoples, some with traditions reaching back to the Pleistocene. The native Hawaiians, for example, have seen their culture wither under the onslaught of progress. Many now speak only the language of their American conquerors, and remembrance has eroded as the places to which words and sensibilities were bound, have come under the bulldozer's blade. Enormous resorts, shopping malls and golf courses (as well as military bombing ranges) have devoured burial grounds, old fishing villages and sacred sites.

I will give just one devastating example. On the island of Hawaii itself, where the active volcano Kilauea constantly creates new land, is some of the richest lowland tropical rainforest left in the island chain (only about ten per cent survives). Even according to the conqueror's laws, the forest, called Wao Kele O Puna, was to be held in perpetuity for Hawaiians to practise subsistence activities and to gather ceremonial and medicinal plants, many of which grow there and nowhere else. Yet in the late 1980s the state government of Hawaii traded the 110-square-kilometre forest to corporate developers who hope to drill into it and tap the volcano's geothermal energy.

To the Hawaiians, however, the volcano is a living being, the goddess Pele. She created and continues to create the islands. Hawaiians have many good reasons to fight geothermal development – its risks, its cost, its violation of native land rights, its inevitable destruction of pristine forest. But the project is above all an assault on the heart of their culture and religion, and thus on a tangible reminder of what it means to be a Hawaiian. As Pualani Kanehele, a respected teacher of the sacred Hawaiian dance, the *hula kahiko*, argued, to cap Pele's steam would be 'putting a cap on the Hawaiian culture... and Hawaii will be dead. Then this may as well be a new California. Because we'll all be *haoles* [whites] with the same goals as the *haoles*: make money.'

Meaning, like ecology, is context: everything is connected to everything else. As strands are pulled from the skein of memory, what it means to be a person within a human community shifts toward some troubling unknown. The experience of the Hawaiians, who have seen their ancestors' bones turned up by machines so that someone else's paradise can be fabricated, lends special resonance to Benjamin's warning that even the dead are not safe when power triumphs.

If, as Czech novelist Milan Kundera has written, 'the struggle... against power is the struggle against forgetting', the need to remember must also inevitably confront power. We may come to need truth commissions to recover our shared memory, like those organized to uncover and preserve the lost stories of disappeared persons in Latin America. Taking responsibility for our past might help us uncover the complex weave of histories that now connect us all in our shared suffering and grandeur. ∎

David Watson teaches, writes and survives in inner-city Detroit.

November 1993

Cephu's choice

Is it natural for human beings to want personal liberty? Or is it a peculiarly Western concern? Nancy Scheper-Hughes draws some conclusions from indigenous cultures around the world.

Imagine a small clearing in the Ituri forest of Zaire. A band of Mbuti pygmies are returning from a hunt. The women have run ahead of the game nets carried by the men to beat the ground and the bushes, terrifying small animals so that they rush blindly and headlong into the traps. The game, collectively caught, is carefully redistributed at the base camp.

But one of the hunters, wily Cephu, has cheated. Running ahead of the group he captured some of the game before they ran into the nets, and Cephu and his wife enjoyed the advantage of an early meal. Found out, Cephu is punished, told that if he does not wish to behave like a human being, that is, like a Mbuti – he is free to go his own way... alone. In other words, Cephu is banished.

But before two nights pass the hunter crawls back to the base camp, shamefaced and repentant. He has learned the lesson: outside the band there is only the 'freedom' of hunger, fear and isolation. Mbuti conceptions of liberty paradoxically imply constraint. Here, liberty means the relative freedom from danger and scarcity through participation in a closed and demanding but reciprocal human community.

This vignette – recounted by Colin Turnbull in his anthropological classic *The Forest People* – reveals a basic paradox in the nature of human freedom. Humans are among the most social of creatures while yet the most self-consciously aware of, and tormented by, the limitations that living in social groups demand. 'Man is double,' wrote sociologist Durkheim, 'individual and social', and there is the rub. Human aspirations for liberty and independence are founded on bio-evolutionary constraints that we are not free to reject, except at a very high cost. These constraints are more visible in small-scale, non-Western societies where human survival is completely dependent on an immediate and balanced reciprocity that requires the subordination of individual goals and desires to larger collective needs.

I think, for example, of a poignant scene from Napoleon Chagnon's ethnographic film *The Feast* about the Yanomami Indians who inhabit a remote corner of the Amazon near the Brazilian border with Venezuela. Fierce raids by renegade bands, as well as by Brazilian miners, have forced the Yanomami into new allegiances with former enemies. The film captures the scene of a three-day feast of dance, food and gift-exchange that symbolizes and solidifies the new bond of trust forged between two former enemy bands.

The headman of the host village calls on each of his fellows to come forward and 'offer up' a prized possession which is given to a member of the other band. One elderly man cowers in the back of the circle of squatting men holding tight to his pet dog, a mangy mutt. But then he, too, is called forward by the headman to surrender his pet as a peace offering. The man hesitates and cries out in protest: 'No, I don't want to give up my dog!' He jumps up and stamps his foot in anger.

No-one says a word, but all stare at the old man fixedly until he realizes that no-one is about to support him and he reluctantly hands over his dog to a man from the other band. As he returns to his place in the circle, the old man shakes his head sadly and mumbles, 'I better get something good next time'.

There never was a 'noble savage' living as a free spirit in an enviable 'state of nature'. On the contrary, many traditional societies lack a conception of liberty altogether for this requires a notion of 'the person' or 'the individual' and thereby 'the self'. Such ideas are often either absent entirely or weakly defined.

Anthropologist Clifford Geertz has argued that Western conceptions of 'the person' as a bounded, unique and separate entity and 'the self' as a dynamic centre of awareness, emotion, judgement and action are actually rather peculiar notions within the context of world cultures. In many traditional societies, instead of individuals there are roles and statuses which particular actors may inhabit for a time but which are eventually passed on to the next 'occupant' of the role. What is valued in collectivist societies is continuity and repetition, not individuation and difference. The Western idea of 'liberty' was developed to protect the latter values and has little meaning in the former.

In Western industrial societies individual personal names have an almost sacred quality and are endowed along with rights of 'personhood' on every infant at birth. But babies in many traditional and peasant societies may go unnamed for the first several months or even years of their lives during which time they are called by such nondescript pet names as 'baby', 'sugar' or 'little bit of nothing'. When finally named they may be given a generic name – such as 'Mary' anywhere in the Catholic world – or be called by some version of 'first born' or 'number one' or 'last born'. This draws attention to the infant's social status rather than to any particular quality of the child as a 'person'.

Perhaps the highest praise accorded to a child in such collectivist societies is to be named simply 'man' or 'human being' as was Ishi, the celebrated last surviving 'wild' Californian Indian, or the late South African founder of the Black Consciousness Movement, 'Stephen' Biko. His actual given name at birth was 'Bantu', simply meaning 'man' or 'people' and the legacy of his personal name was a source of strength to Stephen who sometimes – and only partly in jest – referred to himself by the rather blasphemous term 'son of man'.

Finally, in rural Northeast Brazil, where death claims a great many infants, a new-born is often given the name of the last child that died in the family. This emphasizes the essential social principle that while family and communities are permanent, individual actors are replaceable. The saying 'you can't take it with you when you die' applies equally in these societies to a notion of 'the self'.

Traditional and collectivist views of naming fly directly in the face of

Western notions of individual human rights exemplified in Article Seven of
the UN Convention on the Rights of the Child which reads: 'The child shall
be registered immediately after birth and shall have the right from birth to
a personal name'. Though seemingly innocuous and self-evident, this article
actually stands in flagrant disregard and opposition to the way many non-
Western people view the meaning of human life and death.

The Zinacanteco Mexican Indians think of each 'new' person as not new
at all but rather as a composite, made up of 'soul stuff' borrowed from a
repository of the souls of deceased ancestral Zinacantecos. At death the
soul leaves the body and returns to whence it came – a kind of soul bank
kept by the gods. This spiritual reservoir is used for the creation of new
human beings, each of whom is made up of at least 13 parts from the souls
of former living persons. There is no sense that each Zinacanteco infant is
brand new or a totally unique individual. Rather, each person is but a fraction of the whole Zinacanteco spiritual and social world. This means that
individual 'claims' and demands are not backed up by the cosmological system which support instead a sort of tyranny of the collective, which
anthropologist Laura Nader has labelled 'harmony ideology'. Freedom is
sacrificed for equality, and the seemingly easy and natural consensus that
is reached is often forced and extracted through subtle forms of threat and
group pressure – a common feature of collectivist societies, whether
traditional or modern.

Among Australian Aborigines of the Western Desert, each new person
comes into the world circumscribed by ancestral origin myths about
'Dreamtime' which structure the world and rigidly define the place of all
aboriginal people within it. The myths determine each person's position and
the marriage strategies, kinship ties and friendship alliances that each must
pursue in adherence to the sacred geography and its accompanying moral
economy. 'The Dreaming', wrote William Stanner, 'determines not only
what life is, but also what it *can* be. Life, so to speak, is a one-possibility
thing.' In this indigenous society there is no sense of personal 'agency' fundamental to Western notions of liberty and democracy. Nor is there any idea
of an individual search for personal salvation which Christian missionaries
have tried, but normally failed, to communicate.

Even more striking, however, are Australian Aboriginal ways of death.
Neither individual biology nor personal choice decides the time of a person's death, which is also collectivized. Harry Eastwell, a psychiatrist practis-
ing for a time in the Western Desert in remote outpost clinics, discovered
that certain old and enfeebled persons die according to a social script that is

initiated by a collective 'sing'. When the old or sick person hears the songs that foretell his or her passage to the next world, he or she suffers a 'mortification' process. This begins with a separation from the group (usually by lying at a slight distance, alone on a mat in the sun), moves towards a psychological acquiescence to death, and concludes with the death itself, normally due to dehydration.

Here, the social group decides the timing of the death and the individual is expected to conform graciously and to express the sentiment that: 'This is, indeed, a good time to die'. From social birth to social death, the trajectory of the Aboriginal person's entire life course is predetermined. No wonder the crude designs to assimilate such peoples into Western culture have failed.

However, even in the most collectivist human societies individuals still have choices and exercise certain liberties. Marriages may be prearranged for Kalahari San or Mbuti pygmy girls against their wishes. But they can still make life so miserable for the unwanted spouse that he leaves the hut, so the girls can then choose a subsequent partner for themselves. Similarly, Australian Aboriginal youths born into one camp can, when they reach adolescence, move freely among different camping groups and choose a marriage partner for themselves – as long as she fits the general design of the Dreamtime myths.

Small-scale, collectivist societies like the Mbuti Pygmies, the Kung San and the Australian first peoples are often romanticized as harmonious, balanced and egalitarian – and they are. But, as I have tried to show, this harmony is extracted at a high personal cost, in the absence of or with a low price placed on personal liberty. In putting individual bodies, desires and goals at the disposal of the group such societies necessarily do violence to Western notions of bodily integrity, habeas corpus, personal autonomy and free choice.

Australian Aboriginal peoples – and many highland New Guinea groups too – practice severe forms of penile mutilation, slashing open the urethra, scourging it with abrasive stalks of grass, mutilating the glans or infibulating it. The purpose is to initiate young men to collective life by inscribing the discipline of the group onto the docile flesh of new recruits. Similarly brutal practices of female circumcision – particularly Sudanese 'infibulation' by means of which young girls are made 'women' by cutting away the 'unsightly' clitoris and both sets of labia – have been criticized by human-rights and feminist organizations. But the liberal and progressive world has been strangely silent when the body in question and under the knife has been male.

The very severity of these body rituals – and these are the most extreme examples – are intended to remind young initiates of the awesome primacy of the Body Social over the Body Individual. When indigenous people defend their initiation practices against the liberal, democratic dictates that attempt to abolish or modify them, the traditionalists assert the symbolic and religious charters upon which the rites are based. What ensues is a fundamental and irreconcilable clash of cultures – one modern, individualist and secular, the other 'traditional', collectivist and sacred. It is another version of the dialectic between liberty and equality that Alexis de Tocqueville identified in his travels through America in the 1830s, a dialectic that has tended to be resolved over time in defence of liberty and at the expense of equality in the US.

The dialectic between freedom and equality on the one hand and individual autonomy and collective harmony on the other, remains an unfinished and perhaps irresolvable human project. Human societies and cultures are essentially variable and highly resistant to a single definition of 'the good'. While attempts at building cross-cultural charters and constitutions that promote human rights to life, liberty and the pursuit of happiness are laudable, one should keep in mind that these values may be in contention. The very idea of freedom is culturally shaped, historically situated and highly specific: it can never be reduced to a single, essential or universal meaning. ■

April 1997
The haunted house
The 'work ethic' was bad enough, says **Zygmunt Bauman**. *But its ghost is even worse.*

Whenever you hear talk about 'ethics' you can be pretty sure that someone somewhere is dissatisfied with the way other people are behaving and would rather they behaved differently. This is especially true in the case of the notorious 'work ethic'. Since its emergence in the early days of the Industrial Revolution, the work ethic has served politicians, philosophers and preachers by removing the obstacles to the brave new world they envisaged.

The main obstacle was the basic human inclination to do no more than satisfy one's needs. Why work more than necessary? the individual might ask. For more money? There are so many other worthwhile things to do of which you might lose sight if you spent all your time running after money.

The early entrepreneurs had different plans, though. Shiftless and laggard factory hands were to be taught – or forced if need be – to wish for a better life, to desire more, and to improve themselves by desiring more.

The moral crusade for the work ethic was presented as trying to recapture – within the factory – the commitment and pride that came naturally to the craftsperson. The trouble was that it was the factory system itself which had destroyed these in the first place.

So under the guise of a work ethic a *discipline* ethic had to be promoted. As Werner Sombart commented, the factory system needed part-humans; soulless little wheels of a complex mechanism – and war was waged against the other, now useless, emotional 'human parts'. No wonder critics of that time such as Ferdinand Lasselle spoke in support of 'the right to laziness'.

Finally, for the first time in history, the work ethic prioritized 'what can be done' over 'what needs to be done'. The satisfaction of human needs became irrelevant to the logic of production – and cleared the way for the modern paradox of 'growth for growth's sake'.

Since then, however, something has happened which neither the industrialists nor the critics of capitalism imagined. A century ago Rosa Luxemburg predicted that capitalist modernization could not survive without devouring the ever-shrinking enclaves of non-industrialized life. The tendency of capital to move from already 'modernized' areas and into the 'underdeveloped' territories of the Third World seems to have proved her right.

But what she did not predict was that modernism (or industrialism) would create expanding enclaves of 'post-modern' existence in which people are consumers first – and workers only a very distant second. The work ethic has been replaced by a consumer ethic; the savings-book culture of delayed gratification has been replaced by the credit-card culture that 'takes the waiting out of wanting'. The inhabitants of these enclaves are kept in place not by coercion but by seduction, by the creation of new desires rather than by normative regulation.

Inside these post-modern enclaves the work ethic has lost its obvious and crucial usefulness. There is simply not enough paid employment any more to support the model of full-time jobs for life.

It is tempting to applaud the demise of the work ethic and to rejoice in the post-modern way's recognition of the multiplicity of human existence. The learned classes are always the first to wax lyrical about the blessings of new life. Now they praise liberation from the stultifying monotony of assembly lines with as much ardour as their predecessors a century ago brought to their songs about the glory of factory chimneys. What the songs of praise stifle, however, are the voices of the victims: the new poor, denied the opportunity to follow the rules of the work ethic in a world in which the only access to the resources needed to exercise one's freedom is still through the door marked 'work'.

The idea that the poor – and the rich – will always be with us is not new. But never before has the split been so unambiguous, so unequivocal. The reason is simple. The rich – who happen also to be the most politically powerful – no longer need the poor. They do not need the poor for the salvation of their souls – which they do not believe they have and which at any rate they would not consider worthy of care. Nor do the rich need the poor for staying rich or getting richer – in fact they reckon they would be better off if the poor weren't there at all, making claims on their riches.

The poor are not a reserve army of labour which needs to be groomed back into wealth production. Neither are they consumers who must be tempted and cajoled into 'giving the lead to economic recovery'. Whichever way you look at it, the poor are of no use. This is a real novelty in a world undergoing perhaps the deepest transformation in the long history of humankind.

So the mutual dependency between rich and poor has gone. No wonder the US pollsters of both competing camps informed their respective candidates for the Presidency that the voters wanted cuts in benefits to the poor and lower taxes on the rich. Both rivals did their best to outspit each other in their proposals to cut down welfare assistance and to lavish the saved funds on building new prisons and employing more police. As Pastor John Steinbruck, the minister at Luther Place Memorial Church in Washington, recently summed it up: 'This nation has as its symbol the Statue of Liberty, with the message carved at its base "Give me your poor, your homeless, your huddled masses". But here we are now in this damn country, the richest in history, and we've forgotten all that.'

To a growing number of people the demise of the work ethic comes too early and in too malformed a fashion to be experienced as a liberation. What such people know for sure is that there is not enough work for them in a society that can easily obtain all the goods it needs – and more – without calling on their labour power. But at the same time they are told that in order to get access to those goods they have to sell their labour. They are reminded, day by day, that without 'being available for work' they are not entitled to any part of the social riches, however meagre and pitiable their share may be. In the US they were told recently that they would be allowed to stay out of work for no more than two years during their entire life. Regardless of the reasons for their unemployment, they are derided as misfits, reproached for sloth, dubbed anti-social and stigmatized as spongers.

The fact is that the house of post-modernity is haunted by the ghost of the work ethic, no less sinister in its posthumous life than it was in its halcyon days.

We have two worlds, at opposite poles, which are becoming increasingly out of touch with each other – much as the no-go areas of contemporary cities are carefully fenced off and bypassed by the traffic lines used for the mobility of well-off residents. The inhabitants of the first world, the relatively affluent and employed, live in a perpetual present. These people are constantly busy and always 'short of time'. People marooned in the opposite world are crushed under the burden of abundant, redundant and useless time they can fill with nothing. In their time 'nothing ever happens'. They do not 'control ' time – but neither are they controlled by it, unlike their clocking-in, clocking-out ancestors, subject to the faceless rhythm of factory time. They can only kill time, as they are slowly killed by it.

For the residents of the first world, abiding by the rules of the work ethic and sacrificing their lives to professional success is the supreme test of freedom. They wear the badge 'workaholic' with pride. For the inhabitants of the second, not being able to follow their example is the symptom of failure and carries a stigma of shame.

Those who have the capacity to act out the principles of the work ethic at will are sceptical and ironic about its virtues. But those who can only dream of their share of a chance bitterly complain of their deprivation. If their ancestors rightly saw the work-ethics preachers as the enemies of their freedom, today's unemployed see those who criticize the work ethic as members of a worldwide conspiracy against their right to humanity.

And this will remain the case unless, as Claus Offe suggests, the proper conclusions from the great social transformation are drawn and all lifestyles are treated equally, including lifestyles that do not involve employment or do so in only a very fragmentary fashion. The old distinction between 'anomalous' and 'normal' life situations and modes of conduct needs to be abolished. Not just in word, but in deed, through breaking the link between employment and living resources and establishing material entitlements to all citizens – a 'minimum wage' that is not tied to work.

Exorcising the spectre of the work ethic will take no less than that. ■

Zygmunt Bauman is Emeritus Professor of Sociology at Leeds University in England. He is a leading theorist of Post-Modernity and author of several books including Modernity and the Holocaust *and* Post-Modern Ethics.

April 1997

The drowning child and the expanding circle

As the world shrinks, so our capacity for effective moral action grows. **Peter Singer** *indicates how this may change our lives.*

To challenge my students to think about the ethics of what we owe to people in need, I ask them to imagine that their route to the university takes them past a shallow pond. One morning, I say to them, you notice a child has fallen in and appears to be drowning. To wade in and pull the child out would be easy but it will mean that you get your clothes wet and muddy, and by the time you go home and change you will have missed your first class.

I then ask the students: do you have any obligation to rescue the child? Unanimously, the students say they do. The importance of saving a child so far outweighs the cost of getting one's clothes muddy and missing a class, that they refuse to consider it any kind of excuse for not saving the child. Does it make a difference, I ask, that there are other people walking past the pond who would equally be able to rescue the child but are not doing so? No, the students reply, the fact that others are not doing what they ought to do is no reason why I should not do what I ought to do.

Once we are all clear about our obligations to rescue the drowning child in front of us, I ask: would it make any difference if the child were far away, in another country perhaps, but similarly in danger of death, and equally within your means to save, at no great cost – and absolutely no danger – to yourself? Virtually all agree that distance and nationality make no moral difference to the situation. I then point out that we are all in that situation of the person passing the shallow pond: we can all save lives of people, both children and adults, who would otherwise die, and we can do so at a very small cost to us: the cost of a new CD, a shirt or a night out at a restaurant or concert, can mean the difference between life and death to more than one person somewhere in the world – and overseas aid agencies like Oxfam overcome the problem of acting at a distance.

At this point the students raise various practical difficulties. Can we be sure that our donation will really get to the people who need it? Doesn't most aid get swallowed up in administrative costs, or waste, or downright corruption? Isn't the real problem the growing world population, and is there any point in saving lives until the problem has been solved? These questions can all be answered: but I also point out that even if a substantial proportion of our donations were wasted, the cost to us of making the donation is so small, compared to the benefits that it provides when it, or some of it, does get through to those who need our help, that we would still be saving lives at a small cost to ourselves – even if aid organizations were much less efficient than they actually are.

I am always struck by how few students challenge the underlying ethics of the idea that we ought to save the lives of strangers when we can do so at relatively little cost to ourselves. At the end of the 19th century WH Lecky wrote of human concern as an expanding circle which begins with the individual, then embraces the family and 'soon the circle... includes first a class, then a nation, then a coalition of nations, then all humanity, and finally, its influence is felt in the dealings of man with the animal world'.[1] On this basis the overwhelming majority of my students seem to be already in the penultimate stage – at least – of Lecky's expanding circle. There is, of course, for many students and for various reasons a gap between acknowledging what we ought to do, and doing it; but I shall come back to that issue shortly.

Our century is the first in which it has been possible to speak of global responsibility and a global community. For most of human history we could affect the people in our village, or perhaps in a large city, but even a powerful king could not conquer far beyond the borders of his kingdom. When Hadrian ruled the Roman Empire, his realm covered most of the 'known' world, but today when I board a jet in London leaving what used to be one of the far-flung outposts of the Roman Empire, I pass over its opposite boundary before I am even halfway to Singapore, let alone to my home in Australia. Moreover, no matter what the extent of the empire, the time required for communications and transport meant that there was simply no way in which people could make any difference to the victims of floods, wars, or massacres taking place on the other side of the globe. By the time anyone had heard of the events and responded, the victims were dead or had survived without assistance. 'Charity begins at home' made sense, because it was only 'at home' – or at least in your own town – that you could be confident that your charity would make any difference.

Instant communications and jet transport have changed all that. A television audience of two billion people can now watch hungry children beg for food in an area struck by famine, or they can see refugees streaming across the border in search of a safe place away from those they fear will kill them. Most of that huge audience also have the means to help people they are seeing on their screens. Each one of us can pull out a credit card and phone in a donation to an aid organization which can, in a few days, fly in people who can begin distributing food and medical supplies. Collectively, it is also within the capacity of the United Nations – with the support of major powers – to put troops on the ground to protect those who are in danger of becoming victims of genocide.

Our capacity to affect what is happening, anywhere in the world, is one way in which we are living in an era of global responsibility. But there is also another way that offers an even more dramatic contrast with the past. The atmosphere and the oceans seemed, until recently, to be elements of nature totally unaffected by the puny activities of human beings. Now we know that our use of chlorofluorocarbons has damaged the ozone shield; our emission of carbon dioxide is changing the climate of the entire planet in unpredictable ways and raising the level of the sea; and fishing fleets are scouring the oceans, depleting fish populations that once seemed limitless to a point from which they may never recover. In these ways the actions of consumers in Los Angeles can cause skin cancer among Australians, inundate the lands of peasants in Bangladesh, and force Thai villagers who could once earn a living by fishing to work in the factories of Bangkok.

In these circumstances the need for a global ethic is inescapable. Is it nevertheless a vain hope? Here are some reasons why it may not be.

We live in a time when many people experience their lives as empty and lacking in fulfilment. The decline of religion and the collapse of communism have left but the ideology of the free market whose only message is: consume, and work hard so you can earn money to consume more. Yet even those who do reasonably well in this race for material goods do not find that they are satisfied with their way of life. We now have good scientific evidence for what philosophers have said throughout the ages: once we have enough to satisfy our basic needs, gaining more wealth does not bring us more happiness.

Consider the life of Ivan Boesky, the multimillionaire Wall Street dealer who in 1986 pleaded guilty to insider trading. Why did Boesky get involved in criminal activities when he already had more money than he could ever spend? Six years after the insider-trading scandal broke, Boesky's estranged wife Seema spoke about her husband's motives in an interview with Barbara Walters for the American ABC Network's *20/20* program. Walters asked whether Boesky was a man who craved luxury. Seema Boesky thought not, pointing out that he worked around the clock, seven days a week, and never took a day off to enjoy his money. She then recalled that when in 1982 *Forbes* magazine first listed Boesky among the wealthiest people in the US, he was upset. She assumed he disliked the publicity and made some remark to that effect. Boesky replied: 'That's not what's upsetting me. We're no-one. We're nowhere. We're at the bottom of the list and I promise you I won't shame you like that again. We will not remain at the bottom of that list.'

We must free ourselves from this absurd conception of success. Not only does it fail to bring happiness even to those who, like Boesky, do extraordinarily well in the competitive struggle; it also sets a social standard that is a recipe for global injustice and environmental disaster. We cannot continue to see our goal as acquiring more and more wealth, or as consuming more and more goodies, and leaving behind us an even larger heap of waste.

We tend to see ethics as opposed to self-interest; we assume that those who make fortunes from insider trading are successfully following self-interest – as long as they don't get caught – and ignoring ethics. We think that it is in our interest to take a more senior better-paid position with another company, even though it means that we are helping to manufacture or promote a product that does no good at all, or is environmentally damaging. On the other hand, those who pass up opportunities to rise in their career because of ethical 'scruples' about the nature of the work, or who give away their wealth to good causes, are thought to be sacrificing their own interest in order to obey the dictates of ethics.

Many will say that it is naïve to believe that people could shift from a life based on consumption, or on getting on top of the corporate ladder, to one that is more ethical in its fundamental direction. But such a shift would answer a palpable need. Today the assertion that life is meaningless no longer comes from existentialist philosophers who treat it as a shocking discovery: it comes from bored adolescents for whom it is a truism. Perhaps it is the central place of self-interest, and the way in which we conceive of our own interest, that is to blame here. The pursuit of self-interest, as standardly conceived, is a life without any meaning beyond our own pleasure or individual satisfaction. Such a life is often a self-defeating enterprise. The ancients knew of the 'paradox of hedonism', according to which the more explicitly we pursue our desire for pleasure, the more elusive we will find its satisfaction. There is no reason to believe that human nature has changed so dramatically as to render the ancient wisdom inapplicable.

Here ethics offer a solution. An ethical life is one in which we identify ourselves with other, larger, goals, thereby giving meaning to our lives. The view that there is harmony between ethics and enlightened self-interest is an ancient one, now often scorned. Cynicism is more fashionable than idealism. But such hopes are not groundless, and there are substantial elements of truth in the ancient view that an ethically reflective life is also a good life for the person leading it. Never has it been so urgent that the reasons for accepting this view should be widely understood.

In a society in which the narrow pursuit of material self-interest is the norm, the shift to an ethical stance is more radical than many people realize. In comparison with the needs of people going short of food in Rwanda, the desire to sample the wines of Australia's best vineyards pales into insignificance. An ethical approach to life does not forbid having fun or enjoying food and wine; but it changes our sense of priorities. The effort and expense put into fashion, the endless search for more and more refined gastronomic pleasures, the added expense that marks out the luxury-car market – all these become disproportionate to people who can shift perspective long enough to put themselves in the position of others affected by their actions. If the circle of ethics really does expand, and a higher ethical consciousness spreads, it will fundamentally change the society in which we live. ■

Peter Singer, one of the world's leading and most controversial moral philosophers, is currently Ira W DeCamp Professor of Bioethics at the University Center for Human Values, Princeton University. Among his many books are Practical Ethics, Animal Liberation *and* Rethinking Life and Death.

1 WEH Lecky, *The History of European Morals*, Longman, 1892.

January/February 1999
Betrayal and promise

*The century may be dying but hope of a better world is not. According to Latin American writer **Eduardo Galeano**, we should not apologize for having tried to conquer heaven but should draw strength from the mosquito cloud of popular resistance.*

The 20th century was born under the sign of revolution and it dies marked by despair. Stop the world, I want to get off: in these times of stupor and collapse, the ranks of the regretful are swelling – regretful of political passion and regretful of all passion. There are many who apologize for having believed that it was possible to conquer heaven; there are many who fervently seek to kick over their own traces and climb down from hope, as if hope were a worn-out horse.

End of the century, end of the millennium: end of the world? How much unpoisoned air have we still got left? How many unspoiled lands, how many waters not yet dead? How many non-ailing souls? In its Hebrew version, the word 'sick' means 'without a project', and this is the gravest sickness among the many plagues of our times. But someone, who knows who, wrote in passing on a wall in the city of Bogotá: 'Let's leave pessimism for better times.'

Whenever we take it into our heads to express hope in Spanish, we say: *abrigamos esperanzas* ('we shelter hope'). Nice expression, nice challenge: sheltering it to prevent it from dying of cold in the implacably rough climate of our present times. According to a recent survey carried out in 17 Latin American countries, three out of four people describe their situation as stagnant or worsening. Is it necessary to accept misfortune as one accepts winter or death? It is time for we Latin Americans to start asking: are we going to resign ourselves to enduring life and to being no more than a caricature of the North? No more than a mirror which multiplies the distortions of the original image? The look-after-number-one attitude degenerating into 'let them die if they can't'? Swarms of losers in a race where the majority are pushed off the track? Crime turned to slaughter, urban hysteria elevated to total madness? Have we nothing else to say and to live through?

Fortunately, we hardly ever hear history described as infallible these days. We are well aware by now that history makes mistakes, that it gets distracted, falls asleep, loses its way. We make it, and it looks like us. But, like us, it is also unpredictable. It is with human history as with football: its best feature is its ability to surprise. Against all forecasts, against all evidence, the little guy sometimes leads the invincible giant a merry dance.

However messed-up the warp of reality, new fabrics are being woven on to it, and those fabrics are made up of a weft of many and diverse colours. Alternative social movements express themselves not only through parties and unions, but in other ways too. There is nothing spectacular about the process, and it happens mostly at a local level, but everywhere, on a worldwide scale, a thousand-and-one new forces are emerging. They sprout from the bottom up and from inside outwards. Without any fuss, they put their shoulder to the wheel of rebuilding democracy, nourished by popular participation, and are reclaiming the battered traditions of tolerance, mutual help and communion with nature. One of their spokespeople, Manfred Max-Neef, defines them as a cloud of mosquitoes launched against a system which spurns embraces and forces us to jostle. 'The mosquito cloud,' he says, 'is more powerful than the rhinoceros. It grows and grows, buzzes and buzzes.'

In Latin America, they are a dangerous expanding species: the organizations of the landless, the homeless, the jobless, all the lesses; the groups working for human rights; the white scarves of the mothers and grandmothers who oppose the impunity of power; the neighbourhood movements; the citizens' groups fighting for fair prices and healthy products; those who struggle against racial and sexual discrimination, against machismo and against the exploitation of children; the ecologists; the pacifists; the health workers and popular educators; those who trigger collective creation and those who rescue collective memory; the co-operatives engaged in organic agriculture; community radio and television stations; and many other voices of popular participation which are neither the spare tyres of any party nor chapels subject to any Vatican. These driving forces of civil society are frequently persecuted by the powers-that-be, sometimes by means of the bullet. Some activists fall, riddled with bullets, on the way. May the gods and the devils rest their souls: it's the fruit-yielding trees that the stones are thrown at.

With one or two exceptions, like the Zapatistas of Chiapas and the landless in Brazil, it is rare for these movements to be at the forefront of public attention; and not because they don't deserve it. Just to mention one case, one of these popular organizations, born in recent years and unknown outside the borders of its own country, has set an example which the Latin American presidents ought to follow. El Barzón is the name of an organization of debtors who have joined together in Mexico to defend themselves against the usury of the banks. El Barzón sprang up spontaneously. Initially, they were few. Few, but contagious. Now they are a multitude.

Our presidents would do well to learn from that experience, enabling countries to unite, as people did in Mexico, and form a single front against the financial despotism which imposes its will by negotiating with each country separately. But the presidents' ears are full of the resonant platitudes they exchange each time they meet and pose for the family photograph with the President of the United States – the Mother Country – always in the centre.

It's happening in many places on the Latin American map: people are uniting against the paralyzing gases of fear and, united, they are learning not to bow their heads. As Old Antonio says: 'Everyone is as small as the fear they feel, and as big as the enemy they choose.' No longer cowed, these people are saying their piece. To give another Mexican example, the Zapatistas' Subcomandante Marcos speaks for the unders: the underdeveloped, the underfed, the undermined, the underheard. The indigenous communities of Chiapas discuss and decide, and he is their mouthpiece. The voice of those who have no voice? They, who have been forced into silence, are the voice. They speak through what they say and they speak through their silence.

The official history, a mutilated memory, is a long ceremony of self-praise by those who call the shots in this world. Their reflectors, which illuminate the peaks, leave the base in the dark. The usual invisible beings form part, at best, of the scenery of history, like Hollywood extras. But it is they, the actors in the real history, the denied, lied-about, hidden protagonists of past and present reality, who embody the splendid fan of another possible reality. Blinded by elitism, racism, sexism and militarism, America continues to ignore the plenitude within it. And this is doubly true in the South: Latin America is endowed with the most fabulous human and vegetal diversity on the planet. This is where its fecundity and its promise reside. As the anthropologist Rodolfo Stavenhagen puts it: 'Cultural diversity is to the human species what biological diversity is to the world's genetic wealth.' To enable these energies to express the possible wonders of the people and the land, one would have to start by not confusing identity with archaeology, or nature with scenery. Identity is not something frozen in the museums, nor is ecology reducible to gardening.

Five centuries ago, the people and the lands of the Americas were incorporated into the world market as things. A few conquerors, the conquered conquerors, were able to fathom the American plurality, and they lived within it and for it; but the Conquest, a blind and blinding enterprise like all imperial invasions, was capable of recognizing the indigenous people, and nature, only as objects to be exploited or as obstacles. Cultural diversity was dismissed as ignorance and punished as heresy, in the name of a single god, a single language and a single truth, and this sin of idolatry merited flogging, hanging or the stake.

There is no longer talk of subjecting nature: now its executioners prefer to say that it has to be protected. But in either case, then and now, nature is external to us: the civilization that confuses clocks with the time also confuses nature with postcards. But the vitality of the world, which mocks all classifications and is beyond all explanations, never stays still. Nature realizes itself in movement, as do we, its children, who are what we are at the same time as we are what we do to change what we are. As Paulo Freire, the educator who died learning, said: 'We exist in motion.'

The truth is in the journey, not in the port. There is no truth but the quest for truth. Are we condemned to criminality? We are well aware of the fact that we human creatures are very busy devouring our fellow beings and devastating the planet, but we also know that we wouldn't be here if our remote Paleolithic ancestors had been unable to adapt to the nature they were part of, or not been willing to share what they hunted and gathered. No matter where, how or when a person may live, each one contains within themselves many possible persons, and it's the ruling system, which has nothing eternal about it, that invites our basest occupants on to the stage every day, while preventing the others from growing and banning them from making an appearance. We may be badly made, but we're not finished yet; and it's the adventure of making changes and changing ourselves which makes this flicker in the history of the universe that we are, this fleeting warmth between two glaciers, worthwhile. ■

4

Bringing it all back home: women and men

THE first issue of the **NI** devoted to women came out in 1977. It was a significant moment, since it's fair to say that feminism had not been high on the magazine's agenda up to that point. Maggie Black's keynote editorial for that issue, most of which is included here, described the beauty of a 15-year-old Ethiopian girl she met on the road to Selekleka and mourned the transience of that beauty 'if policies don't change fast enough to avoid her back being bent, her hands calloused, her body broken, by the time she is 30'.

By the mid-1980s, as the implications of feminist thinking and campaigning percolated ever deeper into Western society, sexual politics had become central to the way the magazine looked at the world. The **NI**'s only two independent films – *Man-Made Famine* and *Girls Apart* – both show by their titles that they emerged from this fertile period. Similarly, the first-ever *New Internationalist* book enlisted prominent writers from all over the world to write about women's lives on the other side of the rich-poor divide: the American Marilyn French travelled to India and the Australian Germaine Greer to Cuba, while Egypt's Nawal el-Saadawi covered Britain and India's Anita Desai visited Norway.

Meanwhile the editors of the magazine were increasingly eager to carry articles that challenged Western readers' own behaviour and assumptions. Many of these were written by Debbie Taylor, whose own pieces here exemplify how she tried to push back the boundaries of what was creatively possible in a *New Internationalist* article. It was she who commissioned Emmanuel Reynaud's article on men and sex which seems just as powerful (and as inflammatory) today as it did in 1986.

The initial burst of excitement editors felt at being turned loose on what we at the time called 'personal politics' may have gone but the commitment to an anti-sexist worldview has not diminished. More is possible for more women in the West than was the case when the **NI** began – but all too many are still left behind, not least the modern equivalents of that girl on the road to Selekleka. ■

October 1977
Waking up to women

*Western women's liberation may have turned the spotlight on sexism in the developed world. But it has almost entirely failed to illuminate the problems faced by most women in the Third World, as **Maggie Black** explains.*

With her striking features and her face full of laughter as she shelters from the torrential downpour, the young northern Ethiopian girl has a kind of beauty unusual around here. Under the crumbling Italianate porch, she waits for the squall to pass, her sodden garment of rough cotton cloth showing clearly the outline of her figure. And where does she come in, this teenage girl, to the women's liberation movement, in either its Western or its Third World form?

At the moment, she is less concerned with women's rights than with the favourite preoccupations of all girls her age, as she chats and flirts with the young men streaming down the road in the wet. Shrouded from head to foot in the strange hooded mats they wear as protection against the rain, the men whip onwards their laden mules and donkeys. For it is market day in Selekleka, this one-horse town in the northern Ethiopian province of Tigre.

She carries in her hands her own produce for market: long dark-green *talla* shoots with their roots embedded in an old tin can. It is from *talla* that Ethiopian women brew a thin, bitter-tasting beer in the heavy earthenware jars they use for carrying water. The *talla* leaves ferment, making an intoxicating liquor, but at least a drinking supply that is no longer contaminated. This is just one of their daily occupations, and today they put it to good financial effect in Selekleka: outside almost every hut flutters the little blue rag that signals a *talla* house. Yet should the government and UN experts from Addis Ababa or Axum drive through Selekleka in their pristine landrovers, they would probably see those flags more as a sign of country people's decadence than of 'economic activity' on the part of women. The things women do to help their families survive in this rocky corner of a very poor country are unlikely even to be noticed, are certainly not registered in any survey, and probably not remotely considered in any plan for the area's development.

The young Tigrean girl stands bold and erect, her back not yet permanently bowed from the weight of the great water jars she must regularly carry from the stream. Nor is her body yet flaccid or misshapen from bearing children year after year. But it will be. By the time she is 30, she will look 50 more than likely, and have borne ten children, of which probably only four will have lived past the age of five. Unless by some freak she is one of the minute handful of girl primary school students who get to secondary school and a life in town – maybe as a servant. Or there is, of course, another kind of life in town for girls with her looks, as Addis Ababa's red-light district bears ample witness. Would the experts call *that* occupation 'economically active'? Who can say.

As in most of Africa, market day in Selekleka is quite an occasion. Most of the buying and selling as far as food is concerned is done by the women. They tend to market the produce because they are the ones chiefly involved in growing it. In the town 'square', an occupying force of resolute ladies sit behind a bright array of oddly coloured food-stuffs. There is bright orange *berberi*, or chili peppers, yellow cardamom, greyish peppercorns, chickpeas, beans, greenish berries. Not meat of course: like almost everything to do with cattle, that is handled by men. So is any skilled craft work – the predictable jobs like blacksmithing and carpentry, but also anything to do with cloth. The women pick, clean, spin and card raw cotton, but it is woven by men, embroidered by men, sown by men. Its manufacture is an important job in cold, mountainous terrain like this can be. Any job here which carries status – which denotes a skill or a training that can be marketed for cash – is exclusively a male preserve. Which is why the women's contributions to family welfare are conventionally ignored.

But even the most casual inspection of the Ethiopian countryside – or the countryside anywhere in the Third World for that matter – shows up this attitude as blinkered and absurd. The number of tasks carried out by women, especially rural women, is far greater than that done by men. Women do the cooking, cleaning, care for the children, fetch the water, gather the fuel. They hold responsibility for agriculture side by side with the men, and often have exclusive responsibility for food-growing. They do the weeding, manuring, harvesting, winnowing, shelling, and storing of the crops. They tend domestic and farm animals – with the exception of the cows which they milk but rarely herd or handle for ploughing. They also usually take the produce to and from market, even when it means walking 25 or 30 kilometres with a baby on the back and a child at the side. And the sight of a woman on a bicycle, or pushing a wheelbarrow, is almost unheard of.

There is absolutely no excuse for the consistent failure of those in charge of local administration, or agricultural development schemes, or the siting of schools and health facilities, or any of the other modern innovations of the colonial and post-colonial eras in Africa, to see and take into account the evidence that is in front of their eyes.

Except, perhaps, male bias. As long ago as 1930 a German geographer drew a map which showed that in the whole of the Congo region, in large parts of Southeast and East Africa and in parts of West Africa, women performed every single task in relation to food-production. The single exception was the felling of large trees to make way for the preparation of new land in areas where the traditional agricultural pattern was to farm a patch for a few years, and move on when it had lost its goodness. To be fair, the men did have other things to do in those days: hunting wild game and sending aggressors packing. In many parts of Africa south of the Sahara today, the exclusive concern of the womenfolk with food both before and after harvest still persists.

Africa is the extreme example of a place in the Third World where women's work is never done, and more important, usually disregarded. But even if they do not support the family almost singlehanded like many of their African sisters, women in Asia and Latin America also make a vital economic contribution to their family fortunes, even where they are inhibited by living behind the total seclusion of the veil. Certain home industries – batik in Java, hand-woven carpets in Iran, hand-made cigars in the Caribbean – have been traditionally female preserves. But the pattern of change – call it modernization, westernization, industrialization – of the past 30 years has made things consistently worse for women, not better. Sure, there are more schools and hospitals, maternity centres and family-planning clinics. But conversely the pressure of people on resources means that food is more difficult to grow, or to earn the money to buy; a clean supply of water may be further away, and fuel scarcer. With all the extra work, therefore, that women's daily round entails, where are the ones who have time for the literacy classes and the nutrition demonstrations? The legacy for women of Western colonization is mostly heart-rending…

In view of these vicious effects of modernisation on both women in towns and women in the countryside, what have the relevant agencies – governments, the UN and the voluntary organizations – been doing to help women since they first coined slogans like 'Freedom from Hunger'? First, there was the assumption that development schemes were nondiscriminatory: everyone would benefit. It wasn't thought necessary to consider the existing pattern of sex-roles before rushing ahead with new agricultural ventures, for example.

One small example where this neglect actually wrecked a development project is at Mwea in Kenya. Families moved from their traditional villages to settle there and cultivate rice under irrigation as a cash crop. But the plots provided for the women to grow the traditional family diet were far too small. It was the women, too, who did most work in the rice fields, but as the men were the 'members' of the scheme, they received the cash. More work and less money, therefore, for the women, even though they now needed cash in a way they never used to, in order to buy the food they could no longer grow and the fuel they could no longer gather.

Where development schemes have been devised specially with women in mind, they have usually been concerned with healthcare and safe water. Another way that women have been singled out for attention by well-meaning development workers is in encouraging them to make and sell 'traditional' handicrafts. These particular schemes manage to epitomize with dreadful irony the downgraded position of women in Third World societies. First, they invariably reflect Western bias about women's roles and aptitudes. Often the crafts promoted are in no sense traditional to the particular place, and therefore the materials have to be imported: tie-dying in Tanzania, for example.

Second, even where they do have genuine roots – jute hanging baskets in Bangladesh, traditionally used for storing food away from infested floors – they are no longer a central contribution to the local economy. Instead they are fripperies, made to serve the whims of a tourist or foreign export market, hooked temporarily on ethnic fashion. These totally peripheral occupations reinforce women's position on the outskirts of the outskirts of society.

It was in an atmosphere of growing consciousness that existing development policies were leaving women out of the picture and actually worsening their lot that 1975 was declared International Women's Year. There was always a danger that the spectacle of petticoats descending on Mexico City for a World Conference would be held up for ridicule, and in the event it was too much for the media to resist. The resultant publicity obscured the central debate, bitterly fought out between the women of the developed and the women of the less-developed worlds.

Is the first priority development, or is it equality between the sexes? From the Third World, egalitarian aims appear legitimate and justified, but on the whole women are more concerned with bettering their chances of survival. That most Third World societies demonstrate quite terrible inequalities between men and women is unchallenged and unchallengeable. The sale of small girls into prostitution is still common in parts of Asia, and the practices of polygamy and clitoridectomy still exist quite widely in Africa. But many vigorous champions of women's rights from the Third World still feel that the first steps towards women's liberation in their countries involve life-and-death matters like minimal health services and fuller stomachs. Trivia like 'chairperson' and other linguistic irritations can wait, they feel.

But when someone of the calibre of Elizabeth Reid, a leading member of the women's lobby in Australia, sounds off about the sexist language used by

Robert MacNamara, she is hardly making a trivial point. Referring to his 1976 speech to the World Bank, in which he made some remarks about 'the poorest quarter of the population... the marginal men,' she wrote as follows: 'One cannot but feel that language such as this truly mirrors a perception of reality of a world where many men are, of course, marginal but where the women, if perceived at all, are perceived as marginal to the marginal. Like fleas on fleas.'

The debate within the women's lobby between those who support development first and those who support equality first still goes on. The sisters did not agree in Mexico and they do not agree now, any more than the Population Conference ironed out once and for all whether development follows the pill, or the pill follows development. Resolving the debate is not the main problem. Nor indeed is getting the notion of women-as-a-priority into the development jargon.

Since 1975, the women's issue has received a good deal of attention. It is part and parcel of UNICEF's and other agencies' strategies for meeting 'basic needs' with 'essential services'. It is part of the rhetoric about introducing a New International Economic Order to readjust the unequal balance between the rich and poor worlds. It is part of the fashionable rejection of economic growth as the way to meet human needs for food, education, shelter, and so on. The goal of 'integrating women into development' is heartily endorsed at every international gathering. But what in effect have been the results?

The results, predictably, are yet to come. So far it is not possible to hold out definite hopes to that 15-year-old girl on the road to Selekleka that she is, in fact, travelling the road to the new Jerusalem. But if policies don't change fast enough to avoid *her* back being bent, *her* hands calloused, *her* body broken by the time she is 30, then maybe they will in time for her children. Under the barrage of criticism that is slowly growing, people are waking up to the needs of women. They are just beginning to see that there is no sense in women making jute dollies when they should be making cheap tin buckets. They are starting to realize the futility of learning how to cook new-fangled foods when there is no time or energy left from a daily food-growing, water-carrying, fuel-gathering, child-rearing grind. They may have begun to see and realize. As yet they have not acted. But they will. ■

*Maggie Black left the **NI** editorial team in the late 1970s to join UNICEF, first in East Africa then in New York. She has since worked as a freelance writer. Among her books are* Children First: the story of UNICEF past and present *(1996) and* The No-Nonsense Guide to International Development *(NI/Verso 2002).*

June 1984

A new man

Men are taught that being violent is part of being a 'real man' and **Bob Connell** *was taught to be a man in resolutely macho Australia. But now he argues that we need a new kind of masculinity – a non-aggressive one that takes its lead from feminism.*

Almost all the soldiers in the world are men. So are most of the police, most of the prison warders and almost all of the generals, admirals, bureaucrats and politicians who control the apparatuses of coercion and collective violence.

Most murderers are men. Almost all bandits, armed robbers and muggers are men: all rapists, most domestic bashers; and most people involved in street brawls, riots and the like.

The same story, then, for both organized and unorganized violence. It seems there is some connection between being violent and being male.

There is a common belief that this is all 'natural'. Human males are genetically programmed to be hunters and killers, the argument runs. The reason is that ape-man aggression was a survival need in the prehistoric dawn, while the ape-women clustered passively round their camp-fires suckling and breeding.

Right-wing versions of this argument thus explain and justify aggression, competition, hierarchy, territoriality, patriarchy and by inference private property, national rivalry, armies and war.

The tissue of pseudo-biological and pseudo-anthropological argument on which these doctrines are built crumbles on critical examination. The pre-history is speculative; and a little thought will show that by similar arguments one can 'prove' equally well that men are naturally co-operative, naturally pacifist and naturally democratic.

The truth of the matter is that no such argument proves anything at all. War, murder, rape and masculinity are *cultural* facts, not settled by biology. The patterns we have to deal with as issues of current politics have been produced within human society by the processes of history. It is the shape of social relations, not the shape of the genes, that is the effective cause. 'Male' and 'masculine' are very different things. Masculinity is implanted in the male body: it does not grow out of it.

Once that is seen, we can look at the familiar images and archetypes of manliness in a clearer light. They are parts of the cultural process of *producing* particular types of masculinity. What messages they convey are important because they help to shape new generations.

One of the central images of masculinity in the Western cultural tradition is the murderous hero, the supreme specialist in violence. A string of warrior heroes – Achilles, Siegfried, Lancelot and so on – populate European literature from its origins.

The 20th century has steadily produced new fictional heroes of this type: Tarzan, Conan, James Bond, the Jackal, the Bruce Lee characters. If you walk into a shop selling comics to boys you will find a stunning array of violent heroes: cops, cowboys, supermen, infantry sergeants, fighter pilots, boxers and so on endlessly. The best of the Good Guys, it seems, are those who pay evildoers back in their own coin.

This connection between admired masculinity and violent response to threat is a resource that governments can use to mobilize support for war. A cult of masculinity and toughness flourished in the Kennedy and Johnson administrations in the US and helped commit the country to war in Vietnam. I can remember the process operating on young men of my generation in Australia, whose conservative government sent troops to support the Americans in Vietnam. Involvement in the war was presented as standing up to a threat and opponents were smeared as lily-livered effeminates. In the fullness of time support for napalm raids and carpet bombing by B-52s became the test of manliness.

Yet Western opposition to the Vietnam War did grow and together with the Vietnamese resistance eventually forced the American military to withdraw. The cult of masculine toughness is not all-powerful. This should alert us to some complexities in masculinity and its cultural images – which have, indeed, been there from the start.

The story of Achilles, for instance, centres not on his supremacy in violence, but on his refusal to use it. And what changes his mind is not his reaction to threat, but his tenderness – his love for his friend Patroclus. Siegfried and Lancelot, not exactly gentle characters, are likewise full of hesitations, affections and divided loyalties.

So the image of heroism in modern figures like Tarzan and James Bond is a degraded one. The capacities for tenderness, emotional complexity, aesthetic feeling and so on have been deleted. More exactly, they are split off and assigned only to women, or to other, inferior types of men – such as the effeminates who evaded the Vietnam War.

The detailed research into masculinity has not been done. We know enough to understand that such changes in images of heroism are part of the historical process by which different kinds of masculinity are separated from each other, some exalted and some spurned.

At any given moment some forms of masculinity will be honoured and influential – and other forms will be marginalized or subordinated. In some civilizations the honoured forms of masculinity stress restraint and responsibility rather than violence. I believe that was true, for instance, of Confucian China. In contemporary Western society, masculinity is strongly associated with aggressiveness and the capacity for violence.

Modern feminism has shown us one of the bases of this, the assertion of men's power over women. This relationship itself has a strong component of violence. Wife-bashing, intimidation of women in the street, rape, jealousy-murder, and other patterns of violence against women are not accidental or incidental. They are widespread and systematic, arising from a power struggle.

This struggle has many turns and twists. Even in a society that defines husbands as the 'head of the household', there are many families where wives actually run the show. Bashings may then result from an attempt to reassert a damaged masculine ego. In other cases domestic violence is a direct expression of the husband's power, his belief that he can get away with anything and his contempt for his wife or for women in general.

So there are many complexities and contradictions. The main axis, however, remains the social subordination of women and men's general interest in maintaining it. The masculinity built on that bedrock is not necessarily violent – most in fact do not bash women – but it is constructed, so to speak, with a door open towards violence.

In much of the writing about men produced by the 'men's movement' of the 1970s it was assumed that violence was simply an *expression* of conventional masculinity. Change the macho image, stop giving little boys toy guns and violence would be reduced. We can now see that the connection of masculinity and violence is both deeper and more complex than that. Violence is not just an expression: it is a part of the processes that produce masculinity. It is part of the process that divides different masculinities from each other. There is violence within masculinity: it is constitutive.

Once again, this is not to imply that it is universal. Real men don't necessarily bash three poofters before breakfast every day. For one thing, TV does it for them. Part of the pattern of contemporary masculinity is the commercial production of symbolic violence on an unprecedented scale, from Tarzan movies to *Star Wars,* Space Invaders and World Series Cricket.

It is also very important that much of the actual violence is not isolated and individual action but is institutional. Much of the poofter-bashing is done by the police: much of the world's rape is done by soldiers in the context of war. These actions grow readily out of the 'legitimate' violence for which police forces and armies are set up.

Yet, for all this, we know masculinity is not fixed. Feminism has been reworking femininity. It is at least conceivable that we can rework masculinity in a way that sustains a struggle without reproducing the enemy. ■

One of the world's key academic theorists on the sociology of masculinity, **Bob Connell** *is currently Professor of Education at the University of Sydney. Among his books are* Gender *(Polity/ Blackwell 2002) and* The Men and the Boys *(Allen & Unwin/Polity/University of California 2000).*

September 1984
Women in Africa: until death us do part
Africa will stay poor until its women are free. **Debbie Taylor** *pleads their case.*

Africa, my Africa. If I had breath enough I would curse: once for the day that you bore me; twice for making me a woman. I would spit at the sun for shining on me, merciless, blazing, every day of my life; withering my spirit and turning my skin rough and dark, black as the bark of the acacia tree.

Africa, Africa, what have they done to you? If I had strength enough I would carry my children far away across land and sea to their concrete capitals and I would stand before their ranks of white-faced men and make them see how dull are the eyes of my children, how slowly they blink and turn their heads, how thin are their arms. And I would show them the palms of my hands, the soles of my feet, the skin of my knees – scarred by stones and splinters and thorns – and my breasts and belly – stretched by 15 years of motherhood. And I would tell those men a story that would make them understand at last why my Africa is dying.

Africa is dying because of me, I would tell them. I have been carrying this continent for centuries. But I can't hear the weight any longer. And as I sink to my knees so Africa sinks down too.

Look at me working, I would say: knee-deep in the south Senegal paddy fields where I alone grow all of our rice crop: or bent low over the dusty land in Tanzania where I keep on tending our maize, sorghum and millet half as long again after the men have gone home; or on the jungle's edge in Zaire[1] where four-fifths of our food is grown by my hands.

Yes, I know I'm not alone. Women everywhere are working: doing two-thirds of the world's work, earning one-tenth of its income, owning one-hundredth of its property. I know the facts. But I know I work hardest of all.

Yes, it's hard for my sisters in India; in Indonesia and Indo-China; in

Barbados, Bolivia and Brazil; arms, back and thighs tightening and straining, doing half of all work in the fields. They are bowed and bent by their workload. But mine has brought me to my knees. They do half of all field work. But I do half as much again; and half of all work with our animals; and all of the threshing and winnowing. Then home to sweep courtyards, wash clothing, fetch water, cook supper. Yes, it is hard for them. And I'm sorry. But it's hardest of all for me.

Some days, I would tell them – those men with their suits and statistics – my sons and my daughters go hungry while our granary is half-filled with food. When the rains come at last, sweeping their blessed grey curtains across the parched red dust of my fields, my days are so long that I can't make my arms lift the pestle to grind grain for our porridge.

That is my choice. To work or to eat. If I work there is no time to cook. If I cook there is no time to work. In Ghana and Botswana, in Gambia and Zambia – everywhere it is the same story. Food or work. Work or food. Look at your statistics. They will tell you that on the wide plains of Zambia the food I grow is not what the land will yield, but only as much as my hands can weed and my back carry. This is why Africa is dying.

From behind their wide desks they would look at my children, an uneven row of dusty angled limbs and tight black curls: and at me in my new brown skirt and my faded scarlet scarf. Their eyebrows would raise and I'd know what their thoughts were. Where is my man, then? Why can't he help me? He is why Africa's dying.

Africa, oh Africa, what have they done to my man? Once I could admire him as the protector of our land: the one who cut through the jungle, clearing a space for our crops, the one who drove away invaders, who led our animals to grazing and water, who hunted and brought back our meat.

Where is he now, the person who was once my partner, an Adam to my Eve, with whom I was proud to say 'we'?

Look at him now: puffed and pompous in the city, playing with his power, turning his back on the people who raised him; or hat over eyes in the shade of a thorn tree, drowsy and docile, afraid of the sun; or weaving and stumbling and stinking of beer red-eyed and angry, kicking his woman; or herded like cattle to cut down their sugar, to pick their tobacco, collect their rubber, carry their cotton.

They took him away from me; took him and beat him; imprisoned his spirit; took him and chewed him and sucked out his goodness, stole all his strength; then spat him out and sent him home.

Turn your minds backwards, I'd beg them, those men with their secretaries and reports. Remember how Africa was when you landed, beaching your ships on our shores. You found fields with no fences, work with no profit, crops without owners.

Of course life was tough then. It's never been easy: sun always too hot, rain always too late. Childbirth was painful and babies still died. But he used to help me and we were together. I had time for singing and suckling my children, and rights to the land that I weeded each summer; and when I raised my voice it was heard. And of course he still beat me when I cursed too loudly. But I knew him, he knew me, and we were together.

With your guns and your greed you destroyed a whole continent. Your bullets ripped through his shining black flesh. Your pistols emptied themselves into my belly. You fenced our best land and called it yours. And you took him and chained him and made him your servant; made him grow coffee on land that raised millet, and cocoa and tea where we harvested corn. You sent him to burrow away from the sunlight, to die in your tunnels in search of your gold. And you threw him in thousands in the hulls of your tall ships; spat on him, cowed him and sold him like meat. This is why Africa's dying.

Those men with their pink lips, sipping their coffee; would they still be listening to the end of my story? Open your history books, retrace your footsteps. Know that Africa has had more good food-growing land taken for cash crops than any other continent. Know that Africa's woman has lost her land-rights more than woman in any other continent. Know that in the place where half the world's gold is mined we do not even have a vote.[2]

But the worst thing you did to Africa was to divide us: brother from sister and woman from man. You came from countries where a man works for money and his manhood's his wages at the end of the week; where a woman's expected to maintain his household. And it's men who make laws and own land and hold power. You did not respect our tradition of sharing – in work, land and marriage; in what we grew and what we inherited. You wanted to transform us all in your image. But all you achieved was division, destruction.

My man you have stripped of his sense of belonging. You stopped him from doing the things that a man should. You forbade his hunting and warring and peacemaking and put fences up in the path of his scythe.

You taught him that a man either earns wages or stands idle. But there are few who earn wages in our shattered continent. Some you reward, sure, with power and land rights. But most you've left with nothing to live for, snatching some solace in the bars and the brothels.

And how can I blame him for refusing to help me? His scorn for my work makes him feel like he's human; his pride is a jewel in the deep of humiliation.

Are you listening up there in your chrome and black armchairs? I'm explaining why Africa is dying.

In Botswana's barren scrubland he wants payment for ploughing, and spanning his oxen is all that a man does. In Uganda he mostly refuses all crop-work, deriding the effort I make to grow food. While Gambian man's turned his back on tradition, refusing to take up his scythe to clear land. Africa, Africa, my man is a burden: one more to be carried on my aching hack.

Can't you see what you've done with your planning and plunder? You've created two half-men where there once was a whole one. One half-man leans languid and lost in our villages, stripped of his spirit and reason for living. This one you call 'farmer'; send in teachers to teach him to farm (while I am out growing the food); lend him money for tractors and tillers (while I am out growing the food); promise him fortunes if he'd only raise cotton (while I am out growing the food); buy our land from him to add to your ranches (while I am out growing the food).

The other you call 'worker'. He's lost to my village; forgotten the place where eight-tenths of Africa lives. He sleeps in a dormitory, a stone's throw from the mine; or under corrugated iron a bus-ride from the factory; or within slabs of white concrete a car-ride from the office.

At first he comes home once a year for a visit, sends money monthly, dreams dreams of childhood. But soon he's forgotten his debt to his village. And now I'm alone in one-third of our households, my door ajar for a man who never comes.

Me? I'm just woman. Invisible woman. Doing the work of both woman and man. No, I daren't stop working (who'd feed the children?); I can't use a tractor (who'd lend to a woman without land, without birthright?); I've no time for schooling (I'm needed for weeding); I missed the last meeting (I was out chopping firewood); never been to the clinic (too late, now I'm pregnant); and I won't, won't abandon that thing I was born for: to make sure my children have food in their bellies.

So what will undo all the harm that's been done to us? Will you hold one more summit, write one more report? Or parachute bushels of wheat and milk powder to prove just how completely my Africa is vanquished?

Oh, if I had my way I'd rule over this continent. No-one could turn me away from my duties. How could I forget what I've learnt all my childhood: a woman tends babies, pounds sorghum, draws water; a woman makes sure we have food in our bellies; a woman can never lose sight of her duties. If I only had half of the power you gave to my man. If he only did half of the work that you made him leave me. Then, only then, can we stop Africa dying. Together we can stop Africa dying. ■

Debbie Taylor *was a New Internationalist co-editor from 1982 to 1988. She is now editor of the feminist literary magazine* Mslexia. *Among her books is the novel* The Children Who Sleep by the River *(Interlink 2001).*

1 Now the Democratic Republic of Congo. **2** In South Africa, then still ruled by the apartheid regime.

December 1984
Cheap thrills

Debbie Taylor takes us on an unconventional journey into Thailand's sex industry.

What a grand hotel it is: a white palace, delicately floodlit, fountains playing in the courtyard, trees festooned with white bulbs in the best possible taste. Though it's nearly midnight, eight lanes of traffic stand tangled, hooting and snarling, in the Bangkok street outside.

Up the wide marble steps and in – through huge smoked-glass doors – to the foyer. You stop and blink. It's dark. You step forward, bump into someone, apologize, step forward again, bump into someone else. Then realize you are in a crowd. It's a well-dressed crowd (this is, after all, a grand hotel); their wallets bulge with baht.[1] Their eyes are bulging too. You follow their gaze.

They're looking at a huge shop window lit from the inside. It's the only light in the foyer. Behind the expanse of plate glass the goods are displayed on wide shelves that look like a shallow flight of stairs running the entire length of the shop. Deep-pile rose-coloured carpet, like velvet, covers the stairs, matched by folds of hanging drapes that clothe the walls.

At this time of night business is good and the shelves are emptying fast. The goods are coded by numbers on different coloured discs pinned to each one. You make your selection, pay the cashier, and – before you can pocket your change – your purchase is waiting to take you to your room.

What a bargain. Blue Number 33 has long shiny black hair cut into a thick straight fringe over eyes that are dark and slanting – but not too Chinky. Blue means body massage (not just hands, but Number 33's luscious body rolled all over you) – all the trimmings too, for just 100 baht.

Tourists are bargain hunters, touring the global supermarket, shopping for trophies – trinkets and triumphs – they could never afford back at home. Spain touts sunshine and sangria. Thailand specializes in sex.

The Vietnam War taught many lessons. And Thailand was not slow to learn. Having seen American GIs turn the country into a giant restroom away from the battle zone, Thailand learnt to service the servicemen: service with a smile. The GIs went home in 1976. But the word got around. Now everyone wants the same service.

Today Bangkok welcomes bulges of all kinds: wallets and eyes definitely. And trousers particularly. Bulges mean business.

In 1977 one-and-a-quarter million foreigners had tourist visas stamped into their passports at Bangkok airport. By 1981 the number had doubled and the bulge business had become the country's third biggest money-spinner, swelling currency coffers by over $220 million.

Welcome to Pattaya, just four hours' drive (by air-conditioned bus on a tarmac road built with American money) from the grime and sweat of Bangkok. Walk on the white sand, bathe in the clear blue water, breathe in the scent of a hundred brilliant tropical blossoms, dine by candlelight overlooking the bay. Then walk down the main street and take your pick. Garish signs hang above every doorway: rooms with a view – and a little bit extra.

Then back to Bangkok next day for something even more exotic. Tramp round the temples all afternoon and take a taxi to Pat Pong after dinner. Upstairs in a bar is a bath full of bubbles. Sip your lager and imagine you're that man in that bath. Yes, there's two of them in there with him.

Thailand will satisfy your appetite. Come one, come all.

Japanese? No problem. In 1976 four-fifths of Japanese tourists to Thailand were men: 74,000 of them, travelling without their wives, roaming the neon-lit Pat Pong streets, bumping and apologizing in darkened hotel lobbies, licking lips at leather mini-skirts. With throngs of Singapore men and Malaysians, they come searching for purchases, for bargains that will writhe and sigh wantonly beneath them.

Two weeks of sweat and saliva, then back to their perfunctory, formalized unions with their wives: restrained and reluctant as decent women should be.

German? Dutch? Fleeing from women who demand to be equal? No problem. Thailand will fulfil the tour brochure's promise of bargains without desire for emancipation, but full of warm sensuality and the softness of velvet. For a tiny amount you will feel like Don Juan. Travel with confident anticipation: your purchases, say the brochure, are not especially particular. So no European need fear going to Bangkok for nothing. Money back if not completely satisfied.

The perfect playmates are waiting for you: ardent, carnal craving lurking 'neath an enchanting shy demureness. And the pouting, panting lips can barely speak a word of your language.

Come one, come all.

And they do. Tourists are not the only takers. Thailand's men stalk the shop-fronts in thousands: older businessmen shopping for virgins (the rich man's expensive, rare delicacy); some Chinese Thais prefer hill-tribe play-mates – their strangeness and wild blood puts strength in their veins, they say. And their pouting, panting lips can barely speak a word of Thai language.

Demand now outstrips supply – especially for specialist morsels. Even the flood of young titbits – who left villages for life on the bases, learnt to wear high-heels and lipstick, and to service the servicemen's dollars – are too few to feed all these appetites.

Last year the Thai Parliament (with its 324 men and 10 women members) heard from a Select Committee that there were 500,000 prostitutes in the country – that's one per cent of the entire population. Two-fifths of Bangkok's wage-earning women are for sale in bars, coffee shops and massage parlours; giving the client his money's worth. Satisfaction guaranteed.

Where else can you get such a good deal: a tumble with a honey-skinned siren for the price of a packet of cigarettes? Just pay up and don't ask any questions. Look at it this way: it's not a bad life as a harlot. Average monthly wage was $40 in 1979 – $15 more than being a waitress, on a par with a job in a factory, and a lot more than working the paddy fields. In fact most of Bangkok's bargains are playmates from the paddy fields: 47 per cent are from the north and 49 per cent from the northeast, the two poorest parts of the country.

Of course there are occupational hazards: 70 per cent have venereal dis-ease. And the hours are what you might call 'unsocial', with breakfast at four in the afternoon, into the shop window by five, pouting and panting till five in the morning, and dinner when the rest of Bangkok is at breakfast.

No, it's not a bad life as a harlot. Strange that the Select Committee found one in ten had been forced to take their first man – raped in effect. And there was a fire on Phuket island last January, acrid black smoke billowing above the tourist's paradise. Fifty buildings were burnt to the ground; among them were 14 brothels. And when the smoke cleared they found chains round charred ankles in the debris. ■

1 The Thai currency.

April 1986
Power and pleasure

*A man's greatest sexual hangup is his potency – his power of erection and ejaculation. But **Emmanuel Reynaud** argues that sexual power is the least of a man's problems. His real malaise is the absence of pleasure. And his real sickness is frigidity.*

Men don't really understand sex. What should be an experience of communication and delight is, for a man, just a struggle and a means of asserting his domination over a woman. The language he uses expresses his general attitude perfectly: he 'fucks' and she 'gets fucked'. And it is reflected in the images he has of his penis. He does not really perceive its softness and sensitivity, its fragility and its potential for pleasure. Instead he turns it into the symbol of his power.

Doesn't he feel *potent* when his penis is erect? It is the weapon or the tool he uses to possess a woman through her vagina. And his main concern about his penis is its size. He sees it as a sort of biceps: the bigger it is, the more efficient it must be, and the more powerful *he* is.

Since it is the sexual organ that most obviously differentiates males and females, it is hardly surprising that man associates the penis with power. Indeed in a patriarchal society the penis does actually bestow power on a man. But what about pleasure? What kind of pleasure can one get with a weapon or a tool between one's legs?

In fact man is more interested in power than in pleasure. And he feels sexual pleasure as a threat to his power. This is why he does not allow his sexuality to develop fully and why he likes to think of woman as such a sexual creature – an Eve, a Pandora, with the capacity to experience fabulous orgasms (supposedly nine or ten times as intense as his own). Of course this does not mean that a woman may actually enjoy her supposed extraordinary sexuality in her own way. No, on the contrary. The pleasure that man keeps for himself is – first and foremost – that of power and, in particular, power over woman's pleasure.

Man's sexuality is not a simple expression of 'natural needs', but a relationship of domination of one sex over the other. In fact man does not perceive sexuality as being a relationship between two human beings at all, but as a relationship between one human being – him, a 'man' – and the object he uses, a 'woman'.

He gets his sexual pleasure through the use of a woman[1], instead of experiencing it in the sensual meeting of two *individuals*.

This sexual use takes different forms. The more sophisticated one consists of giving pleasure to a woman: using her as an instrument that produces sensuality. The most common image is of a man playing music on a woman's body with his hands and penis. She produces harmonious notes but, without the musician and his bow, she is nothing but a curvaceous object, a mere promise of music. She quivers but cannot choose the rhythm or the melody. She is totally dependent on the musician, on his skill, his mood and his sensitivity.

The comparison is striking and it has been frequently used in art and literature. But not everyone is a virtuoso. So a man does not generally take the risk of trying – and failing – to be sophisticated. The result is that he usually just ignores woman's pleasure altogether and reduces his own to mere ejaculation. His sexuality becomes a simple question of needs to relieve, and he regularly relieves himself by imposing conjugal rights on his wife or by going to a prostitute.

Sometimes a man will try to enhance the poverty of his sexuality by living out fantasies. He seeks in his mind what he does not feel in his body. Another way he tries to increase the intensity of his pleasure is by means of violence.

Because he is, first and foremost, a 'man', and therefore sexually inhibited, his way of experiencing intensity has little to do with sensual pleasure. When he gives in to his desires he frequently feels the urge to brutalize or rape. At times he does it on a large scale: when he is at war, for instance. Between 200,000 and 400,000 women were raped in Bangladesh by Pakistani soldiers during the nine-month conflict in 1971. And when the Japanese invaded Nanking in China in 1937, there were over 1,000 rapes a night during the first month of occupation. But man also seeks his pleasure in rape and violence on a more daily basis. Even when he does not actually commit violence, it can nonetheless be on his mind. According to the Hite Report on US men, between seven and eleven per cent regularly fantasize about rape and one in two admit they have sometimes wanted to rape a woman.

Rape is the 'pleasure' of violence, but it is also a means for man to use a woman without having to give her anything in return, as he does in marriage or with a prostitute. It enables him to satisfy his needs without giving up any of his power. In fact it is the very expression of that power. In that sense rape is the archetype of masculine sexuality: when man desires, woman is not to desire or refuse. She must only acquiesce.

This is man's sexual paradox: he uses women to get his pleasure, but in doing so he restricts the pleasure he could get. He is missing the rich sexuality that lies in the meeting of two persons, in the merging of two pleasures: a relationship where one's pleasure is reinforced by the feeling of the other's pleasure. The sad fact is that, however obsessed by sex man seems to be, his sexual pleasure is desperately weak. Hanging on to the notion that his penis is an instrument of power, and to his perception that the sex act is an act of domination and use, he experiences a profound frigidity. And this frigidity is all the more serious because he does not really know that he is frigid.

A woman can be frigid or not. But frigidity is not perceived to be the issue for a man. He just has to be potent. He feels that his problem is not the experience of pleasure, but the ability to express his potency and fulfil his desires through his erect penis. Likewise, woman is not supposed to be potent or have any desire, but she is expected to feel pleasure. This traditional view is reflected in modern sexology. Woman's problem is presented as the absence of pleasure – frigidity – and man's as the inability to express his desires – impotence. But surely the sexual problems of the two sexes are really just the reverse? Surely woman is all the more impotent because her impotence is unrecognized, and man is all the more frigid because his frigidity is ignored?

Modern sexologists do not understand male sexuality at all. They assume that ejaculation automatically brings about sexual pleasure in the male; they even consider ejaculation to be synonymous with male orgasm. This assumption was questioned by sexologists of the past – Wilhelm Reich, for example, or Kinsey – but sexology today considers that ejaculation equals orgasm. And, on this principle, it defines normal male sexuality as being the capacity to ejaculate and – at the same time – to give the woman an orgasm with the erect penis. From this definition 'naturally' follow the corresponding sexual problems: absence of ejaculation, premature ejaculation, difficulty with, or absence of, erection. And the treatment consists in fixing the man in such a way that he is able to give a woman an orgasm. Sexual pleasure for her, ejaculation for him.[2]

But ejaculation has little to do with sensual pleasure. It can perfectly well be triggered off in a man who will not let himself go the tiniest bit in experiencing pleasure. And this is man's biggest sexual problem: his inability to let himself be really carried away by sensuality.

Man is afraid of letting himself go. In his struggle to dominate, he feels that every sexual pleasure is a threat and he wants to control it. He dare not abandon himself to his sexuality. When he embraces a woman, he does not feel enveloped and overwhelmed by pleasure. He penetrates and wants to 'possess' her, projecting into her as if he hoped to draw from her the sensuality which he is reluctant to experience for himself.

His mind fixed on the objective, his penis aimed at the target, he does not allow himself to be caught up in the experience of two bodies discovering each other. He is afraid of losing his way; he controls and channels his sexual feelings to prevent them from spreading and causing him to lose control of himself and the situation. Instead of letting his whole body be sexualized, he confines his sexuality to his penis. He stems the tide of pleasure at its source for fear it may submerge him if he allows it to swell. His ecstasy then becomes no more than a series of wavelets: four thrusts of the pelvis, a few drops of sperm, and it is all over. ■

Emmanuel Reynaud's book, Holy Virility *(Pluto Press, 1983), caused an uproar in France when it first came out in 1981.*

1 I am speaking here of the dominant sexuality – i.e. heterosexuality – but a man can also sexually use another man or child. 2 For a general view of modem sexology see W H Masters and V E Johnson, *Human Sexual Inadequacy*, Churchill, 1970.

October 1987
Childless by choice

Mina is 16 and lives in Nepal. If she doesn't get pregnant soon, people will think there's something wrong with her. For Mina there is no choice. **Kathleen Muldoon** *is 35 and lives in England. If she doesn't get pregnant soon, people will think there's something wrong with her too. Does she have a choice?*

'Wouldn't you like a nice little baby like that?' The question popped up so regularly I was getting used to it 'She's beautiful,' I said, stroking the soft, downy cheek. 'And I'd love one. But not yet. Maybe in a year or so we'll stop using contraceptives.' At first everyone had been smiling, thinking how right I looked holding the baby. But then the smiles had given way to whispering. The words themselves were tactfully disguised, but their gist was clear: no childless, married woman uses contraceptives, so I – poor thing – must be trying to cover up my barrenness.

For Mina – who, at 16, was exactly half my age at that time – there was no question of postponing motherhood. She desperately wanted a child. She told me that she couldn't be happy until she'd given birth and, in the course of time, I began to understand what she meant. She was married to the eldest son in the household where I lived, high in the Himalayan mountains of Nepal. They'd been betrothed since she was two and, when she reached puberty, she'd left her home village several miles away and come to join her husband and his extended family.

The early years were misery. She'd never been away from home before and her new husband and in-laws were virtual strangers. They didn't treat her badly, but she was made to feel a burden. She was always the first to start work in the morning and the last to stop at night. She rarely spoke and, when addressed, she replied in a whisper, eyes averted. At festivals she went back home and often stayed away for several days, despite the knowledge that her late return would meet with an endless round of angry curses.

One day Mina was taken to the spirit medium because she wasn't getting pregnant. He assured her that she would, in time, give birth. But he told another woman, barren after five years of marriage, that she was a witch. Mina's sister, too, was childless and her husband had humiliated and rejected her by marrying a second wife.

Eventually Mina did have a baby – a son – and the family was jubilant. A family with sons had wealth and status. There would be an extra pair of hands to tend the sheep, to trade, to work the land, or go to school then work in the city and send money home. With sons the family would be a powerful voice in village politics. With sons they'd be cared for in their old age, their death rituals would be properly performed and their souls would rest, satisfied.

And Mina was right. She blossomed in motherhood. No longer feeling the need to escape at every opportunity to her parents' home, she talked and laughed, openly relaxed. At last this was her home and family; this was where her son belonged and she belonged beside him.

True, contraception was virtually unobtainable in this remote village. But this is not the main reason why women like Mina give birth so frequently or so young. Far more important is the value of children, particularly sons. To ensure that the desired number of sons reach adulthood – allowing for mis-carriage, stillbirth, infant death and, of course, daughters – a woman has to be pregnant as many times as possible.

Twenty years from now, Mina's body will undoubtedly be depleted by con-tinual childbearing and it will become progressively harder for her to keep up her agricultural and domestic work throughout each gruelling pregnancy. She will probably often feel ill and exhausted, and giving birth will become more and more dangerous for her.

Several older women, desperate about this situation, came to me for con-traceptives (which I didn't have). The only contraception that was on offer (though sporadically) was for use by men, whose interests were arguably bet-ter served by the birth of another son than by their wives' good health. (When a visiting paramedic distributed free condoms, the children blew them up and played with them like balloons. And when a team of doctors came to per-form vasectomies, they were sent away, their services unused.)

In a society where a woman's very livelihood depends on her affiliation to a man, her ability to determine her own life's course is negligible. At two Mina was passed from father to husband. As a mother she was reprieved. The rewards of motherhood made it her main source of self-esteem and satisfaction. Small wonder, then, that at 16, she 'desperately' wanted a child, that her own 'personal desire' coincided exactly with society's requirement of her.

As a woman in my mid-thirties, living in England, there is an underlying assumption that I, unlike Mina, am self-determining in my choices about sexuality and motherhood. Until now, I have unfalteringly exercised that choice to postpone motherhood. Now I realize, with growing apprehension, that my fertile years will soon be over and that the time has come to make another choice. The issue is now no longer *when* to have a child but *whether* to have one.

Despite the urgency, the question numbs me. How do I decide rationally when I hear a thousand different voices screaming contradictory advice? In calmer times I try to analyze, weighing up the pros and cons. Surprisingly, I find that all my reasons for postponing giving birth still apply: I don't particularly like children; I value my independence, the freedom to come and go, the open doors; I want to write, and literary history tells me that my chances of succeeding as a writer and a mother are pitiful; I hate and fear the nuclear family, the stifling atmosphere, the exploited wife and mother, the generation gap.

Occasionally these voices come across loud and clear. But then the hubbub starts again, and other voices ask me what I'll do in 20 years' time. Will my life be bleak and empty? Will I dry up, bitter with regret? I must be mad wilfully to deny myself this ultimate creative act, this absolute satisfaction, the most passionate love affair of many women's lives.

The persuasive power of these latter voices is astonishing, When they speak, I feel the force of history bearing down on me. They are commanding and authoritative, bloated with conviction that their advice is right, the best thing for me.

In the Nepalese village, the pressures forcing women into motherhood are clear and tangible. Here they are more subtle. There a barren woman is a potential witch and punished with low status and harsh treatment Here, too, to call a woman 'barren', or even 'childless', implies that – whether she can't have a child or simply doesn't want one – she is somehow wrong and unnatural. In Nepal, only a sick or crippled woman fails to marry and if the female population exceeds the male, men will marry twice. Here, too, the word 'spinster' evokes an ugly, lonely woman who has failed to get her man.

One day there will be a word for a woman without a husband or children that is not pejorative; a single word that conjures up the image of a strong, sexual and feminine woman who revels in her voluntary freedom. When that word becomes common currency, then we'll know that the present stereotypes have lost their stranglehold. Until then our sexuality and fertility are not our own: they are the property of a patriarchal society which fears women's freedom and penalizes deviants like spinsters, lesbians, unmarried mothers and the childless.

Until any woman can stand up and say freely, without the fear of social reprobation, that she doesn't want a child, then no women is free to 'choose' to have a child either. ■

Kathleen Muldoon *is a writer and anthropologist who lived in Nepal for three years.*

January 1992
The real woman

What is a woman anyway? **Nina Silver** *charts a course through sex roles, paganism and love for her dog.*

'You walk like a soldier.' The sneer in the accusation startled me. Focused on my inner world and stepping determinedly, my body was free to let my arms swing the way they are supposed to when you walk.

This was in the late 1950s, before women's liberation. The words were spoken by my mother, who had been brought up to believe that if a woman didn't suppress the natural impulses of her mind, body and heart she wasn't being a lady – and was therefore not worthy or redeemable as a human being.

Even before that childhood challenge to my sex identity, I'd thought a great deal about what it means to be a woman, what is really entailed in being a man. As a little girl I was keenly aware of the sex-role stereotyping in our culture and hated it.

I observed my mother submerging her intelligence and opinions beneath my father because, according to her, his ego was fragile and needed boosting – and should be boosted because he was a man. In kindergarten the boys were assigned to play with electric trains while the girls could only potter with miniature kitchen sets. This made me very indignant. I ignored the tiny stoves, sinks and pots, and taught myself how to read bigger words.

The world has changed somewhat since I was a child but the same questions have remained with me. What is a man? And what is a woman? Apparently, my possessing female genitalia wasn't enough to qualify me for being a woman. It also involved other things I needed to learn.

I failed miserably. Particularly in those early years. I was accused of embodying qualities that offended both the existing norms and the people who made the accusations. At different times my accusers charged that I looked like a boy (when I kissed another girl); looked like a girl (when I was developing breasts); thought too rationally (like a boy – my father called me 'Univac' after the first computer); was too emotional (like a girl); was a lesbian (because I was assertive); and – after all that – acted as though I weren't human.

In high school, when my budding sexual desire for female classmates was unhappily still relegated to the realm of fantasy, the mother of a nice senior boy I was dating warned him about me. She'd heard I was on drugs (which wasn't true) and that I was a lesbian (which wasn't true – yet – either). I felt amused by the first allegation and complimented by the second. To me, being regarded as gay meant that people saw me as someone who had enough personal identity not to need males or the male-dominated culture to define me. A lesbian, unconcerned about securing a husband, was exempt from most role-playing at being a 'sweet young thing' who shouldn't get her hands dirty, sprint across the street, fix the faucet or tell somebody off.

By the time I entered college, cataloguing people's similarities and differences had become my passion. I decided that I couldn't do anything about the language or what people thought, but I *could* try to develop my strengths so that whatever people said about me wouldn't have any power. If people wanted to equate a female adult or a lesbian with being 'mannish', who cared? Those qualities made me more, not less, of a woman. I met many lesbians who were vibrant, strong, women-identified women. And these women were saying that what our culture defines as 'feminine' is in its own right strong, necessary and good.

This challenged me, for despite the fact that a woman is not supposed to possess the stronger characteristics attributed to men, I had actually found it easier to exhibit traits relegated to the 'non-female' end of the spectrum. I would now find the perfect balance and support in the gay community. I rejoiced in eager anticipation.

Alas, in communing with the gay world I discovered to my horror that the polarized butch-femme roles of gay women I'd always heard about did indeed exist and my precious theory was shot to hell. I saw how in some lesbian and gay relationships – just as in heterosexual ones – the rigid sex-typed roles of 'man' and 'woman' kept people prisoners of culturally acceptable human behaviour. Both partners were – as far as I could tell – genitally women. *So what then did constitute a real woman?*

By now I was a psychology student and reading voraciously. I discovered enthralling facts that only complicated my research. Some African cultures reversed roles. That was great, I thought, but wait a minute... that meant there were circumscribed rules to follow. That couldn't be very good, could it? Men who acted as women do in our culture, and women who were male-like? What was the use of role reversal as long as there were still roles to reverse? Why couldn't people simply act as they felt?

By the time I graduated college there were lots more studies out on both humans and animals. I read, fascinated, about the male seahorse which gestates the eggs that the female seahorse lays in his pouch. Another article reported that the tropical clownfish changes its sex according to the reproductive needs of its community.

What men investigators had determined was natural, aggressive, sexual behaviour in some adult male primates was countered by women who were showing – surprise! – that many female monkeys were sexually assertive and promiscuous, even when they were already pregnant.

And on it went. By this time, even the local newspapers were featuring stories stating that men had hormonal cycles as well as women, who now shouldn't have to take all the bad press for being emotional during 'that time of the month'. When I read that male monorail operators in Japan were given time off during the sensitive points in their cycles, I was overjoyed.

Meanwhile data was coming out that the maternal instinct is stimulated by the mother's smelling of the newborn and I struggled with the possibility that maybe there was something to biology after all. But no; that would give men power to call women weak and emotional, power to relegate women back to the kitchen. I collected more data, grateful for my 'male' analytical mind and hating myself for even thinking in those terms.

Maybe underneath my passion for learning was an inferior female body. But that couldn't be. Trying to calm my whirling brain, I had just treated myself to New York City's Big Apple Circus and seen the only two-women trapeze act in the world. One of the women had to be as strong as a man in order to hold herself in the air and her partner, too.

If my outward genitals didn't qualify me as a woman, then it must be more subtle biology. Enter John Money, Johns Hopkins University psychologist and sex researcher, who said that the XX and XY chromosome myth was very nice – tying the sexes into neat packages – but untrue.

We have assumed, he wrote 'that there are two quite separate roads, one

leading from XY chromosomes at conception to manhood, the other from
XX chromosome at conception to womanhood. But scientists are uncovering
a different picture. There are not two roads, but one road with a number of
forks where each of us turns in either the male or the female direction. You
become male or female by stages. Most of us turn smoothly in the same direction at each fork.'

I read, fascinated, about how the many different forks could produce:
females with internalized male organs; women with an 'overabundance' of
testosterone which gives them muscular strength greater than the average
female; hermaphrodites possessing an XX chromosome pattern born with
both male and female internal organs; and the extremely rare case of males
possessing XX chromosome patterns.

This was interesting, but left my basic question unanswered: how could I
determine what a real woman or a real man was if biology was so varied?

Meanwhile my world was rearranging itself at a dizzying pace. All around
me, lesbians were buying houses and having children together via artificial
insemination; my feminist friends were growing their hair long again and
becoming more 'feminine'; and open transsexuals joined the women's, gay,
and bisexual liberation movements.

Frantic, I focused the bulk of my affection on my dog and decided to be
celibate for a while.

Clearly, the sex of the person one relates to didn't have a thing to do with
one's own sex. Neither did chromosomes, times of the month, hormones,
whether or not someone lactates, how one earns a living, or what they do in
their spare time. There had to be a fresh insight apart from the books I was
reading or the people I was talking to, something that would end my search
once and for all.

I got interested in the pagan movement and finally, one day, I invented
a transcendental experience. My awareness took the form of a voice. It was
– and is – my own voice. It has authority, this voice that somehow got lost
in the shuffle of turning book pages, discussion groups, questions. For a
long time this voice has needed to know that it exists. How can we know
who and where we are until we sort through everything that *isn't* important, *isn't* real?

I remind myself that we are all bound together by our humanity: we laugh,
cry, eat, grieve, pee, yell, feel joy, have orgasms. Embracing the life force
inside myself that grants us these feelings is the most I can ask of life. And if
I feel my own energy, and act according to my desires, then that's who I am.
If I am considered a woman, it's because I'm a human being who happens

to have *observable* female genitals. But that's as far as it goes. We're constantly inventing ourselves, or allowing ourselves to be invented by others.

When I'm in the present, labels don't cross my mind. I'm too busy simply... being. ■

Nina Silver is a counsellor, writer, singer and composer based in the north-eastern US.

January/February 1999

Domestic murder and the golden sea

The battle for women's rights – from the vote to sexual autonomy – was well and truly joined in the 20th century. But it was not only fought in the West, as **Urvashi Butalia** *explains.*

One hot summer afternoon some 20 years ago, my mother looked out of her window at the house across the road. She noticed, first, the smoke billowing out of one of the bedrooms and then suddenly became aware of a commotion – loud voices, muted screams. Within minutes, Hardeep Kaur, a young woman who had recently married into the family, was brought out wrapped in a sheet and rushed to hospital.

Later we found out what had happened. Hardeep hadn't brought enough dowry – enough, that is, to satisfy her in-laws' greed. They asked for more, repeatedly, and continued to harass and threaten her. One day, they decided to kill her, make the death look like an accident, keep what she'd brought and offer their son in marriage to another woman – thereby acquiring another dowry.

My mother found this difficult to believe. Was it possible that people could so easily dismiss a woman's life? She resolved to help Hardeep. She visited her in hospital, gave evidence against the murderers in court, joined anti-dowry demonstrations, refused to accept that domestic violence was a 'family matter' – and thus began her journey into one of the most empowering and significant ideologies of all time: feminism.

In some ways, my mother had always been something of a feminist – though, like many other women, she had never admitted this to herself. Years later, when I asked her about this, she said: 'Well, it was so simple. Had it not been for the many women who had gone before me, I would never have had the courage to live the way I have – to resist being cast in the role of the Indian mother.'

Today, as I stand at the end of the century and look back on the women who have made feminism a reality for us, I realize, with something of a shock, that they are far more numerous than I ever imagined. I'm reminded of some of the landmarks of our history...

The year is 1910. Bhikaji Cama, an Indian nationalist and feminist, addresses a meeting of the Egyptian National Council in Brussels. She says to the assembled men: 'I see here the representatives of only half the population of Egypt. May I ask where is the other half? Where are your mothers and sisters? Your wives and daughters?'

Bhikaji Cama, I realize with the knowledge born of hindsight, isn't just conjuring up imaginary Egyptian feminists, for things are happening in Egypt too. In the same year that she speaks, Huda Saharawi opens the first school for girls in Egypt. Later, during the nationalist agitation of 1919, she organizes women to demonstrate against British colonialists. But her most important step comes a year after the founding of the Egyptian Feminist Union (1923) when Saharawi goes to Rome to attend an international conference of women. On her way back, she takes the bold step of casting her veil upon the waters, refusing ever to wear it again.

The year is 1911. In America, Carrie Chapman Catt, a leading feminist and suffragist, is bemoaning the shortsightedness of men. To them, she says: 'the woman movement is an inexplicable mystery, an irritating excrescence upon the harmonious development of society. But to us... there is no mystery. From its source... we clearly trace the course of this movement through the centuries, moving slowly but majestically onward, gathering momentum, with each century, each generation, until just before us lies the golden sea of women's liberty.'

A year later, suffragettes in England explode into militant action, breaking windows in London shops and even at the Prime Minister's home. Some 150 of them are arrested, including Emmeline Pankhurst, and in prison they continue their protest, refusing to eat, driving the prison authorities to force-feed them. Shortly after she is released, Pankhurst addresses a gathering at the Royal Albert Hall in London. 'It always seems to me,' she says, 'when the antisuffrage members of the Government criticize militancy in women, that it is very like beasts of prey reproaching the gentler animals who turn in desperate resistance when at the point of death.'

Egypt, India, the US, England – a mere handful of countries, and such a short space of time. How many more names and issues would we be able to line up, I wonder, if we were to take stock of the whole century? For it is true that in many ways, the 20th century can be called the age of women: all over the world their rights and wrongs, their wishes and desires, have been the subject of fierce and heated debates.

Where, then, does one find a beginning? 'It was in the United States – at Seneca Falls, New York, in 1848 –' the Vintage Book of Historical Feminism tells us, 'that the first organized movement for freedom for women was founded.' As an Indian feminist, I react to this statement: this, I tell myself, is only an American beginning. For the women's movement internationally has many different starting-points, many trajectories.

The key feminist issue in the West in the early years of the century was the fight for women's suffrage. The first country to offer women the vote, New Zealand, did so as early as 1893, but in other countries there was no sign by 1900 that their rights were being taken seriously. As British feminists made world news in their battle for the right to vote, they inspired their North American sisters across the waters.

Elsewhere in the world too, suffrage became a key issue, although most of the early attempts – Iran in 1911 and 1920, Philippines in 1907, China in 1911, India in 1917, Japan in 1924, Sri Lanka in 1927 – were unsuccessful. But women beyond the West were also waging another kind of battle: against colonialism and for independence. Joining hands with men, they demanded their rights as citizens. That did not mean they ignored women's issues: they worked on both fronts, giving solidarity to men when it was needed and questioning their dominance when it seemed necessary. Nor did the inspirational examples in these early years all come from the rich world. One of Indonesia's leading feminists, Kartini, talked, for instance, of the influence on her of Pandita Ramabai, an extraordinary Indian woman whose life she found inspiring: 'I was still going to school when I heard of this courageous Indian woman for the first time. I remember it so well: I was very young, a child of ten or eleven when, glowing with enthusiasm, I read of her in the paper. I trembled with excitement: not alone for the white woman is it possible to attain an independent position; the brown Indian too can make herself free. For days I thought of her and I have never been able to forget her. See what one good example can do! It spreads its influence so far.'

In the West, the years following the First World War – after partial suffrage had been won in some places – are generally seen as marking a lull in feminist activity. So too, in other parts of the world, women retreated into the home after the success of anti-colonial campaigns in the 1950s and 1960s. The empire had ended, in many places independence had been won – the new nations would be free, egalitarian, democratic...

It took many years for a different reality to sink in. Freedom, democracy, the rise of the proletariat – none of these delivered to women the promised 'equality' or dignity. Little changed, at home or in the workplace. Men still held all the cards.

Each step along the way brought more questions. How was it that trade unions hardly had any women leaders? What gave a union member the right to speak about workers' equality on the one hand and come home and beat his wife on the other? It began to become clear that politics was not confined to the outside world; instead it entered the home and was acted out in the most intimate of domestic interactions. It was, in fact, a very personal affair.

It took the women's movement to bring this important – and difficult – fact to the notice of the world. Yet very few people, both men and women, were willing to accept such a frightening truth: as long as politics could be kept somewhere 'out there' they could cope. But the moment it entered the home and touched on all those things that made up one's very being, it signalled an overhauling of intimacies, relationships, family life. How could this be accepted? The feminist slogan 'the personal is political' – for women the most empowering of slogans – was as troubling for activists on the Left as it was for conservatives.

In 1925, a year after Lenin's death, the German socialist Clara Zetkin recorded her memory of several conversations with him on the subject of women. 'I have been told,' he complained, 'that at the evenings arranged for discussion with working women, sex and marriage problems come first... I could not believe my ears when I heard that. The first state of proletarian dictatorship is battling with the counter-revolutionaries of the whole world... But active communist women are busy discussing sex problems and the forms of marriage!'

The 'second wave' of the women's movement all over the world, from the 1960s onwards, was marked by just such discussions on what had hitherto been seen as taboo subjects including, specifically, female desire and pleasure in the form of the female orgasm. The campaigns were not without their lighter moments. In Italy feminists coined a slogan that upheld the greater importance of the clitoral orgasm, saying thereby that the penis was not necessary for women's enjoyment of sex. 'Col dito, il dito', the slogan said, 'l'orgasme sara garantito' (with the finger, the finger, the orgasm is guaranteed), to which a group of men replied, 'Con cazzo, con cazzo, e un altro andazo' (with the penis, with the penis, is another experience altogether)!

By the 1970s, it was becoming clear that the women's movement was one of the most dynamic and vibrant movements of all time. Everywhere in the world, it was women who were in the forefront of campaigning. In the peace movement, women occupied bases, exhorted countries to stop the arms race, advanced the issues of livelihood and survival. In the environmental movement, it was women who led demonstrations and marches and clung to trees to stop them being felled. In the labour movement they demanded that attention be paid to women's rights...

With every campaign came a new lesson. At one time winning the vote seemed to be the crucial issue. Yet once the vote was won it became clear that there was a long road ahead. At another point, education seemed the most desirable goal. Yet, as education began to spread, women all over questioned its usefulness and validity.

Then it seemed that class differences were an insurmountable barrier, but this too was not the only answer. Soon religion came to displace class since, for women in the Majority World, religious dogma and practice seemed to reinforce patriarchies – until it became clear that religion, like class, was not a force that was easily wiped out.

Perhaps the most empowering insight came only gradually – that emancipation did not mean the same thing all over the world; that for every group of women, perhaps even for each individual woman, the idea of liberation differed. At a conference in London some 15 years ago, a panel of women discussed their understanding of women's liberation. Toni Morrison, the black American writer, located it within the context of racism in the US; Petra Kelly, the German peace activist, saw it in the context of the struggle for peace; Ellen Kuzwayo, the black South African activist and writer, spoke of women's struggle against apartheid's pass laws; while a member of the audience identified homophobia as women's most pressing problem. It was the US writer Adrienne Rich who pointed out that each of these points of view had its own validity; that at this moment, for these women, liberation meant winning their particular struggle. Later, at another time, in another context, it might mean something different.

Long years ago, when single issues dominated the women's movement, such a view would probably have been considered lunatic. Yet today, as we look back on a century of women's activism, this recognition of difference, this understanding of its infinite variety, this turning of the gaze from the North to the South and back again, is perhaps the most valuable contribution of the women's movement the world over.

It was this understanding too that lent new meaning to the slogan 'Sisterhood is global', for while that nebulous thing called sisterhood allowed one woman to feel another's pain, no matter that they were divided by geographical, religious or other borders, it also brought home the realization that each woman's life had different priorities, different needs. The internationalization of the women's movement worked, as an activist in Pakistan put it, to 'give it a universal and specific dimension'.

Today, more and more hidden histories of feminist activism are coming to light: women are coming out of the shadows, abandoning the margins. And as men and women alike look at this exciting development, there's cause both for optimism and concern.

Will humanity as a whole prove equal to the promise of the women's movement in the 20th century? Or will it be – as has happened in small ways – that women will move ahead, leaving men behind? Will people create new and different relationships? Or will they reject what the movement has to offer, making that terrible word 'backlash' a reality?

It's difficult to say. What is clear though, it seems to me, is that from the point at which we stand today there is no going back. We may not have quite arrived at the 'golden sea of women's liberty' envisioned by Carrie Chapman Catt nearly a hundred years ago, but its waters are certainly beginning to lap at our feet. ■

Urvashi Butalia works in Delhi with Kali for Women, India's first feminist publishing house, which she co-founded in 1994. She is a regular columnist for the New Internationalist.

5

The cosmic ark: earth resistance

IN the world of the mid-1970s, concern about the environment was very much a fringe concern. Of course it still seems that way now if you take your bearings by the stars of the White House or the compass of the corporate lobbyists. But back then ecological campaigners struggled to be taken seriously even by those committed to social justice who might have been expected to be their natural allies.

To its credit, the early **NI** was not among the doubters, possibly because its stock in trade was to look at the earth as a whole entity, as One World. An early environmental editorial (from 1975) asked: 'You are driving along a narrow winding road in the dark when suddenly the headlights fail. Do you brake or accelerate? If that question seems slightly mad, it is perhaps worth reviewing the mental health of those who are driving our earth-vehicle with its four billion passengers in the back... In a million different ways, from aerosol sprays to supersonic planes, from Vapona fly-strips to DDT, we are taking risks with our delicate, vital and beautiful environment without anything like adequate knowledge of the consequences. In short, we have our heavy boots firmly on the accelerator of material progress without any headlights to see whether we are proceeding safely on the straight and narrow or about to go crashing through flimsy safety barriers and plunge exhaust-over-combustion-engine down the nearest cliff.'

It was followed by regular thematic magazines, from *Trash and Grab: the looting of a small planet* in 1976 through *Assault on the Earth* in 1982 to *What if the Greens achieved power?* in 1987. But even within our own committed ranks the key environmental issues became ever more central as the century wore to an end, utterly inseparable from our other core concerns of poverty and social justice. One day the Great God Economic Growth will be pulled down from its altar, and when that happens it would be nice to think that our explorations of alternative ways forward – of green economics and sustainability – made some contribution to its downfall. ■

June 1976
A tale of two crises
Peter Adamson's *editorial from the first* New Internationalist *theme issue on the environment.*

There are really two crises of the environment. For the majority in the developed world, there is an environmental crisis of 'too much' – too much consumption of raw materials; too much pollution of air, earth and water; too much waste of non-renewable resources; too much packaging, noise and stress.

This year alone, over 500 million metric tons of iron ore and two million metric tons of oil will be taken from the earth's finite stocks; 200 million tons of industrial wastes will be poured into the rivers and one million tons of oil will be smeared on the seas; 6,000 new chemicals and 400,000 tons of pollutants will be introduced into the environment; 200,000 cars will be abandoned on the streets and 60 billion metal bottle caps will be thrown away.

The consequences of 'too much' are already beginning to weigh heavily on the industrialized world. Resource problems are reflected in political and economic conflict; low-level pollutants are becoming a serious hazard to health; obesity has been promoted to the rank of major killer; noise is one of many new factors contributing to stress; and increased consumption seems to be exacerbating social tensions. When Barbara Ward says 'There are limits to the amounts of material goods which man can absorb – it does not benefit us to consume more and more if the result is an ever-increasing need for tranquillizers and mental hospitals' and Aurelio Pecci adds that 'there are reasons to believe that these limits have been surpassed' they are not indulging in idle talk. Half the hospital beds in Europe and North America are now occupied by the mentally ill.

For the majority in the developing world on the other hand, the environmental crisis is a crisis of 'too little' – too little food and fertile soil; too little clean water and safe sanitation; too little energy to meet everyday needs; too little adequate housing and too little employment to invest in environmental improvements at either social or personal levels.

The consequences of 'too little' are even weightier. Lack of food means that 450 million people, according to the FAO, are 'actually starving'; waterborne diseases kill an estimated 25,000 people per day; and a guessed-at 100 million people are forced to become squatters.

When one group of people suffer from 'too much' and another group from 'too little', whether it be within or between countries, it does not take a degree in economics to suggest a broad solution. It cannot be framed in fewer words than Shakespeare's: 'So distribution should undo excess and each man have enough.'

It is in this way that the problem of the environment is inseparable from the problem of development and the need for a fairer distribution of the earth's resources.

Put in today's jargon, the environmental problem is one of 'inner and outer limits' – how to meet the inner limits of basic human needs for all people without transgressing the outer limits of the environment's tolerance. That framing of the question also points down the path towards redistribution – it is 'too much' which threatens to step over the outer limits of the environment and 'too little' which already does step over the inner limits of basic human survival needs for millions of people alive today. Again, the now-fashionable problem of inner and outer limits was summed up 30 years ago by Mahatma Gandhi when he said simply: 'The earth has enough for every man's need but not for every man's greed.' ■

April 1990
The cosmic ark
Jeremiah Creedon heads off to the Arizona desert to probe the Western world's obsession with economic growth. In his quest he discovers new wisdom from old sources.

In the Arizona desert north of Tucson, at the foot of an arid mountain range, scientists and entrepreneurs are building history's first utopia under glass. Called Biosphere II, the airlocked enclosure is intended to be a self-sustaining ecosystem, a tiny model of the complex biological web that forms Biosphere I – otherwise known as Earth.

The two-acre microcosm contains seven distinct 'biomes', including an ocean 30 feet deep, a rainforest, a savannah, a farm plot and a human village. Crops and small animals will provide food for the eight 'biosphereans' due to be sealed inside the structure for a two-year test beginning this September.

The $30-million project has been privately financed. The allure for investors is apparently more than a chance to learn something about the environment. One major investor, a Texas oil magnate, expects to see a profit from such systems in the near future when the new pioneers establish permanent space stations and colonies on other planets. This faith in Biosphere II is based on the surety that life on Biosphere I is deteriorating

– that pollution, overcrowding and scarce resources will soon push humans out of the earthly nest.

Last year I made an effort to visit the project. Though it has been widely covered in the press, my own attempts to gain access as an independent journalist were not encouraged. I was going to be in the area anyway and I resolved to visit the compound unannounced. I had convinced myself that I had to see it.

My interest was less in the project's scientific significance than in what it stood for as a social symbol. Biosphere II seemed to epitomize the advanced expression of a technocratic mentality whose adherents were now turning their energies towards escaping the mess they had made on Earth. Many claimed this experiment would yield profound ecological insights. It may. But beneath the ecological rhetoric I sensed a powerful counter myth, a fantasy of the cosmic ark, with a man who made his fortune selling fossil fuels playing the modern Noah.

Such myths contribute to global warming and other environmental problems in a crucial way. Throughout history, various peoples have used myth to justify their own values and behavior. Western societies are no exception; they are constantly seeking ways to explain, among other things, their obsession with economic growth. The scenarios for exploring space are only the latest narratives to 'heroicize' a technological world-view. The idea that underlies every such story is both simple and absolute: growth is good. Which happens to be closely related to another, perhaps older, Western conviction that nature is bad.

The tie between these two concepts must be understood before the latest, and thus least visible, rationales for unlimited growth can be seen for what they are. One can easily recognize that felling the wilderness in Europe six centuries ago, in North America two centuries ago, or even in the Amazon Basin today, implies a view of nature based on aggression and fear. It is not so easy to detect these same impulses at work on a project like Biosphere II. But the basic mindset bears many similarities. The belief endures that nature must be literally 'manhandled' into subservience if human society (that is, Western society) is to progress.

The idea that society must progress to survive is one of the ruling principles of Western thought. According to the Marxist anthropologist Stanley Diamond, we 'cannot surrender the notion of Progress without destroying the rationale for... civilization.'[1] Progress, a euphemism for growth, is how well a society transforms raw resources into consumable goods. The image of a shark comes to mind, a primitive omnivore that can't breathe without moving forward. Western societies are like sharks swimming through time, impelled by the fear that to pause is to die.

The mathematical expression for this dynamic (widely recognized since the Club of Rome's 1970s study, *Limits to Growth*), may be even more disturbing. It is the exponential curve depicting what the world consumes – hurtling upward, ever steeper, toward an apocalyptic collision with a fixed ceiling of resources. If humanity really possesses something like the collective unconscious, the exponential curve may one day rival the mushroom cloud as the era's most profound contribution to the legacy of archetypal symbols.

In the great urban centers, mass anxiety about rampant growth seems to become more palpable year by year. There are moments when the individual, observing the sprawl of a place like Mexico City from the air, can almost feel progress accelerating in the uncontrollable fashion of a nuclear meltdown.

But others maintain these gloomy intuitions are unfounded. Only a few months ago, for instance, an editorial in the *New York Times* looked back at the prediction offered by the Club of Rome in *Limits to Growth* and declared: 'The Club was right to tell industrial countries they had to pollute less, but it underestimated the power of technology to raise the limits to growth, and the vast flexibility of economic systems to respond to shortages with new sources of supply.' This view is shared by the World Commission on Environment and Development, which called for 'a new era of economic growth, one that must be based on policies that sustain and expand the environmental resource base'. The Commission sees 'sustainable' growth as 'absolutely essential to relieve the great poverty' in the Third World.

Such thinking may be pragmatic, even laudable, but it also neatly severs the causal link between global problems like greenhouse warming and the underlying ethos of growth. Pollution is viewed as bad, of course, but growth remains good – in fact growth is championed as the tool through which such problems can be solved. This faith in technology and growth also imposes a future on the developing world that looks quite similar to the industrial world. 'Sustainable growth', for all its virtues, is still the conceit of a ruling economic order seeking to remodel all societies after its own image.

Politicians, journalists, financiers – the custodians of the industrial present – are not the only ones who accept the ideology of progress as an absolute truth. Social scientists base their definition of society on progress. As a result, modern anthropologists and historians have colonized the past as well, imposing the standard of Western progress on earlier peoples whose visions of the cosmos may actually have been quite different.

In other words, at the very core of a science dedicated to the rational understanding of society, the 19th-century positivists implanted a bit of pure speculation – their faith in progress. As John Stuart Mill noted, the European mind had already chosen between two visions of history: as a cyclical 'orbit' or as a linear 'trajectory' in which no event was ever repeated. Mill saw the notions of trajectory and progress as synonymous.[2] No-one could dissuade the industrial West from envisioning its own destiny as a missile streaking into the future.

The wealth of Western society has created whole classes who spend their lives gleaning insights into nature and the universe. Their achievements are stunning; but so are their misperceptions. Take the theory of evolution, which held the potential to shatter forever the Western idea that humans stood apart from nature. Instead, evolution itself was interpreted as a progressive program whose final achievements – merging with the godhead or colonizing the universe – would be triggered by an act of human will.

The social Darwinism of the 19th century thus never disappeared; it simply became the metaphysical Darwinism of the 20th. Meanwhile profound modern problems like exponential growth and global warming can be rationalized as the consequences of a grand plan. According to this design, the species may be multiplying in such great numbers as a way to generate the freak genius in a billion who will take the mission forward another small step. The Earth in turn is but a chunk of raw energy, a propellant that humans will reduce to ash in launching the ultimate voyage to an unspecified Somewhere Else.

Around the time I intended to visit Biosphere II a newspaper in Tucson ran a feature on it. A photograph showed a young woman emerging from a small test module after 'five days in isolation'. She was wearing the sort of jumpsuit favored by astronauts and waving at a small crowd beyond the camera's frame. The caption said they were applauding. Other articles have mentioned that choosing biosphereans for the longer experiment will be a highly selective process. Only certain people are apparently suited for such confinement. The same could be said of the organisms that an entomologist and 'vertebrate co-ordinator' are planning to select, including a bat colony and 250 species of insects.

My own efforts to reach the cosmic ark were not successful. After driving for hours one day I found myself at the end of a dirt road surrounded by dry hills. I got out of the car. Two ravens swept down from the hills, following the contour of the land. The slopes were covered with a shrublike tree I did not recognize. They were spaced in an equidistant pattern – the arid land was perhaps incapable of supporting them any closer together. I assumed this system of order, the ecological lattice, extended far beyond what I could see. And I suddenly realized that for all my effort I didn't really want to find Biosphere II. I never had.

Biosphere II is one expression from a technocratic people looking for the way out of a profound jam. But the growing numbers who are beginning to listen to the advice of the Earth itself represent another. Once again, the West has arrived by brute strength at the threshold of a choice between different visions. Just as some say that modern physics has come full circle, rediscovering the cosmological wisdom of the Chinese sages, so also has industrial society in general stumbled on a 'new' knowledge of the Earth that until recently they were forcing primitive societies to renounce.

This rediscovered awareness is at once so simple and so radical it is hard to imagine an urban people choosing it. And yet many are. The great value to the emerging dialogue over issues like green politics and 'deep ecology' is that it promises to recover certain ideas that we in the West long ago buried. Some scholars may cringe at the cavalier way that bits of Native American and Taoist thought are combined by the deep ecologists and others. Some claim such eclecticism has no coherence, and maybe in a formal sense it doesn't. But such thinkers, despite their many faults, are in the forefront of a new discipline: an archaeology of lost ideas. And one day the philosophical potshards they are now finding may be pieced together into the real vessel – call it Paradigm II – that will bear us into the future. ■

1 *In Search of the Primitive: A Critique of Civilization*, Stanley Diamond (Transaction Books. 1974). **2** *John Stuart Mill on Politics and Society*, edited by Geraint L. Williams (International Publications Service, 1978).

April 1990
The denial syndrome
Faced with monumental change, we all tend to convince ourselves that our lives will continue unscathed. But in the case of global warming that very basic human trait – the psychology of denial – may bring about our downfall. **Anuradha Vittachi** *explains.*

Once upon a time there was a frog which was dropped into water so hot that it leaped out, shocked – and saved itself. Later it was dropped into tepid water, which it found very pleasant. Then the water began to warm up, but only imperceptibly, so the frog remained lulled and relaxed, becoming more and more warm and sleepy... until it was too late to escape and it was boiled to death.

I was told this story three times in a single day by a Norwegian activist, a US politician and a Soviet scientist, at the massive Global Forum conference in Moscow earlier this year. Each of them stressed their anxiety that human beings were still swimming around relaxedly instead of taking urgent action to save the planet from the effects of global warming. And it does seem that public interest has been waning since the initial shock of awareness in the summer of 1988. Yet unless we spur ourselves into action soon, it may be too late to act at all; we will drowse, like the frog, to a dismal death.

Why are we so inert? At the Moscow conference, *denial* was offered as the chief explanation. Denial is the psychological process by which a painful truth is pushed out of an individual's consciousness. We use denial as a defence mechanism, to protect ourselves from the force of a truth we imagine will be too shattering for us to cope with. When someone we love dies suddenly, for example, for many months we may keep expecting them to come home as usual. We 'deny' their death, because we can't cope with the loss.

And that may be what is happening in our response to global warming. Certain high-consuming humans (like ourselves in the West) have been putting huge amounts of greenhouse gases into the atmosphere. And now the terrible consequences of this behaviour are beginning to show, we suspect the imminent loss of our high-consumption way of life. Rather than acknowledging that loss and beginning to come to terms with it, we choose to deny the reality of the greenhouse effect.

Humans are chronically attached to the past. We don't like separation from what's familiar: it makes us feel deeply insecure. It always has done, from the moment of birth when we had to leave the womb, or the time of weaning when we had to leave the breast. Courage and psychological strength are needed to face an unknown future – especially when the future seems to be governed by forces beyond our control. But also we don't want to change our pattern of living because we high-consumers have been having a pretty good time. We like our 'modern' high-tech lifestyles, full of gadgets and glitter.

This is where denial comes into its own as a way out. It's a lot easier than thinking up a series of individual excuses – just deny the whole problem exists. Perhaps it won't happen, this greenhouse effect. There isn't any really hard evidence yet, is there? ('The water's just pleasantly warm,' said the frog, dreamily.)

Some scientists and politicians are experts in denial. A few centuries ago they knew the earth was flat. In the 1970s they knew that chlorofluorocarbons (CFCs) were harmless. And now some scientists know greenhouse warming is not a problem. Kenneth Watt, professor of environmental studies at the University of California, calls the greenhouse effect 'the laugh of the century'.

Is Professor Watt right? Or is he denying a truth he finds uncomfortable?

But let's be charitable to those who deny. Denial isn't always bad. A woman who cleans the house all day to make it inviting for her devoted husband may one day discover a letter revealing a rapturous affair. She may stop cleaning, call a lawyer, throw her husband out and get a job – or she may go on polishing the furniture with redoubled vigour telling herself she misread the letter. But the period of denial may be an important shock absorber: while superficially she denies and polishes, she may be gathering strength to make her break and go back out into the world. Perhaps we too, as a society, are going through a period of shocked denial while we adjust. After all, the psychological changes we are being asked to make are sudden and profound.

We are being asked, for example, to dethrone the god of growth after centuries of apparent industrial success. We are being asked to believe that the Cold War is over and that national sovereignty is no longer the highest good, despite centuries of personal sacrifice in nationalistic wars; to hold 'earth patriotism' as more valuable than nationalism; to see 'the enemy' not as Soviets (or Americans) out there but to reconstruct it mentally as our own inner fear and greed.

And we are being asked to see nature not as a form of life secondary to humans, submitting willingly to our domination and exploitation, but as a complex, wondrous, universal system, of which we are just one small, integral part – and a rather disreputable part at that. These are just a few of the fundamental changes of perception being thrown at us, and during a very short space of time. After all, it isn't long ago that Ronald Reagan was saying: 'A tree is a tree. How many more do you want to look at? If you've seen one, you've seen them all.'

No wonder we are finding it so hard to adjust. But my sympathy for us shell-shocked consumers starts to fade when one particularly nasty form of denial rears its ugly head, and that's the *displacement* of our responsibility for the damage we've caused onto those who are not in a position to argue back. Ronald Reagan, for example, apparently claimed that 'trees cause pollution'. How's that for blaming the victim? Fortunately, not many people took Mr Reagan's views seriously. Far more worrying is the veiled victim-blaming indulged in by influential environmental experts who ought to know better. They seem to be reactivating the 1960s population-bomb bogey, blaming future greenhouse disasters on consumption caused by population growth among the poor, instead of consumerism-led consumption in the West.

But an average Briton uses 50 times as much electricity as an average Indian. So even if the population in poor countries doubled to eight billion people by the year 2030 and the rich countries' population remained static at one billion people, the rich would still be doing far more environmental damage through consumption than the poor.

And even if, by some political and economic miracle, every one of the poor eight billion people were allowed to earn and consume twice as much as they do now, the small numbers of the rich would still be consuming the lion's share. Added to this is the fact that several Western European countries are actively encouraging population growth (at least of white babies, though not of black) in their own high-consuming nations. Clearly, it is not consumption per se that worries the West but who gets to go on doing it.

A little serious energy-saving by the rich would make far more difference than any heartbreaking, subliminally racist manipulation of the poor. But this kind of practical information is not always welcomed by First Worlders (whichever country they were born in: being a member of the First World depends on your state of mind and your bank balance, not on geography). This is because it forces them into changing their own ways of behaving.

When, for example, an Indian delegate at the Moscow conference pointed out that some of the panelists' sentimental whimsies (like: 'We should see the birds and animals as delegates here') might not be as useful as vegetarianism, he was clearly regarded as a crank rather than as a man with a simple, practical suggestion. He was urged from the platform to let individual freedom rule: people should have the right to change their diets only when and if they wanted to. Fine. Just as mothers and fathers should have their individual freedom to have children when they choose – and not according to the panelists' preferred population figures.

To sum up, there are two main threats at present to the stability of the global temperature: massive damage caused by the rich world's consumption levels, and some damage caused by the poor. Both of these threats could be mitigated straightforwardly by a willingness in rich consumers to stop denying or displacing the problem. The outcome would be not only a safer planet but also a cleaner, greener, fairer life for everyone, rich and poor alike. ■

Anuradha Vittachi was book-reviews editor of the NI in the 1980s. She left to work as a counsellor and writer, eventually becoming the first editor of One World Online. She is now director of the One World Trust.

April 1992

The scars of *umlungu*

Ravaged land. Scarred faces. **Sindiwe Magona** *meditates upon her South African legacy.*

My people have their own ways of doing things. We have always had our ways of doing things. 'The ones scrubbed in hot water' could not see this when they came. They came – 'the ones with coloured eyes' – and found my people living worthwhile lives that were satisfying to them. But the newcomers saw only indolence, ignorance and superstition. They saw nothing commendable, nothing worth preserving, least of all emulating. For them our being alive held no lessons whatsoever. It proved nothing. They had their ways. And, in their eyes, these were far, far superior to ours. So began the destruction of my culture. So began our dying.

My people are a wise people. I do not claim God accorded them special preference in the allocation of grey matter. That would be absurd; as absurd as the claims of superiority made by 'the ones without colour', the ones we came to call *umlungu*.

But my people are patient. We have a saying: 'These mountains were here when we were born. They will be here long after we are gone.' Patiently my people observed the world of which they knew they were a part – equal with the land, the rivers, the trees, the mountains and every other living thing.

Thus my people knew how to flow with nature's rhythm, dance to its tune and harness its forces for their good. They knew about using and using up. They knew that rest is the beginning of restoration, that it brings healing.

How can one stand under the heavens one night, look up at the sky, point out one star and say: 'That star is mine!'? My people would have thought anyone mad who suddenly pronounced themselves sole owner of such and such a mountain, valley, river or any other piece of the earth.

They had not learnt the greed that brings fences with it. When, later, the newcomers cut up the land, cut it up until it bled, the stakes driven hard into its very heart, the barbed wire strangling it of breath, my people found themselves lessened, reduced. They were fenced in. They could no longer heal the land.

The strangers had come with new laws to the land they had 'discovered'. They imposed these laws on the people they found there and made sure they themselves were not bound by them. They were exclusively for my people. Makhulu used to say to me: 'Grandchild of mine, a person has a definite nature, and if something is good you can be sure they will keep it for themselves.'

My people could no longer heal the land. They could not restore it when it was exhausted. The law forbade them to move pasture. A person's place of dwelling became their place of dying. We lost freedom of movement – the land lost the right to rest and restoration.

Fenced in. Forced to till exhausted land, we could not feed ourselves. But, you see, even that was no accident. The no-colour people had planned it all. They did nothing without planning it through and through – years in advance.

To feed his children, to feed his wife and his aged parents, a man was forced to go to the ones with eyes that have colour. And beg them to use his strength as they would use a horse. For that they would give him the shiny buttons without holes they had brought with them. This had become the only thing of value. It was hard to come by it. The scrubbed ones made sure they kept it under lock and key all the time. And never gave my people enough to get the things it was supposed to give them: food, clothing, medicine, anything. You could be dying, but without this button *umlungu*, the ones without colour, would not give you medicine.

Umlungu law said we could not dig for roots: it said we could not gather healing herbs. 'Miserly is the white man, indeed. He withholds ochre which he, himself, does not use. *Uyabandeza umlungu. Ude abandeze imbola engay-iqabi,*' exclaimed my people, flabbergasted. For this kind of stinginess was new to them.

Ochre is the red powder with which we adorned ourselves. Now it was illegal to dig the ground for it. Resistance was strong, there were infringements galore. But by the time my own mother was a young woman ochre had already become a thing of the past.

Umlungu had an even better way of weaning us from our ways. Backward. Heathen. Things of the dark. Those are some of the labels he gave all things essentially us. The things that defined our uniqueness. In time we learnt to hate them ourselves. To scorn those who adhered to them, who refused to 'go with the times', those we saw as hesitant 'to enter the world of electricity, the world of light'.

Instead of ochre and herbs, roots and other powders we started using *umlungu*'s creams. They promised us 'eternal youthfulness, glowing, wrinkle-free skin'. We didn't stop to think that our skin was already free of wrinkles, well into grand old age. We were being civilized. And happily did we stretch out our necks for the yoke.

Umlungu's ways have an essential ingredient called Progress. Where Mama started with Metamorphosa, graduated to Karroo Freckle and Complexion

Cream and Bu-tone Cream for a Lovelier Complexion, now, in her nineties, she is on Oil of Ulay, that bona fide fountain of youth.

But Mama is far, far luckier than I am.

I am a true product of *umlungu's* enlightenment. My face never was touched by such crudity as ochre or any of those things rural women – whom, basking in our new-found sophistication, we called backward – used on their faces. I started on Pond's Face Cream as a pre-teen. I was into Karroo Freckle and Complexion Cream by my adolescence. And in my early twenties, like millions of African women my age, I was breaking new ground. By this time, Progress had brought black people an elixir. Skin Lightening Creams.

And *umlungu* said he was doing what he was doing for our own good. He couldn't understand our gross stupidity. He had a duty to stop us from doing harm to ourselves. The yawning *dongas*[1] crisscrossing the land told *umlungu* it was the women digging for their cosmetics that were to blame; it was our large herds of cattle, the women gathering firewood. So said the dongas to *umlungu*.

But, to my people, the bleeding soil sang a different song; a song of mourning. And, in the manner of our tradition, my people passed the history on:

'These white people and their fences! They have killed the land.'

'They came with no cattle. But today we are the ones without cattle, while they boast ever-swelling herds.'

'Our land has been stolen. We live in fenced-in toy plots. Look at their farms! You can ride across them for a whole day without reaching the other side.'

With hearts more sorrow-filled with each dying day, my people watched their cattle getting thinner, their herds dwindle – and the youth of the nation die in rock falls in the mines of the colourless ones, who made them dig for gold they would never own.

'The land died with the coming of the *umlungu*,' said my people. And the mothers wailed: 'We lose our sons in mines of greed, mines our eyes have never seen, for gold we never touch.'

Young women, their husbands away too long, swallowed by the mines, fretted: 'Do not forget me, my love, in the land of gold. Do not forget me, beloved. My heart, daily, yearns for you.' We became part-time parents to our children.

The fences built for the colourless ones were not yet finished. There was more to come. *Umlungu* didn't care about the problems he made for my people. What did it matter that a mother, for lack of firewood, could not cook for her children? *Umlungu* had a bigger problem: deforestation.

We had no experience of hoarding, of planning scarcity when there was enough. We had not learnt that one person might exact a price from another. We gave freely what God had already given.

Umlungu said he was not starving us. We could always buy firewood. Go to the shop and use the button without holes, he said. His brother who owned the shop wanted plenty of that button. But the button didn't like my people at all. It took one look, made a sharp U-turn and went right back whence it came. The coloured-eyed people hoarded it all. And the gold. And the land. To own. While we still wondered: how can a person claim a star as a personal possession?

Our fathers and our brothers, they toiled hard for that button without a hole. They suffered insults, broke their bodies and lost their lives. The button remained unmoved by our sacrifice. It was of one mind with those who had brought it. It would never change allegiance.

Poor as we were – my generation of women – we used a lot of buttons without holes buying the creams that bleached our skin. We listened to *umlungu* promises of a better life. If only we could rid ourselves of our colour, scour it off, like some dirty foreign matter. How we pursued the dream! At last we would be like them, the people who had brought us all these things of light. How we 'chased' the mirage: Ambi Skin Lightening Cream, Super Rose, Clear Tone, Astra... and others too many to list here.

Like the fences on the land the creams made *umlungu* plenty, plenty of buttons without holes... and killed our skin. Just like the fences had killed the land. Today thousands of us walk around with ugly, dark blotches on our faces, a disfigurement. The land has the scarring *dongas* and we have these hideous marks.

We have no name for this disease in my language, or in any of the indigenous languages of the land. 'Chloasma' *umlungu* calls that which sits on our faces like fungus on a plant. Chloasma. And he has a cure for it. If you can give him many, many buttons without a hole. ■

Sindiwe Magona is a South African writer currently working for the United Nations in New York. Among her books are the autobiographies, To My Children's Children *and* Forced to Grow, *and the novel* Mother to Mother.

1 Steep-sided gullies created by soil erosion.

November 1994
Inheritance of absence

What do you see if you look at the world through a gunsight? Not a lot. And what if you approach your emotional life in the same way? **Susan Griffin** *brings to the surface some deep connections.*

There are stretches of land scattered throughout the United States that have become so desolate they are the stuff of legends. Chain-link fences and signs warning trespassers away set them apart from the rest of the countryside – deserts in California, Nevada and New Mexico; pastures, fields, forested land along creek beds or rivers in Tennessee, South Carolina, and Washington State.

It is as if these patches of earth have been erased from existence, or at least existence as it is configured in the public mind of the last half-century of this nation. These are the dumping grounds for the United States military, places where the unintended excrescences of wars real and imagined have been hidden, shed, stored.

There are shell casings, live bullets, unexploded mines and grenades, countless chemicals and radioactive waste. Toxic substances bubble to the surface destroying vegetation, turning it brown or fluorescent. Underneath, subterranean waters are fouled and carry their poisons unobserved past the gates and sentries into the surrounding countryside, towns, cities.

The effects where they have been observed are devastating. Cancers, childhood leukemias, whole communities uprooted, farms abandoned, unworkable. Armies are supposed to defend the people against early, untimely death from unseen enemies. And over centuries the most sophisticated equipment has been devised for this task. Heat-sensitive photographs taken from satellites, every kind of radar, computerized projections made from the slightest evidence. How is it then that these visible marks on the land, and the countless less visible traces of danger, escaped notice?

I am thinking of the military body. The body of a good soldier. Trained to respond quickly to danger. And yet at the same time educated away from fear and other more subtle responses. Toughened of course against discomfort, pain, fatigue, cold. Tuned to the highest possible pitch of aggression, mastery, control. This is the masculine ideal. Ramrod straight and orderly.

But there are losses. The posture does not allow for peripheral interest. Whatever is in the background disappears in the focus of a gunsight. And the quick reactions necessary in battle make the soldier speed past so much texture, detail. To identify the enemy in time one must not be looking at minute variations, only the uniform.

Of course, these habits of perception would not prepare the mind to see the intricate levels of existence in a field, valley, stretch of desert, forest, at the edge of the stream. Each of hundreds of species of birds, insects, grasses, cacti, fade into what is called background. If there is learning to be had from the land, from the ancient texts of rock, tree, or 'layers of pollen in a swamp' – as Gary Snyder names them – these are books unread, lessons ignored.

So this mind would not be prone to detect the path of a watershed. Not even know that water is running underground, much less that it will reappear thirty, or a hundred, or even several hundred miles later, and enter the life cycles of plants, the mouths of animals, or other people.

And as for the death of an owl, a coyote, a species of small insect that might be a harbinger of danger, how can one expect the soldier to observe these with grief? Everything in his training tells him it is his life or the life of the enemy. The other. Everywhere he looks he must make this distinction. One or the other.

And since birth he has been taught another attitude. An approach going back centuries to at least the Roman Empire where whole forests were destroyed to build the ships and palaces of expansion. Perhaps armies are the most intense evocation of this state of mind. Initiated early in life, the soldier has already learned to think of what he calls nature not only as background but also as other, and even enemy, or prey.

He has been raised with the belief that other life forms are without spirit or souls. The life or death then of a small eco-system, a pond, a hundred square miles of hot sand, red rock, inhabited by lizards, snakes, mice, has no cosmic significance and means nothing to him. Or so he believes. And if the meaning of these deaths are somewhere in him, he has learned to bury this in an unconscious region. Unclaimed as the lands set off by sign and fence.

I am remembering G. He was the lover of a friend in our last year of high school. Just returned from Korea, he still wore a khaki uniform. Our circle was a group of rebels and no-one could quite understand our friend's attraction to him. Nor his to her. He gave the appearance of a leathery skin, thick neck, imperviousness to any delicacy. Talked to us for hours about the Japanese women he had had as lovers. How attentive they had been to his needs. How obedient they were to his demands. They would cook elaborate meals for him, give him massages, walk on his back, and make love to him exotically, passionately, all with no demands of their own, no complaints. None of these women had names or histories he could tell us. They fell into the background as part of a general category: Japanese women.

But at the same time he was obsessed and in love with Japan. And we all liked this in him. He took us all to Japanese restaurants. Introduced us to new ways of eating fish, a different beer; showed us poetry, water colors. Nothing in California pleased him as much as this more delicately sensual world. Because of the quality of intense presence he had whenever he spoke of Japan, one was drawn to him in these moments.

It is certainly possible to be someplace, any place and not be present in this way. By the time I was born, my mother's father had become a kind of emptiness in himself. Most of the time he seemed scarcely present, adding little to family conversations. He had a sweet side though, through which he seemed to come alive solely for me. At these times he would tell me about his childhood or watch the Westerns with me and joke and laugh.

The unclaimed regions of a man, which military training walls off more effectively. To reveal hesitation, sensitivity, fear – above all fear – occasions ridicule. He is likened to a woman. Or a faggot. There is a subtle heritage that connects the military repression of homosexuality with negligent pollution. The inheritance of absence.

So much of modern warfare is not present to itself, takes place in the mind as if nowhere. Almost hypothetically. On a computer screen in an airplane miles above the target. Or in a room with computerized controls set to launch rockets. But this only mirrors a much older divide by which the soldier walls himself off from his own compassion, remorse, terror.

And if there is evidence? Trace deposits, toxins, as yet unkindled fire of all that has been avoided. It is best to ignore it, he reasons with himself.

But the logic is circular. Ignoring place, earth, his own knowledge, the fear in his body, the delicacy of his own perceptions. He is oddly dislocated. He is like a computer screen floating in air. Where is the ground of his being? What is his purpose? Only a marching band with a strong martial rhythm and the sound of his feet indistinguishable from the lockstep of a battalion which follows the clipped, familiar shouts of a commander, can give him back some sense of direction.

And if the parade is marching off to war, some war which he can hardly understand, which means nothing to him, he already has a sense of loss. And grief and rage because of it which will now be useful while he fights over possession of some small stretch of land, two or three acres, over which the victor will one day draw a boundary. ■

North American essayist, poet and playwright **Susan Griffin** *is author of more than 20 books including* Pornography and Silence, Woman and Nature *and* A Chorus of Stones.

April 1996

Building a green economy

The global economy is going from bad to worse and the old solutions don't seem to work any more. **Wayne Ellwood** *goes in search of a better way.*

More and more these days I get the feeling that something is wrong. It's an odd sense of unease, a dim registering that the world is 'out of joint' as Shakespeare might have put it. It happened most recently on a trip to my local corner store in Toronto, a family-owned greengrocer where the *signora* always gives me a welcome smile and her husband invariably drops cigarette ash onto the check-out counter as I pay for my milk or cold-cuts.

Today, when I ask him if the local strawberries have come in yet, he gives me a shrug and mumbles: 'Too expensive. California strawberries are cheaper and they last longer.' This seems odd to me but I let it pass and don't really start to put the pieces together until I'm fumbling around for a few cloves of garlic and notice the words 'Product of China' on the side of the box. China. This gives me pause: from where I'm standing China is approximately 15,000 miles away. These little, white bulbs have been harvested, transported overland, packed and shipped across the Pacific Ocean, then freighted three-quarters of the way across North America.

It's at moments like these that the spectacular lunacy of the global economy comes crashing in on me. California strawberries and Chinese garlic have muscled local produce out of the market for one reason only: they're cheaper. And in terms of actual cash out of my pocket here-and-now that's true. Economists argue that consumers like me are simply maximizing self-interest by buying from more efficient – i.e. cheaper – producers. That's the reason Chilean grapes fill supermarket shelves in Minneapolis and Dutch butter is half the price of local butter in Kenya.

But this word 'efficiency' is a double-edged sword. In fact, what's efficient in market terms is almost always damaging and costly in other ways – to employment, to social cohesion and to the environment. That's because the real costs of getting those mutant California berries onto breakfast tables in Montreal and Philadelphia are hidden. Or, as economists would say, 'externalized'.

Modern industrial agriculture is based on cheap, non-renewable fossil fuel: to run tractors and harvesters, to produce pesticides and fertilizers and to transport produce to market. That massive subsidy is not factored into final food costs any more than are the environmental costs of this high-tech approach to farming. Increased output per hectare over the last 50 years has come with a steep price: soil erosion, groundwater pollution, salinization of soils and diminished genetic diversity, to say nothing of the carbon dioxide and other greenhouse gases vented into the atmosphere. And this is a vicious circle. When soil fertility declines more fertilizer has to be dumped onto fields just to maintain yields. At the moment half the fertilizer used on US farmland is to replace nutrients lost to soil erosion.

So much for the hoopla about the 'efficiency' of the market. Ecologist and business consultant Paul Hawken argues that markets are good at setting prices but lousy at recognizing costs because they give us the wrong information. 'Whenever an organism gets wrong information, it is a form of toxicity,' writes Hawken. 'A herbicide kills because it is a hormone that tells the plant to grow faster than its capacity to absorb nutrients allows. It literally grows itself to death... Our daily doses of toxicity are the prices in the marketplace.'[1] Hawken's metaphor is apt: industrial society, too, is literally growing itself to death.

That's because there is a basic, potentially lethal, flaw at the heart of today's market-based economics. The varied and complex natural ecosystems, on which all life depends and on which the human economy is based, are treated as both limitless and, for the most part, free. The more oil we pump from the ground, the more forests we clear-cut, the more land we till, the more minerals we blast from the earth, the more the economy grows – and the richer we become.

At least that's the theory. Except that, as every economist knows, treating capital as current income is a recipe for disaster. Any business that operated along those lines would soon be bankrupt. For production to be sustainable, capital that is consumed (depreciated) must be replaced by investing some of the production. It's only what's left after this investment that can be counted as income.

A century ago this destruction of natural capital wasn't such a problem. The earth's bounty seemed infinite and its natural systems resilient enough to absorb whatever waste we could throw at them. That situation has changed dramatically over the last four decades. Since 1950 global economic output has jumped from $3.8 trillion to $18.9 trillion, a nearly fivefold increase.[2] We have consumed more of the world's natural wealth in this brief period than in the entire history of humankind.

And the Great God Growth continues to hold sway at the centre of economic policy. Every year at the World Economic Forum in Davos, Switzerland, the world's financial leaders, in a spasm of myopic optimism, close ranks in their quest for renewed economic growth. This year Renato

Ruggiero, Director-General of the new World Trade Organization, stressed the need for a 'universal system of free trade' which would be an 'unprecedented force for economic growth, for both rich industrial countries and the developing world'

What's so depressing about this view is that it is widely shared by the power élite. There are few politicians, trade-union leaders or business bosses advocating anything other than growth as the key to prosperity and the solution to global poverty. Yet there is irrefutable evidence that growth is not the solution but the core of the problem. A central assumption of economists on both the Left and the Right has been that the 'carrying capacity' of the earth is infinitely expandable. A combination of human ingenuity and advanced technology will allow us all, eventually, to live like middle-class Americans – if only we can control our impatience and keep the economy growing.

Unfortunately, reality shows otherwise. It's clear there are limits to growth – and there is startling evidence that we've already breached them. According to University of British Columbia ecologist William Rees: 'Total consumption by the human economy already exceeds natural income; humankind is both liquidating natural capital and destroying our real wealth-creating potential. In this light, efforts to expand our way to sustainability through deregulation and trade can only accelerate global decline.'[3]

It is now estimated that 40 per cent of what ecologists call the 'net primary production' (NPP) of the earth's natural ecosystems is diverted to human activities. If global economic growth continues at the current rate and the earth's population doubles in the next 35 years (as would happen at the current pace) human beings, one species out of millions, would corral 80 per cent of NPP for their own use. Of course in some ways that's pure speculation. For the simple reason that a combination of environmental and social collapse will almost certainly kick in before we ever reach that point.

The iconoclastic American economist Herman Daly argues that we have moved from an 'empty world' to a 'full' one in what amounts to an historical eye-blink. But it is politically convenient, Daly says, not to admit to problems of carrying capacity because that would imply a limit to growth. And if growth is limited, Daly continues, 'then poverty must be dealt with, either by redistribution or by population control, both of which are taboo'.[4]

In his pioneering work on what he calls our 'ecological footprint', William Rees estimates that four to six hectares of land are needed to maintain the consumption of the average person in the West. Yet in 1990 the total available productive land in the world was an estimated 1.7 hectares per person. The difference Rees calls 'appropriated carrying capacity'. The Netherlands, for example, consumes the output of a productive land mass 14 times its size. Most Northern countries and many urban regions in the South already consume more than their fair share, depending on trade or natural capital depletion for their survival. Such regions, Rees says, 'run an unaccounted ecological deficit – their populations either appropriating carrying capacity from elsewhere or from future generations'.[5] There are other more resonant names for this process, imperialism being the most obvious.

We don't have to search far for proof that growth-centred economics is pushing the regenerative capacities of the earth's ecosystems to the brink. The worry is not the one raised by the Club of Rome's *Limits to Growth* report of 20 years ago. There is no immediate shortage of basic non-renewable resources. Even at current rates of consumption there is enough copper, iron and fossil fuels to last centuries. More pressing is the concern that those basic life-support systems which we take for granted – the water cycle, the composition of the atmosphere, the changing seasons, the assimilation of waste and the recycling of nutrients, the pollination of crops, the delicate interplay of species – are everywhere on the verge of disintegration.

There is a now a large, unimpeachable body of research documenting this precipitous decline. Deserts are spreading, forests being hacked down, fertile soils ruined by erosion and salinization, fisheries exhausted and groundwater reserves pumped dry. Carbon-dioxide levels in the atmosphere due to our extravagant burning of fossil fuels continue to rise. On average we deposit 5.6 pounds of pure carbon into the atmosphere with every gallon of gasoline we burn – nearly six billion tons a year in total. And that doesn't include the estimated one to two tons released into the atmosphere every year from burning forests and grasslands. In September 1995 the Intergovernmental Panel on Climate Change, a select group of nearly 2,500 climate scientists, stated baldly that climate change is unstoppable and will lead to 'widespread economic, social and environmental dislocation over the next century'. Meanwhile, oceanographers examining deep-ocean sediments have confirmed that rapid, unpredictable shifts in climate can take place in as little as three or four decades.

So it seems the production of goods and services in the human economy cannot be detached easily from biophysical reality. Yet the powerful myth that more production and greater consumption equals progress remains firmly entrenched. But 'progress' measured in this way is both relative and narrowly economistic. At the beginning of the industrial revolution in Britain the poet Oliver Goldsmith made an observation in verse that might just as easily apply today:

'Ill fares the land, to hast'ning ills a prey,
Where wealth accumulates and men decay.'

We have a growth that impoverishes rather than enriches. The dominance of the business perspective and an addiction to the 'bottom line' as
the defining goal of human society have twisted the concept of community
and perverted the notion of the public good. Thus in our modern economy
the central purpose of life is shopping; the purpose of the family is to raise
compliant future workers and consumers; the purpose of schools to teach
marketable job skills; the purpose of government to boost business; and the
purpose of Third World nations to provide cheap labour, raw materials and
new markets.

Instead of an economy in service of community we have the reverse. In
the original Greek, economics (*oikonomia*) means 'good housekeeping'
and it is that broader humanitarian vision that has vanished. 'True economics,' writes Herman Daly, 'studies the community as a whole and
locates market activity within it' in a quest for 'the long-term welfare of the
whole community'.

Nor is our modern economy capable any longer of providing jobs and
improving living standards for the majority. The evidence – and it's there for
any who care to look – is unequivocal. The gap between rich and poor is
widening in nation after nation. Real wages are declining as employment
growth sputters. There are now more than 30 million unemployed in the
West with no sign of the oft-promised outpouring of new jobs. Mainstream
economists say this wrenching transformation to the new information age
(what some have labelled the 'creative destruction' of the marketplace) will
be worth it in the end. Don't count on it.

The truth is corporations are in the business of cutting jobs, not creating them. Witness the recent announcement by telecommunications giant
AT&T that it would cut 40,000 jobs over the next three years. (The company's stock on the New York Exchange immediately rose $2.62 a share.)
Or data that shows the top 500 companies in the US cut their workforces
by 4.4 million between 1980 and 1993; this at a time when corporate assets
more than doubled and the salaries of corporate executives increased
more than sixfold.[6]

In the Third World, employment in the modern sector continues to grow
in a few isolated enclaves. Chinese and Indonesian factories churn out an
unending stream of Nike running shoes and Barbie dolls from non-union-
ized workers, often women, working 50-hour weeks for a few dollars a day.
In Mexico – the lab test for economic globalization – it's been all downhill

since the North American Free Trade Agreement (NAFTA) was signed three years ago. Over two million Mexicans lost their jobs after the 1994 peso devaluation and another two million peasants have been forced off their land since NAFTA.

Meanwhile, urban slums in the Third World proliferate, the total number of poor grows and overall living standards plummet. According to the World Health Organization a fifth of the world's nearly six billion people live in extreme poverty, almost a third of all children are undernourished and half the planet's population lacks access to basic essential drugs.

The global economy is not a total balls-up of course. It is working perfectly fine for some people. Like the world's 358 billionaires whose combined wealth now exceeds that of the world's poorest 2.5 billion people. And *Forbes* magazine tells us the number of non-Japanese, Asian multi-millionaires will double to 800,000 this year. The same article neglects to mention that 675 million Asians will continue to live in absolute poverty.

Orthodox economics and its seers have a lot to answer for in all this. As Canadian social critic John Ralston Saul notes: 'If economists were doctors, they would be mired in malpractice suits.'[7] He's right of course. The advice of economists has been treated as gospel when it should have been dismissed as self-serving cant.

And today's standard free-market prescription for economic health – deregulated markets, lower taxes for the wealthy, privatization and government cutbacks – is simply more of the same. It's a bit like rearranging the deck chairs on the Titanic. Instead of this stale dogma we need a new vision of economics which puts people back at the centre of the human economy and subsumes economics to the interests of the public good.

I don't want to be naïve about this; it's not going to be a stroll in the park. Those profiting from the current set-up will not cede power voluntarily. Thankfully, there are hundreds of organizations and millions of people around the planet who share my deep sense of unease about the direction in which we're heading. And many of them are working hard to sow seeds of change, to develop a practical, realistic strategy for forging a new economy.

There's even a new discipline called 'ecological economics' which is attempting to challenge mainstream growth-centred economics from within academia. Though you may not have got wind of it yet, there is a movement brewing – a movement which is attempting to turn conventional economics on its head by redirecting its focus from the narrow concerns of growth and efficiency to the broader concerns of community solidarity, democratic governance and environmental sustainability. The movement doesn't have a name or a leader or a headquarters. But it does have momentum. And more importantly it has a vision of a new green economy. ■

Wayne Ellwood is the New Internationalist's *longest-serving co-editor, having worked in the magazine's Toronto office since 1977. He is the author of* The No-Nonsense Guide to Globalization *(Verso/New Internationalist 2001).*

1 *The Ecology of Commerce*, Paul Hawken, HarperCollins, New York, NY, 1993. **2** *When Corporations Rule the World*, David C Korten, Kumarian Press, West Hartford, CT, 1995. **3** *Alternatives Magazine*, Vol 21, No 4, Oct/Nov 1995, University of Waterloo, Waterloo, ON. **4** *For the Common Good*, Herman E Daly and John B Cobb Jr, Beacon Press, Boston, MA, 1989. **5** 'Ecological Footprints and Appropriated Carrying Capacity', William Rees and Mathis Wackernagel, from *Investing in Natural Capital*, Eds Jansson, Hammer, Folke and Costanza, Island Press, Washington, DC, 1994. **6** From 'An agenda to tame corporations, reclaim citizen sovereignty and restore economic sanity', a speech by David Korten of the People Centred Development Forum, 3 September 1995. **7** *The Unconscious Civilization*, John Ralston Saul, Anansi Press, Concord, ON, 1995.

March 2002
Rush to nowhere
Richard Swift says it's time we slammed on the brakes.

The Titanic and its sad fate have become a metaphor for human foibles and arrogance towards the power of nature leading to disaster. What is less well known is that the White Star Line built the ultramodern Titanic in part to compete in an obsessive effort to break the steamship record for crossing the North Atlantic. The record had passed back and forth between the German Lloyd Line and the British Cunard Line. After the accident, both George Bernard Shaw and Joseph Conrad wrote in anger about the foolishness of a ship's captain ploughing into an icefield at full throttle. The enquiry into the sinking of the Titanic identified pressure to keep up with increasingly unrealistic schedules as a cause of the disaster. Criticism of the mania for speed records became common currency on both sides of the Atlantic.

Now that we have Concorde, which also famously crashed, the era of leisurely travel in steamships may feel archaic. But the preoccupation with speed that cost 1,500 lives in the icy ocean that fateful night in 1912 still drives us relentlessly on. Today we see it in the speed-up associated with almost every aspect of life. This is particularly true in the industrial heartland of the global economy. We drive fast cars. We are expected to 'multitask' and some people have even come to enjoy it. Children are rushed to grow up. We are under ever-increasing pressure to work faster and faster. Some people work themselves to death. The Japanese have even created a diagnosis for it. They call it *karoshi*: death by overwork. We gobble fast food – it is the aim of McDonald's to have a restaurant within four minutes of everyone in the US. We sleep less than we used to; more car accidents are caused by sleepy drivers than by drunk ones. We take energy drugs to keep us going. My favourite stimulant is coffee, but there's a new range of energy-based soft drinks with names like 'Jolt' and 'Surge', or Edge2 and Edge2OJ orange juice with caffeine added to keep us 'up to speed'. Added to this there are lots of pills, particularly amphetamines, and special vitamin diets.

Many people have daybooks so crammed with commitments that you'd have a better chance of getting an audience with the Pope. There is even a new craze for 'the nine-minute date', so that singles in a hurry can check each other out. The preoccupation is with control. A whole industry has evolved based on managing time. Drugstore bookshelves are crammed with titles on how you can do this. In his classic study *American Nervousness* George Beard identifies the dread that 'a delay of a few minutes might destroy the hopes of a lifetime'. There is a macho ethos of speed that goes with it all. It's like the Michael Douglas character in the Oliver Stone movie *Wall Street* says: 'Lunch? Lunch is for wimps.' It's an idea that has fortunately been slow to catch on around the Mediterranean, though even some holidays are packaged to rush from place to place.

Time is at a premium. But where are we going?

The modern disaster – the modern Titanic, if you like – is economic development, particularly the mega-project form of it. Dams, roads, highrise buildings, port facilities, airports, pipelines, power-generating stations are slapped up with little thought as to the consequences. Dangerous corners are often cut to meet deadlines. Forests are despoiled. Toxic chemicals pumped into the air. Debt mounts. Local people, on the Yangtse River, in the Narmada Valley, in the jungles of Sarawak, have their lives uprooted. Their protests are studiously ignored.

Some management consultants say that 'it is better to be 50 per cent over budget than to be six months late'. Gigantism and speed go hand-in-hand as mega-projects tie even the most remote parts of the world into a global economic web. Globalization is the product of a kind of turbo-capitalism that utilizes technologies to project itself through trade, investment and speculation at ever-faster speeds to ever-farther horizons.

Marx, who admired capitalism more than he should have, called it 'the most revolutionary' of social systems. And so it has proved. Dynamic. Aggressive. Technologically innovative. Always thrusting into the future. It is propelled forward at market-driven haste fuelled by competition – or fear of it – and acquisitiveness. The faster capital is turned over, the faster it can realize a profit. The faster that profit can be reinvested, the faster it can expand in its turn. This quick turnover of capital is of course connected with volume – more widgets produced, more energy used, more money in circulation, more infrastructure needed.

The key to the process is to speed everything up, whether in production, transport, the circulation of money or – nowadays particularly – consumption. Historically this meant a shift towards factory mass-production and away from artisans, who were too concerned with the quality of their product. Then came the evolution of the assembly line, where workers were cued to perform particular tasks at precisely timed intervals. Techno-innovation spurs it on and is in turn driven by it. In our 'wired world' billions of dollars can be made or lost in hours. Stock markets are open 24 hours a day. Volatile online and day trading have become a norm. It's like a giant, global Las Vegas.

In production it's all about 'just-in-time' inventory control, downsizing to keep labour lean and quick, computer-driven systems of 'command-and-control' and the constant input of data on the supply of raw materials, capital markets, market conditions, consumer preferences. Slowing up is simply not on the cards. Workers are asked to be endlessly flexible in their jobs and to engage in 'lifelong learning' in order to prepare themselves for what the labour market might next demand. 'Time-wasting' has been cut to a minimum and all the 'components' of production are on site in the 'three factories' of the free-trade zones of south China. Young women workers live on one floor, production takes place on a second and inventory is stored on a third. For 'security' purposes the women are locked in – factory fires have taken hundreds of lives.

Genetic engineering, the 'bio-wing' of turbo-capitalism, is even speeding up the 'natural' world. Many crops are made to grow and ripen faster. Turkeys, cattle and other farm animals are fattened at spectacular growth rates through gene manipulation, special feeding programmes and the use of antibiotics. Industrial agriculture is based entirely on its ability to get products to the market quickly. The consequences for food safety are just beginning to be felt.

As always, advertisements best reveal what is at the heart of the matter. Whether you are selling cars, travel, an internet service, a courier company or the 1,000-channel universe, speed is of the essence. Help people rush through life with as little 'hassle' as possible. Make buying convenient. And make it frequent.

The national economies of the West – particularly that of the US – are awash with consumer credit. In addition, turbo-capitalism depends on consumer markets expanding into new areas, like the huge Chinese market. But here, as in so many other areas, speed creates instability, an inevitable contraction in the economy means highly 'leveraged' people and companies just can't afford to pay off their creditors.

What is this time we are so concerned to save through speeding up? Over centuries humankind has measured time in relationship to natural cycles. Planting and harvest times were key markers for agricultural societies. The place of the sun in the sky dictated the tasks and pleasures of the day. Some societies, like the Mayan people of Central America, had highly sophisticated calendars based on everything from a woman's period to the number of layers believed to exist in heaven. The habits and migratory movements of animals (not only essential for survival but also endowed with religious significance) were crucial indicators of time's passage. The Trobriand Islanders of eastern Papua New Guinea begin their year when a certain Pacific marine worm spawns. In different parts of Africa, time may be measured by how long it takes to cook rice or how long to fry a locust. You don't get told what time it is, but what kind of time it is.

With the advent of industrial society we pulled time out of nature. The perceptive social critic Lewis Mumford saw that 'the clock and not the steam engine is the key machine of the Modern Age'.[1] The historian David Landes goes a step further by claiming that the clock 'helped turn Europe from a weak, peripheral, highly vulnerable outpost of Mediterranean civilization into a hegemonic aggressor. Time measurement was at once a sign of newfound creativity and an agent and catalyst in the use of knowledge for wealth and power.'[2]

So the imposition of industrial time has had pride of place in the history of empire. The repetitive racist discourse about work-shirking 'natives' (slothful, unreliable, no sense of how to plan ahead) repeats the history of enclosure during the late Middle Ages in Europe, when work time was imposed on a reluctant agricultural population. The adoption of Greenwich Mean Time in 1884 as the international standard shaped the first wave of the global economy. Local times and methods of telling time were swept away. The same process continues to this day. It became a condition of Mexico joining the North American Free Trade Agreement that it adopt Daylight Savings Time.

Some kind of standardized time-telling is obviously here to stay. But the obsession with 'saving' time through speed-up, frenetic living and the constant, neurotic measurement of nanoseconds is doing both human culture and the natural world a severe disservice. For what we lost when we pulled time out of nature was a respect for the natural rhythms and ecological balance on which we depend to survive. Our data-based culture has replaced contemplation and critical thought with a narrow, instrumental form of reasoning, no matter how it gets dressed up with cyber-babble about 'lateral thinking' or 'virtual intelligence'. Basic assumptions seldom make it to the table.

There is a different way to think about time – not as a commodity but as a continuous flow. In his fascinating book *Faster, The Acceleration of Almost Everything,* James Gleick concludes that one should 'at least recognize that neither technology nor efficiency can acquire more time for you, because time is not a thing you have lost. It is not a thing you ever had. It is what you live in. You can drift in its currents, or you can swim.'[3]

The currents of time-gobbling turbo-capitalism are at the moment threatening to sweep us away as a species if we do not find a way of swimming against them. It is perhaps in their ecological consequences that this is felt most sharply. The unsustainable pace of development is based on the concept of 'mining' natural resources. Mining is quicker and provides bigger yields than the more careful process of sustainable cultivation. The consequences: collapsing fisheries, falling water tables, shrinking forests, eroding soils, dying lakes, crop-withering heat waves and species extinction. Mining transforms renewable resources into non-renewable ones.

A clear example can be seen in the sophisticated and wasteful trawler fleets that have so laid waste to the world's fish stocks that 13 out of the world's leading 15 fisheries are now in decline. More than a third of the global catch is simply dumped, dead, back into the ocean.[4] The way we use, and misuse, water provides plenty of other examples. The worldwide consumption of water has more than tripled since 1950. From the US Great Plains to the Punjab, aquifers have been drained to feed industrial agriculture and its unsustainable yields. In 1995, 92 per cent of the world had relative sufficiency in water, but this is projected to decline to 58 per cent by 2050, when two billion people will be living in a situation of water scarcity.[5] Conflict over water rights, particularly where it involves trans-border rivers, is already acute and likely to increase.

Demand for paper has gone up more than sixfold since 1950. The use of lumber has doubled, firewood tripled, adding to the pressure to 'mine' (i.e. log unsustainably) forests worldwide: 'Another 10 per cent of the world's forests may be lost by 2050. Almost all the forests in Africa and China may be wiped out. There is a danger of severe loss in Southeast Asia and South America. Old undisturbed forest is in decline almost everywhere.'[5]

Soil erosion and exhaustion are threatening our ability to produce food.

Biodiversity is being lost. Thousands of species are pushed over the edge every year as habitat is gobbled up by development. And while population growth is a factor, the global economy is growing faster (in many places much faster) than population.

Turbo-capitalism is highly energy-intensive. Worldwide energy use is expected to rise 46 per cent by 2010. In places like California the energy grid is so over-stretched that rolling 'blackouts' have become commonplace. The highest energy use is in the industrial North, where economies gobble up more than four or five times the energy used in the South. Most of the growth in future will come from a further expansion in the use of fossil fuels.

What does this heavy energy use sustain? The world automobile fleet continues to grow, with its attendant problems of pollution and congestion, particularly in places like China and India. Since 1950 the number of people per car has dropped fourfold. As the hurry-up lifestyle is exported, the US-based fast-food industry is growing at a phenomenal rate. The top ten chains now operate over 100,000 outlets around the world. There are predicted to be 1.6 billion cellphone users by 2005 with internet access also showing spectacular growth.[6]

All of this indicates the spread of the speeded-up lifestyle turbo-capitalism needs for the quick turnover of capital. Its global 'utopian' vision is predicated on our ability to drive to the nearest Taco Bell as we chat on our cellphones. The US, with only 6 per cent of the world's population, consumes about 30 per cent of global resources: extending its unsustainable lifestyle to the rest of the world is a deeply malevolent fantasy.

That is not the full extent of the problem, either. There are many signs that the speed of turbo-capitalism is causing a profound cultural and political disorientation. You can see it in the spate of book titles announcing the end of almost everything: *The End of Democracy, The End of History, The End of Sex, The End of the Family, The End of God, The End of Equality, The End of Affluence*. Other titles announce the 'death' of everything else, from Modernity or the Nation-State to Ageing, Work and – perhaps most tellingly of all – Certainty. Since most of these things haven't actually 'ended' or 'died', what they speak to is a rapid, disorienting form of change. People no longer feel the firm ground of institutions or even solid belief-systems beneath their feet. The family, a secure job, public services, personal safety, even meaning itself are all thrown up in the air by turbo-capitalism and its disposable, 'post-modern' culture.

Opposition can easily be undermined when it is shaped more by reaction than by transcendence. An increasingly desperate fundamentalism clings to repressive old certainties in the face of the constant uprooting of beliefs and ways of life. The Left is slow to abandon the industrial dream-turned-night-mare and clings to a politics of ghettoized 'identities'.

The gravest danger lies in trying to out-race turbo-capitalism. A failure of state socialism was its attempt, and its inability, to keep up with the glitz and the goodies, the missiles and the Mercedes, of its opponent. What we need to put forward is an alternative that is happy to 'fall behind', that measures life by slow quality, not fast quantity. It won't be easy. As a species we have never really chosen to slow down. The habits of speed are deeply ingrained in all our psyches – particularly the urban ones. The love of the rush is real enough. But the stakes are also pretty high. The iconoclastic scientist Stephen Jay Gould points out with wry wit: 'If we continue to follow the acceleration of human technological time so that we end in the black hole of oblivion, the earth and its bacteria will only smile at us as a passing evolutionary folly.'[7]

There needs to be a playfulness in our resistance to the time-gobblers. A clear refusal, a kind of 'time guerrilla warfare'. After all, whose time is this anyway? The writer Douglas Adams caught the flavour of refusal: 'I love dead-lines. I love the sound of them as they whoosh by.' The Cuban writer Paul Lafargue, in his pamphlet *The Right To Be Lazy*, opposed the preachers of work-dogma and called for a three-hour working day. And that was back in 1880. Dance, festival, contemplation, laughter, riot, love, are all part of a nas-cent culture of 'go-slow' we must surely embrace. A conscious movement to slow down everyday life is starting to take hold – what we might call 'slow activism'. After all, the world's fastest animal, the cheetah, lives for just 15 years, while the lugubrious tortoise can keep going for 150.

There is an old sundial in an overgrown garden I know well. It says on its face: 'Measure only the hours that are serene.' A tall order. But this too has to be part of our resistance. For what we do with our time is in the end what we do with our lives. ■

1 Jeremy Rifkin, *Time Wars*, Henry Holt, New York, 1987. 2 David Landes, *Revolution in Time*, Harvard University Press, 1983. 3 James Gleick, *Faster: the Acceleration of Almost Everything*, Vintage Press, New York, 1999. 4 Lester Brown, 'The Acceleration of History' in *State of the World 1996*, Worldwatch Institute, Washington. 5 Ian Pearson, *The Atlas of the Future*, Routledge, London, 1998. 6 *Newsweek*, 7 August 2000. 7 Stephen Jay Gould, 'Scale Models' *Forbes ASAP*, 30 November 1998.

6
Stories from life: the personal world

THE heyday of personal or confessional writing in the *New Internationalist* would seem from this selection to have been the 1980s – all but two of the pieces that follow date from that decade. Certainly there was then a surge of interest in publishing material with a more personal flavour. In part this was simply an attempt to offer readers a variety of writing styles, but it was also a reflection of the influence of sexual politics, to which a whole section of this book is dedicated.

But why would interest have waned again in the 1990s? The commitment to presenting varieties of tone and texture was certainly then no less great. But perhaps there was a general move away from the kind of subjects that are particularly conducive to an autobiographical approach towards addressing the headline concerns of globalization and the environment.

I make no apology for selecting two pieces by women struggling bravely, creatively, to cope with the impact of cancer on their lives: these are certainly among the most poignant articles the magazine has ever carried, speaking to each of us much more deeply than any overview of cancer in society could manage. Besides, a personal story can enliven almost any theme. Gerry Dawson's fascinating account of a day in the life of a general practitioner appeared in an issue mainly concerned with primary health care in the Majority World. While Mo Bo's *I was a teenage Red Guard* brings home the realities of the Cultural Revolution in China much more graphically than a straight historical piece would have done.

Some journalists do little else but write about themselves. But often the best personal writing comes from those to whom it does not come so easily, whose normal journalistic voice is more detached. There are two articles here which certainly fall into that category – and they are companion-pieces, in a way, since while the one talks about the experience of becoming a parent the other concerns the struggle to be a good father. Both Wayne Ellwood and Dexter Tiranti have countless editorials to their name but neither of them have written more engagingly and powerfully than about their children's impact on their lives. ∎

September 1983
Doctoring

Gerry Dawson is a doctor. Here he describes one day in his South London practice: a day, like every other day, in which he is forced to grapple with the question of whether the medical profession has a part to play in keeping people healthy.

It is 7.45 in the evening and I have been doctoring all day. Forty-three consultations, 430 decisions, four or five thousand nuances, eye-muscle alterations and mutual misunderstandings have left me emotionally drained and so exhausted that it is a considerable mental effort to remember quite how to double-lock the surgery door. But don't pity me. I get paid – quite well by my patients' standards. Pity the patients instead.

There was the batty woman who 'has always suffered with her legs'. A forklift truck driver with asthmatic attacks to whom I explained three times the action of sodium chromoglycate in stabilizing mast cells – until we both agreed I should give up the effort and he should keep taking the pills. There was Mrs J, making light of the fact that her devoted husband, as well as herself, now has cancer, asking with genuine feeling about my family, and insisting on giving me $2 'for the holidays' which she could ill afford but I could ill refuse. A man with a brain tumour who hasn't told his wife and who keeps this agonizing secret with me and his hospital doctors. An ex-services amputee who clanks his tin leg against the chair, and a widow still in tears ('we'd been together since the General Strike').

And so it goes on. Wax in the security guard's left ear, a nasty childhood eczema; several sore throats and coughs; two of which are selected for the five-star anti-smoking tirade; one of whom tellingly replies that he will give up his cigarettes the moment someone stops the pollution from lorry exhaust fumes that blackens the air of local streets.

Why haven't I got the time or energy to refuse an old dear the sleeping pills which one of my colleagues commenced, on a strictly temporary basis, 15 years ago? Am I really making anyone happier, except perhaps the drug companies whose overpriced, crudely advertised ('Narcoxyn 500 Has the Power') – and occasionally unsafe – products I have been prescribing all day? I once heard a consultant colleague, who meant it as a compliment, describe general practitioners as 'specialists in highly skilled reassurance'. I would much prefer to be a highly skilled specialist in making patients angry: because these so-called medical symptoms have causes – and cures – far beyond my sphere of medicine. We're not trained in the installation of handrails or the delivery of meals on wheels. That's somebody else's business – despite the fact that any major improvements in health have been because of political and social reform rather than 'medical breakthrough'.

Today – against my better judgement – I referred for specialist investigation a bus conductress with a run of 'funny tummys'. I wrote her a comprehensive referral letter and she was carefully and competently examined by a specialist physician who, in turn, wrote a comprehensive and illuminating letter back to me explaining he too could find nothing specific and suggesting she might wish to try bran on her breakfast cereal. Were we maintaining a show of professionalism to mystify our patient or simply justifying the existence of the technology at the specialist's teaching hospital? Or did the bus conductress simply want a little time off to postpone facing yet another new brain-bending fares scheme?

Probably my time was better spent visiting a recently bereaved wife whose husband's ghastly death is still vivid in both our minds. And I would certainly do better if I were to bully the housing authorities to forbid a neighbour breeding pigeons next door to a diabetic man with life-threatening asthma, than I would by increasing his broncho-dilator dosages still further.

But then again, just as one has almost talked one's own profession out of existence, along comes a good, old-fashioned emergency, calling for high-tech hospital medicine and some very fancy clinical management – but fast.

It came this morning with the unpredictability which is so typical of general practice. It should have been an easy visit: just another case of chicken-pox. Some common-sense advice, a bottle of calamine, maybe a squint in the ears, and you can usually be out of the door again in a couple of minutes. This time I was greeted by two kids running barefoot down the length of the council-house corridor – naked but for grubby towels, and covered from the soles of their feet to the roots of their mouths with weeping scabs. Inside, their baby sister lay face down on the carpet like a discarded doll, with a burning fever, rigid neck stiffness, swollen eyelids shut tight over her eyes and with skin almost obliterated with pox craters.

Trying, while on the phone, to make light conversation, I asked where Dad was. He was, his wife explained, on remand in Brixton Prison on a charge of attempted murder. Oh, and since he had suffered brain damage in a road accident he was now so deranged that he literally tore his cell apart if not visited every day by his wife. So would I be able to arrange for her to speak calmingly to him over the phone before she accompanied her daughter in the ambulance?

A bad day; we all have them.

It only becomes a futile day when I get home and try to unwind in front of the TV set which is celebrating, yet again, that profitless and very expensive adventure in the South Atlantic.[1]

I doubt if I have 'saved' more than half a dozen lives in my life or, to be perfectly honest, prolonged or greatly improved the quality of more than a very few. Yet instead of tackling housing and working conditions, our society has instead perfected weapons which can blow a cruiser full of teenage conscripts out of the water, which publicly gloats over those boys' deaths and which boasts its ability to blow the entire world into a desert of radioactive dust. What price then the stabilizing effect of sodium chromoglycate on mast cells?

Perhaps I should have the courage of a colleague who recently – and with a certain icy logic – gave up her medical career to work full time for nuclear disarmament: perhaps the single most fruitful measure of preventative medicine that modern society could take?

Obviously this is not my conclusion. I remain more convinced now than I was ten years ago, as a rather naïve young hospital doctor, that if we are to have a society genuinely enjoying good health – rather than a medical sector snuffling after the causes of sickness like a baffled bloodhound – we need fundamental changes in the way our society is owned, ordered and organized.

Healthcare according to need rather than wealth is not just a good moral principle. It has been shown to work. And to be more efficient and effective than the commercial medical sector in North America. This is ground which must be held against governments who make no secret of their wish to return to the old two-tier medical care of charity and minimal medicine for the majority with a lucrative private sector providing VIP care to those who can foot the bills.

But if I ever get complacent about what can be achieved by medical measures alone, I need only go as far as I did this lunchtime: to the local supermarket. There I will almost certainly know half a dozen shoppers and will be able to see the trolleys quaking with pop and sugar, cheap cosmetics and ciggies: not because my patients are bad people. But because those products are cheap and filling and quick and keep the kiddies quiet. And it's then, not in the consulting room, that I renew my practical and intellectual commitment to social change.

In this respect it is conventional to think of doctors like Ernesto 'Che' Guevara, Norman Bethune and Josuah Home. But I have more affection for those flaming words of Sylvia Pankhurst (whose mother-and-baby clinic – a converted pub called The Mothers Arms – was only a stone's throw away from where I practise today) to the judge sentencing her, once again, to jail for sedition: 'I have sat up with the babies all night and tried to make them better. But this is the wrong system and it cannot be made better. And I would give my life to see it overthrown.' ■

*We have lost contact with **Gerry Dawson** but would be intrigued to know if he is still persevering as a general practitioner after all these years.*

1 The Falklands/Malvinas War between Britain and Argentina.

October 1986
Connectedness

*They disturb your rest, cost a fortune, inhibit your sex life and turn you grey worrying about their own – why on earth do parents have children? **Wayne Ellwood** has become a father twice over in less than a year. This is how and why he did it.*

I'm bolt upright in the half-light. Confused. The crazy herring-gulls are screaming in the park across the street, on their early-morning detour from the shores of Lake Ontario.

But the gulls are not the only ones trying to raise the dead this morning. My son Robin has just released a high-pitched yelp, his version of reveille. No bugle needed. I lurch drunkenly past formless humps of furniture, sweep into his room and scoop him up before his protests reach our third-floor lodger.

He is like a coiled spring in his urgency, hands grasping for the bottle. Fwap! – he's got it, the nipple is nestling in his perfect mouth. Instant bliss – for both of us.

Am I losing my mind? It's five o'clock in the morning. I'm looking into this six-month-old baby's face. He's grinning like I'm the world's funniest stand-up comic and I'm lapping it up.

By now you've probably gathered that I'm a new father – I exhibit the identifying signs of the type. The bags under my eyes are a little blacker than normal. My shoulder is spotted with curds of cheesy baby puke. I bore my childless friends senseless with tales of my son's antics. Yet six months ago I was a normal 37-year-old male, not knowing that my days as half of a childless couple were numbered.

How did all this happen? My partner and I had been trying to have a kid for years. We went through the round of fertility investigations but realized after some years that the chances were slim that we would have our own baby. We still wanted to be parents. It's hard to say why. It was a kind of existential urge – it just felt right.

In the end we decided we would try to adopt. In Canada almost all adoptions are through quasi-state agencies. An exploratory phone call got us to the first hurdle. A group of nervous would-be mums and dads were called together for a talk with slides. All the babies you'd never want? Spina bifida, hydrocephalic, cleft-palated, learning-impaired babies. Black, brown, male, female: these choices didn't matter. But neither of us were quite ready to take on the awesome responsibility of a severely handicapped child. And unlike natural parents we weren't obliged to run the risks of genetic roulette. One slight advantage, we thought, in being adoptive parents: couples who chose to adopt a handicapped baby would do so knowingly.

When we got over the application hurdle, we were assigned our social worker. That's when the hard part started. We actually had to think about *why* we wanted to be parents. None of this locking loins and letting nature take its course. We had to show we were serious and that we knew what we were getting into.

And it was hard work. Our social worker forced us to open our minds in a way we would never have done otherwise. We talked about our own childhood: how our parents had treated us and what our feelings were towards them. We talked about each other and our relationship. How would we describe our feelings for each other? What attracted us to each other in the first place? Why did we stay together? We talked about our domestic lives and our work lives. It helped that our social worker was a thoughtful human being and not a disengaged bureaucrat.

Was it a good thing? In retrospect I think it was. Natural parents have nine months to search and probe and come to terms with their coming parenthood – though how many of them actually do is another question. Although we were being exposed to strangers' scrutiny – an ordeal biological parents don't have to undergo – we couldn't feel resentful. The questions seemed to make sense.

In all we spent ten hours going over our family dynamics. Not to mention detailed responses to a six-page questionnaire, and supporting letters from three friends. They also checked our police record for any record of child molesting.

It was wearying and demanding, but worth it. We got the OK and joined the queue. All we had to do was wait. Six months, a year, five years – we didn't know. We just had to cool our heels. And wait.

I was counting the grey hairs in my moustache the other day thinking grand thoughts. You know, the kind Woody Allen makes films about: big, deep, serious ones.

I remembered what Marshall McLuhan called c-o-n-n-e-c-t-e-d-n-e-s-s. He was referring to the timeless echoes of history, the infinite chain of being that joins us to the past and future. To the Huron Indians who lived where I do 400 years ago, to the Buddhist empire that built the remarkable Borobodur temple in central Java 1,000 years ago, to my Scots and English ancestors – rough peasants in sod huts whose penurious lives made mine possible.

This naked, powerful feeling of intimacy with the past was prompted by the arrival of my son. I actually feel *connected*. Long chains of parents having children who themselves become parents having children... *ad infinitum*, corkscrewing endlessly into the past and inexorably into the future. The world is a process; history is all around us. And I am an actor in it.

And so is my son. That he is not a product of my genes somehow doesn't matter. He is a little boy: totally helpless (so far) and totally dependent. He needs us. We are his link to life. It is that simple – and it is that primal. We care for him and by doing so immediately become part of Parents International. Parents and children are transcultural. The look in my son's eyes is a language understood in any country.

In fact our son is more an actor in the creation of human history than he knows. He's soon to have a sister: this time a biological one. Don't ask how. All we know is that something meshed less than a month after the adoption. Body chemistry moves in mysterious ways and our son seems to have been the catalyst for his sister's conception. Another spiritual link.

Connectedness... it may sound silly – a flight of fancy conjured out of the early-morning mist. But it has been important to me, and it's an experience that came with becoming a parent. ∎

April 1987
I was a teenage Red Guard

*Fanatics ready to commit violence and denounce anyone in the name of communism – or heroes who sacrificed personal comfort to work for the greater good? Conflicting images of the Red Guards summed up Western confusion about Mao's China. **Mo Bo** remembers what it was really like to be a Red Guard.*

When the Cultural Revolution reached my school in 1966 I was 14. In the beginning, classes were interrupted from time to time; the teachers began to get worried and did not know what to do. Then, overnight, wall posters appeared everywhere. We all took it for granted that the senior students wrote the posters and that the only thing we could do was admire them.

Most of the posters were just empty slogans but one depicted our geology teacher as a 'dirty bourgeois intellectual' because he would make sure that the water temperature was exactly the same as that of his body whenever he washed. He was also criticized for his 'yellow' diaries, which were searched out by the active 'rebels' (he was so eccentric that we all thought there must be something bourgeois about him). In one of his diary entries he recalled his experience of sitting beside a plump lady in a bus. The poor bachelor wrote that it was 'very comfortable' to feel that lady's flesh.

Then, following the example of the students in Beijing, we formed an 'Organization of Red Guards'. Everybody wanted to join the Red Guards because nobody wanted to be 'unqualified', 'backward' and 'non-revolutionary'. I was one of the first to join because, being from a poor peasant's family, my background was supposed to be 'clear'. We all enjoyed having no classes and degrading the teachers. 'The teacher takes the student as the enemy and uses examinations as weapons to attack the student' – the fact that it was Chairman Mao who had said this meant a great deal.

In the past our teachers had been intimidating. Now the situation was reversed: whenever teachers came across a student they would lower their heads. This kind of experience was so intoxicating that some of us went off our heads. But, like most of the Red Guards, I never appreciated the beating-people-up business. The farthest we went was when the most unpopular teacher was made to kneel down and confess his 'crimes' to the students. One student hit the teacher's heels with a brick – I couldn't bear to look. This student was one of the rough boys who would call their fathers 'bastard' and perform badly in exams. Chairman Mao gave them the chance to get their own back – at least that was how I understood it then and it is how I understand it now.

Then I was selected as one of the representatives to go to Beijing to see Chairman Mao. I was very proud and excited. We saw him in Tienanmen Square when his car passed us like the wind. Some Red Guards cried with joy: 'the happiest moment in my life,' said one. But I just felt nonplussed: I could see Chairman Mao better by looking at his portraits.

Then we went to Beijing and Qinhua universities to copy posters. We were supposed to 'learn revolutionary experience and then to spread the revolution all over the country'. After a fortnight several of my notebooks were full of slogans and posters. But I had no better understanding of what was going on.

Later on all the Red Guards started going to Beijing or somewhere else to 'establish the revolutionary links'. But what most of us really wanted was to travel. It was wonderful because we didn't have to pay for anything: hotels (very primitive), food and transportation were all free. Special centres were set up where Red Guards could borrow clothes and even cash in an emergency. I remember I once borrowed coupons worth 80 kilos of rice and I was never able to return them. Nobody asked me to return them and I did not know how.

Nobody understood Marxism. After all who would bother? The only things we believed were that Chairman Mao was the great banner-carrier of Marxism-Leninism; that Russia had turned to Revisionism and that the Third World needed guidance for their struggle against Western Imperialism and Hegemony. We also believed that Western society was rotten and decadent and that the only way to create a new society was to destroy the old one in China first. The 'academic authorities' in the fields of philosophy, history, literature and art (not science!) had to be re-educated because they stood for the Old Ideology. Temples were destroyed because they were thought to be part of feudal superstition.

I think I believed all this. But that did not lead me to beat people up or to destroy buildings. I wrote hundreds of posters but I never attacked anyone in them whom I knew personally. Some people destroyed things simply because they liked being vandals. Later on, when things were getting chaotic, the whole of society got involved, whether they were Red Guards or not. By then nobody could tell who did what – let alone for what reasons.

I felt at a loss when I came back from Beijing to find my school closed. It meant I had to go back to the countryside – when I really wanted to continue my formal education. I found Chairman Mao's idea of 'young people going to the countryside to learn from the peasants' uninspiring to say the least. But then I was from a peasant family.

For the city-dwellers things were different. Few did not want to go to the countryside. Some youngsters ignored their parents' anger and volunteered to go before the required age. Of course several years later most of them regretted it and wanted to return to the city. The sheer physical labour and material deprivation was enough to strip them of the romantic sentiment of the Great Helmsman's call. A lot of the 'educated youth' were sent to state farms where there were no poor and lower-middle peasants anyway. Those who were sent to poor villages began to despise the peasants as soon as they got there. For them, the people in the country were illiterate, ignorant and unhygienic. When an educated youth went to visit a poor peasant's home she might have enough revolutionary sense not to use her handkerchief to wipe off the dirt from the bench that was offered – but that meant she had to remain standing for half an hour, pretending to talk with and learn from the peasant.

The peasants, on the other hand, treated these 'foreign students' as temporary guests. Their instinct told them that things might come and go but their life would always be the same. However, they did look at the young urban people with great interest. The 'educated Shanghai youth' became well known all over the country for their good-looking hairstyle and clothes – and young Shanghai women with their white skin were constantly hunted by the 'local bosses'.

But this is only part of the story. Quite a few students settled down in the rural areas and contributed to the improvement of the country. When I went to university in 1973, we former Red Guards met to exchange our experiences. We agreed that our stay with the people in the country had taught us the value of things – and of life itself.

Looking back dispassionately, whatever motivated Mao to launch the Cultural Revolution, some of the ideas which emerged from it are still valuable. The 'barefoot doctor' and 'barefoot teacher' system is certainly good for a country like China. The country people, especially the children, suffer from simple and common diseases. Great improvements were brought about by training local people in basic methods: a school leaver with just three months' medical training is capable of dealing with many of these diseases. Similarly with education. Basic things like how to read, write and calculate can be taught very cheaply if they are organized by the local people themselves.

At the beginning of the Cultural Revolution I feel the ordinary people were exhilarated by their new right to criticize and even to attack their bosses. The suppressed humiliation that one suffers at the hands of a faceless bureaucracy builds up a resentment that is like the surging tide blocked by a dam. When the dam crumbles the destruction is horrendous. That was what happened during the Cultural Revolution.

Now resentment is building up again. The bureaucracy problem was never solved. And when the old bureaucrats and local lords were invited back to power as heroes after the Cultural Revolution had been denounced, their prejudice was confirmed and their stupidity encouraged. And their misuse of power was intensified by the urge for revenge and a wish to make up for lost time.

But again this is only part of the story. There is something deeper and more permanent going on as well. When the leadership launched a campaign against 'cultural pollution' in 1983, the response of the people was very revealing – there was simply no response. Meetings were called. But I recall vividly that all we said at the meetings were things like 'well, well…' and then 'the price of fish is 2.50 *yuan* per *jin*'. The end of the campaign was also untypical in Chinese politics: no documents, no theoretical summary and justification in the *People's Daily* – just a natural death.

But for the Cultural Revolution this would not have happened. After that unforgettable ten years we don't believe official propaganda any more. I myself have developed a peculiar habit. Whenever I read from the paper or hear over the radio something like 'another great achievement…', 'such and such project has been accomplished with great success…', 'the statistics show that…' I say to myself 'rubbish!' But whenever I hear bad news reported I say 'this may be true, more of it!'

We are more cynical, more sceptical and more practical. The age of ideological romanticism is gone, perhaps forever. Because of this, no leader or ideology will ever again give us such inspiration; and hopefully there will never again be such horrific suffering either. ■

*At the time he wrote this piece the author was studying linguistics in Britain. But the name **Mo Bo** was anyway a pseudonym to protect him from possible retribution when he returned to China.*

September 1987
The absent father comes home
More and more fathers are taking an active interest in their children. Instead of leaving everything to the mother, they are present at the birth and enter more into the intimacy of child-rearing. Is the experience changing them? **Dexter Tiranti** *looks at the example he is setting his own children – and at what they are teaching him.*

'Dad, can I watch *The A Team?*'
'No.'
'Go on.'
'No, I'm not having you lap up that violent American rubbish. The world's not about fighting, guns, flashy cars and street chases.'
'But it's interesting.'
'Too bad. Can't you amuse yourself any other way than by watching TV?'
This kind of dialogue goes on regularly between me and my eight-year-old

son. I try to control the values our children are exposed to on TV, rather like King Canute. Yet they accumulate insidiously, be they in praise of violence, crass materialism, junk food or rigid sex stereotyping,

When I was a boy myself I was given, at my own insistence, a gun for every birthday and Christmas. As I got older my toy cupboard looked like an arms dealer's warehouse: Colt 45, Luger, shotgun, submachine gun, Magnum .38. Yet today toy guns are banned from our household. This is because we are trying to create a better world now, I hastily reassure myself. Fathers were different when I was a child. There was no lip service paid to sexual equality. Everyone knew their place in the family, and Dad's was usually behind the newspaper.

Nevertheless one of the more uncomfortable sides of being a father, I've learnt, is exploring the nooks and crannies of my own hypocrisy. 'Do as I say, not as I do' is an uncomfortable tenet to live with... and I wonder at my own inconsistencies. As someone seriously concerned about the sexism in our society, the fatherhood model I provide for my son and daughter will be their biggest teacher. And these perceptive little people will soon notice if I'm not doing my share of the cooking, caring and concern.

For the greatest teacher is personal experience, and kids will imitate what they see and hear around them, not least Dad's example. So by hanging in there and not diving for cover, by being about the home while the children are still up, fathers can do their children (and partners) a great service. They might be helping themselves too. By spending time with my offspring, thoughtful nine-year-old Ann and turbulent eight-year-old Gabriel, I've learnt a lot about myself and them. And I've changed as a result. Of course there are trade-offs. My paid work is not quite as full-time or as good as it should be. My tennis doesn't sparkle as it would, I delude myself, if there were more time for practice. And goodness knows I get tired, irritable and hassled by my children's demands.

But I've had my eyes opened too. Privacy is not so important, not after sitting on the lavatory and discussing Jesus Christ, the *conquistadores*, Gary Lineker, Margot Fonteyn or the various merits and drawbacks of penises and vaginas with little people determined not to leave you alone. Nor can I value material things too highly – after all, when a toddler has savaged the sofa with a saw, what can you say but 'never mind'? Not least I've learnt to live amid chaos, to spend less time on clearing up than on the serious business of playing or cooking with the children.

In return I've been given golden moments. My daughter Ann took to ballet dancing like a swan to the lake. The beauty of this 'frilly' world surprised me. And at her first public dance in a church hall, with my bottom aching from the small wooden seat and nostrils twitching from the dust heavy in the air, when she danced and smiled... for me, the moment was magical.

Opting into children is opting into laughter too. It doesn't have to be sophisticated. Twisting garden hoses that unexpectedly drench you, dreadfully silly jokes ('When you're driving, where do you stop for refreshment? At a tea-junction.') are part of the credit side of the ledger to make up for interminably going through the times table or separating bickering siblings for the umpteenth time.

Goodness knows we've struggled to provide a range of non-sexist options for our children. Santa Claus, for instance, provided teddies and dolls, racing cars and spaceships without any sex discrimination – so Ann and Gabriel simply traded them on Boxing Day. For despite my daughter's able goalkeeping and my son's deft cake-mixing their interests are on the whole pretty conventional.

Disciplining is not easy, particularly where Gabriel is concerned. I probably resort to smacking and frogmarching him to his room more than I should and pay the price of guilt at my own violence. But I love him dearly and thrill to his sliding tackles on the football field. I've also learnt to play the advantage rule at home, to be diplomatically deaf where necessary. And when the bust-ups occur, as they do regularly, we make it up with kisses and sit together reading. It's all over.

Of course I'm far from perfect. When our two were babies I dreaded the treadmill of heavy nappy buckets and continual feeding, all the dirty bottoms and sleepless nights. I helped, but I didn't do my fair share. Now I've grown more and more resolved to spend time with them. Too often I've heard men say: 'They grew up so quickly – I never really got to know them.' Or, from the other side of the generational divide: 'He was always away, always somewhere else. I never really knew my father.' I promise myself it's not going to be like that with our children. Memories of them growing up are not going to be just regrets about lost moments.

With a bit of luck there won't be just memories either, but lasting friendships. Friendships which will be a reason for living in old age, as we defuse the cold war between generations and see the world through fresher, younger eyes. But I am not waiting for future returns on present emotional investment. Fathering has changed me, here and now. I've become a little less sharp, a little less self-centred, a little less goal-orientated, a little less materialistic and hopefully rather more sensitive to the needs and wishes of those about me. I've learnt a lot about patience and, not least, I've had the excuse to be a child again myself.

For my son Gabriel, I hope his father's input will have helped to make him more gentle and loving, able to form lasting relationships and be a good father in his turn. For my daughter Ann, perhaps my contribution to her upbringing will have taught her some irreverence for authority, self-confidence, helped her to fend for herself and feel every bit the equal of the males in her life.

In the meantime: 'Dad – Can I watch *The A Team?*'

Things don't change overnight. ■

Dexter Tiranti was recruited for his marketing skills and was part of the team which launched the New Internationalist *as a national magazine in March 1973 – as well as laying the groundwork for the magazine's launch in Australia and New Zealand in the ensuing years. He worked as a co-editor of the magazine for a decade before concentrating on other products and publications, notably the* One World Calendar *and* One World Almanac.

August 1989

White flowers and a grizzly bear

Living with cancer, by **Dian Marino**.

When I woke up in the recovery room in November 1978 my doctor was waiting to tell me the results of the biopsy. It couldn't happen to me; I was just 37 years old. But it had – I had breast cancer. My feelings ricocheted all over the place. I was afraid, angry, grateful and sad all at the same time. I remember thinking: 'I've been a caring person, how could this happen to me? It's not fair, it's so arbitrary.'

I cried, wailed and curled up into a ball but I also continued to work – it seemed like my sanity depended on returning to 'normal' as quickly as possible. A month of radiation treatments began a long series of checkups, more biopsies and finally surgeries. My last surgery was in 1983 – a lymphectomy; afterwards I was put on a hormone blocker. Last summer, I was nearing the famous 'five year' marker which meant that statistically I had a much better chance of surviving. Then I had a bone scan and they discovered bone cancer in two places. I was put on another hormone blocker and given more radiation. I had the summer to put my life into a new framework: 'The best we can do is slow it down,' they said.

Writing this is difficult. It brings up complex and contradictory memories. But it does add both a clarity and simplicity that wasn't there at the time.

Perhaps this article should be written by my husband and daughters who know what happens when someone you love gets cancer. Or by my friends who've shared my fears, anger, frustration and even the small moments of beauty that have come from trying to make sense of cancer.

I have resisted putting words on paper for fear of getting back on an emotional rollercoaster. Also because what has helped me to understand and live more calmly with cancer may not work as a 'prescription' for others. The sense of loss of control is so great with this illness, that it is a time to be very careful about issues of power and control. While waiting in clinics and hospital corridors I have found that many people are not as enthusiastic as me for knowledge about their illness and for playing an active role in their healthcare. Death is such a responsibility that I hesitate to project my keenness to be clearer, to understand better, onto others who share my illness. I write not to prescribe but to describe and wonder aloud about some difficult times.

For me there is irony in the act of reflecting on cancer since I'm the kind of person who might easily have left these thoughts until five minutes before death. I too frequently gallop into new projects without sufficient time for contemplation. But in trying to make sense of cancer I think it is important to speak out in a straightforward manner. The knowledge gained from coming to terms with this disease too easily remains in the hands of medical professionals. So I stumble for words to speak of problems, responses, speculation, small rearrangements.

As a visual artist and teacher I use many kinds of language. For me the meaning of words changes with time and place. How we use words indicates our values and priorities. I have found most writing about cancer disempowers those of us who have the disease. One example is the use of militaristic or war-like metaphors. Phrases like 'fight', 'beat' and 'win the war' are commonplace. But if I get into a 'war' with my cancer, I can only interpret myself winning if my cancer 'loses' or is 'defeated'. This kind of either/or thinking reduces all experience to win or lose. A person like myself with a 'terminal' cancer has automatically lost.

We do need a language of resistance in our struggles with chronic illness, but it needs to be a language free of militarism. I found it wonderfully healing to spend quiet time in nature – a form of resistance perhaps but hardly a battle. Even supposedly alternative language can be infuriating. The 'new age' philosophy of illness is a good example. At first, I would go out and buy these latest self-help books only to find the basic message was: 'You made yourself sick so you can heal yourself.' So simple but so damaging. It fits all too well with mass-media messages that bombard us daily: problems are individual, not social. We're kept disorganized with a simplistic presentation of blame and responsibility.

I began to think about how I got cancer. I read and asked around. There were many possible explanations – heredity (my grandmother died very young from breast cancer), occupational hazards (for the previous 20 years I had made silkscreen prints using highly toxic paints and clean-up solutions), poor diet, lack of exercise, too much stress, birth-control pills and many more. Often I read that one or another of these factors was the primary cause. I found this completely immobilizing so gradually I developed a map, a kind of ecology of possible causes. This allowed me to deal with those dimensions that I had some control over. I didn't feel like I needed to have a 'scientific map' but could elaborate my own open map so that as my experience grew I could alter it.

By the time cancer was diagnosed I had an excellent relationship with my doctor. He trusted me as an expert on my aches, pains and feelings; I trusted him because he was able to tell me what he didn't know as well as what he did. He also knew how to cry. Most doctors see surgery as a response to unhealth, he told me. So advice from a surgeon must be seen from this critical vantage-point. He was open to my exploring alternative health support (like massage therapy) and would ask me whether they were having any effect. It was important to me to understand the limits of medical knowledge and to recognize the intuitive as a legitimate part of making decisions.

When I shifted from Princess Margaret Hospital to the Sunnybrook cancer clinic, a doctor introduced herself as the head of my team of seven different specialists. She then gave me a physical exam. The usual response of a new doctor was to admire my many incisions and scars and ask which surgical artist had given me this or that wonderful piece of handiwork. She said simply: 'I can see that you have been through a lot.' In a simple sentence she affirmed that I had a history and was not merely an example of her peers' technical skills. I told her that she had a lot to teach her colleagues.

Last summer I wanted my bone-scan results quickly because I needed to spend time with my oldest child who was going off to university. Most doctors wouldn't have bothered trying to speed up the bureaucracy. Fewer still would trust that I was the best judge of when I needed to know something. She told me over the telephone which wasn't easy for either of us. It gave me an extra week to let my daughter know how serious it was this time.

In the first five years, I had four surgeries. Whenever I asked the experts what the odds of survival were for different cancers, they would at first answer ambiguously. As I insisted they would get more precise. Later I learned this was called 'staging', a way of finding out what patients really wanted to know. Some doctors withhold information based on whether or not they think you can handle it. I would say you should lose those characters fast. If they can't trust you, how can you ever trust them?

I needed to know as much as possible so I could get the most out of the time I have left. It doesn't mean that I wasn't overwhelmed and anguished when I heard cancer had returned. But knowledge and understanding helped liberate me from self-destructive fear, anger and sadness. These feelings are always close by. But now I have learned to treat them as reminders of my current agenda – to figure my way as creatively and peacefully as possible through the last part of my life.

You can read my face like a book. If I am happy, worried or frightened you know immediately. We told the children in as calm a way as possible and tried to keep open the lines of communication on the subject. I would get extremely tense and agitated before routine check-ups. I learned to tell the children the reason for my short temper. It was important that they 'felt in the know' as much as any of us. My daughters (now 21 and 18) both realize the transition from a parent-child relationship to more of an adult friendship has happened earlier with us than with most families. They feel good about giving support. Instead of feeling powerless in all this my daughters feel they have some control over events.

Family and friends make all the difference. I was surprised, delighted, shocked and often healed by how they reacted. My husband ditched his jeans and dressed in a three-piece suit to look like a doctor so he could sneak into the hospital at 7.00am to bring me capuccino and the newspaper. Another friend called me at home and asked: 'How are you feeling?' 'Terrible,' I replied, 'I'm depressed.' 'Good,' she said, 'I thought you were going to avoid this part.' I burst out laughing.

For me, irreverent stories and fumbling attempts to connect were far better than never responding for fear of doing 'the wrong thing'. A few people told me about their friends' ills (back pains for example) as a way of connecting. As much as I appreciated their concern I always wanted to say: 'Hey, wait a minute, this disease is life-threatening. I'm afraid I'm going to die too soon.' Even now friends I only see every few years will call to say hello and find out the latest news. In moments of crisis I find it healing to know my friends are not denying my most recent diagnosis of cancer.

I'm afraid. I fear my cancer will isolate me socially. People with the best intentions will treat me as incompetent and exclude me. I fear people will feel sorry for me and patronize me – denying the energy and intelligence I bring to this current phase of my life. Recently a person I considered a close friend did just that. He told me he was close to me because he felt sorry for me and that I was naïve to think otherwise. I felt betrayed and angry to be treated in such a cold and clinical fashion. It is one thing to feel sad. But if you feel sorry for me you distance yourself from my pain in a way that denies my status as an actor in my own life. Friends like this are toxic and I will resist being any one's social-work project or charity case.

Last summer, during my bone scan I could tell by the way the technician responded that something had shown up. He went out of the room and when he reappeared he said: 'You look a lot younger than you are. Do you have any children?' I said: 'You checked my file.' To which he replied: 'Yes.' I was pretty sure that they had indeed identified some cancer.

That same day I went to my massage therapist. I decided this was a unique moment in my life when I could look into my psyche. When I am very frightened I sometimes have the courage to face or to see the unseeable. So as my friend did his work I decided to let go and see what images would surface. The first image was very surprising to me. There was a field of wild carrot (white flowers composed of many smaller white flowers) surrounded by pine trees. Strolling through the field was a huge grizzly bear. He looked strong, confident and curious as he moved through the field of flowers. At one point he stopped and picked a handful of flowers which I knew symbolized my essence, even as the whole field was me too. Then, in my flower form I made him sneeze and laugh and I flew back into the ground except for one small white flower which landed on his shoulder. Together we strolled away.

The next day bone cancer was confirmed. Almost immediately my husband and I (we have been separated for four years but are still fine friends) began to look for a cottage or a place for me to be still. I sometimes feel my cells vibrating from too much work or not enough sleep and I imagine that I can see them all jangled and in motion. I told Chuck that I had a recurring dream that I needed to spend the last part of my life on a lake surrounded by trees with a beach. This became a guide for us. We found an island we liked called Cranberry Island and Chuck had a cottage built. The day after we bought the property we went to look at it again and much to my delight in the middle of the cranberry bog was a large patch of white flowers. The lake is called Kahshe, which I later found out means 'healing waters'. I am keeping my eye out for the grizzly. ■

Dian Marino was teaching in the Faculty of Environmental Studies at York University, Toronto, when she wrote this. She died in 1993.

November 1989

On the terrace

Bombay's flamboyant gays find elaborate ways of surviving a hostile world. But what goes on inside their hearts and minds? And what hope is there of liberation? **Dinyar Godrej** *recalls his first gay party.*

Ramesh's building towered over all others in that area. His family had access to the terrace and that is where Jamshed had his birthday party. It was an area of such nondescript middle-class high-rise housing that it dispelled every one of the several fantastic notions I had crafted in anticipation.

This was to be my first gay party. As Jamshed and I climbed the tortuous staircase up to the terrace, carrying food we'd brought in a cab, we met Ramesh's mother. Severe in her starched white sari, she stood at the entrance of their flat, surveying all arrivals. She did not approve, but would not state her disapproval. Her presence was confirmation that there was no secret, magic realm awaiting me on the terrace. That enjoyment would have to be wrung out of fantasy. On the terrace it seemed that even night had been pulled down tight over us.

We tried desperately to transform the space into what it was not. A gay world had to be created and it had to be an area not of discourse – time was too short for that and the situation, perhaps, too difficult – but of a curiously predictable kind of freedom, the freedom of imitation and travesty, a freedom familiar to all who have no personal leeway within the stifling social systems. In the next few hours almost every aspect of heterosexual social intercourse was enacted either with sincerity or mockery.

Here I met Rohinton and later that night we went to his flat. He was a sturdy, hirsute man with a bewitching cleft in his chin. Although I found him physically attractive, he exuded something worse than body odour – machismo. However, as he danced he wiggled his hips in the screen-siren fashion you see in Hindi films and moved his hands like aquarium fish. This, he told me, was to express 'the feminine side of my personality, which is usually suppressed'. Such exaggerated 'femininity' could only, I felt, have been conceived by a Male Chauvinist Pig. This Rohinton was. On his dressing-table, stuck to the right side of the triple mirror, was a picture of his girlfriend. It kept his mum from asking questions and represented the all-too-familiar dream – wife, two kids, apartment, car. He brushed aside my queries about fairness to the woman with 'she will have to accept my other side'. We shared some sincere lust and his parting words were 'keep in touch'.

A few months later he was married and when I ran into him and his wife one evening at the theatre she had already acquired the ability to recognize a gay man and to react with disgust.

The next time I saw the couple she was very obviously pregnant. Rohinton looked fulfilled, she tired. To me he had not married the woman but a concept of morality.

As it was his party, Jamshed skipped from guest to guest with ballerina steps. His large frame was swathed in a long garment of shimmering brown stuff. It was a *pathan* suit, the dress of the ruggedly handsome men of the north-west frontier. The Bombay queens loved its voluminous drapes, the way it emphasized every gesture with rustling sounds if one got the material right.

On Jamshed's chest a gold angel glittered – a birthday gift from his sailor lover. It was perhaps an appropriate symbol of the nature of their relationship, for Jamshed was garrulous to the point of boredom about his sex life (mainly exploits of the so-many-men-so-little-time variety) which made one suspect that he had none. He affectionately referred to the other queens as 'eunuchs' *(bijdas)* and himself as 'the eunuchs' mother'.

This terminology derived not from an intuitive sympathy with Ms Greer's conceptualization of swaddled female sexuality. In India eunuchs are all too visible. They dress in women's clothing and assail passers-by with ribald remarks. They beg in groups, threatening to expose their mutilated genitals should someone be recalcitrant about parting with small change. Despised by most, they are also feared.

Such a position of strength gay men do not have. Their 'defences' against social hostility are either camp ebullience or self-negating invisibility. Jamshed and the 'girls' excelled in the former. Never shopping without the benefit of an audience, Jamshed cast himself in the role of The Irresistable Tease and addressed salesmen with an air of haughtiness and sexual invitation. As they could not dismiss a potential customer, they either humoured him or teased back. But being unable to match his acid-and-steel verbal style, they slapped him and pinched him.

On the terrace among his friends he was Mother Hen, provider of courage and food. He leaned out over a parapet and called to a domestic washing up in a kitchen of the next building to come up and join the fun. Behind such boldness lay the traditional assumption of a master-servant relationship, an imbalance of power which is sometimes sexually exploited. Poor gay men often extend services beyond the call of duty to their employers. It is a complex relationship. On one side there is the fact of having sex with a person who has a social and economic advantage but who will not share its benefits. On the other there is the advantage of being in the employ of someone who understands the pressures of being gay and who may thus be more sympathetic than others.

Friendship, however, lies among social equals. In Bombay a gay domestic would in all probability know every other gay domestic on the block. Knowledge of a shared sexuality brings togetherness and working-class gay men often move in groups. Sex is, at the best of times, difficult. Parks (few and far between), public toilets (usually brightly lit and filthy) and alleyways are the usual settings. Police harassment is not unusual. Few arrests are made – however, money or sexual favours or sometimes both may be extorted. Physical assault by gangs of gay-bashers is another hazard.

Togetherness means an increased degree of protection – not only does news travel swiftly down the gay grapevine but it also means that in a situation of conflict it does not have to be every man for himself. Supported by such a network 'cruising' becomes more blatant. At night groups of gay men travel up and down on the suburban trains camping it up, alighting from carriages to be greeted by friends hanging out at the station. Their banter is often a modified version of the dialogue from the commercial Hindi or Marathi cinema – witty, self-conscious and not a little grandiose. Their flamboyance and self-dramatization come easily after a day's work is done and the demands of a largely heterosexual environment are at some distance. It is positive and shot through with comic asides. It also helps emotional recovery in stressful situations.

Feroze, however, had been injured too much. 'Discovered' at 14, his parents had marched him to a psychiatrist who electrified his brain. The 'treatment' continued until he was 18, by which time he had been rendered an obsessive fantasist. His parents suffered him, his brother hated him. I taught him at college. In an exam his composition piece read like a Mills and Boon romance, a dream of bliss and security in the arms of a blond man with blue eyes. Feroze, like many others, idealized the West. For him the possibility of his love's survival was 'out there'; he could only be rescued by a White God.

A few other men I knew had a similar admiration for white men, mostly a mixture of curiosity and mild xenophobia. Everyone knew gay tourists would be travelling light and that love if it happened would be a hopeless mess – immigration laws do not recognize gay relationships. But then even within our own people we were convinced that love could not withstand demands from the family, from the social environment which expected coyness and discretion even from the heterosexual relationships it sanctioned. As long as we did not love each other and we married women in the end, we could mate like rabbits. When, despite the odds, gay people set up house together they quickly became media fodder.

Activism was almost non-existent. Instead we partied, lived for the moment and trapped ourselves in the stereotypes straight society had created for us. Gay friends in journalistic circles advised me not to put my neck on the chopping block by writing about ourselves, and martyrdom had no place in my plans for the future.

Ramesh, however, had written and survived. I sought him out in order to discuss the possible ways in which gay people could press for rights. Whereas men were getting it on in the parks, toilets, crowded suburban trains, they were achieving little. The majority took it as a given that it was too troublesome to attempt to change social restrictions.

Ramesh advocated separatism – gay people should interact economically only with other gay people. But apart from being impractical this would do little to alter traditional male notions of the female which both gay and straight men share. Nor would it help us to escape the heterosexual stereotypes that we both imitate and revile. And it would mean acknowledging that we belonged to a ghetto.

Ultimately if there is a movement for the decriminalization and social acceptance of homosexuality in India, it will have to uphold the flexibility with which gay men have been interacting, despite belonging to mutually exclusive communities. This the traditionally minded will view as betrayal. There will also have to be the recognition that the man one has sex with is one's social equal despite his economic status. This the middle class will resent. In a land of a myriad of orthodox cultures, a movement would split up before it even began.

Perhaps knowing this, the Bombay gays partied all the time. This capacity for enjoyment and comic deflation of very real problems was about all the self-determination we felt we could achieve. So what if things hardly changed on the outside – there was camaraderie and lust. At Jamshed's party, my first, I wanted almost everything to be different. That was five years ago. It's still the same. ■

At the time he wrote this **Dinyar Godrej** *was studying in Britain and writing poetry. Later he became an* **NI** *co-editor and currently works for the magazine from a base in Rotterdam, the Netherlands.*

October 1995
How shall we live?
Amanda Hazelton describes her search for healing beyond 'slash-and-burn' medicine and makes a connection between cancer and clowning.

I knew something was wrong when my blood-test result came back indecently fast and my GP asked me to 'pop along after surgery'. It was 'terrible news', she said: I had leukemia. It felt like being struck by lightning. It was 1985 and I was nearly 28. Oddly enough I spent much of the consultation mopping the doctor up. Contrary to popular imagination GPs rarely have to tell young patients that they have potentially fatal diseases. It was her 'first time', and I remember thanking her profusely for being so brave.

'It means a lot of hospital for a long time,' she said, and sure enough I spent the next morning in haematology outpatients being prodded and pushed and having unspeakably horrible things done to get a bone-marrow sample. They were very nice at the hospital and took the trouble to explain. Leukemia is a form of cancer. No-one knew exactly why, but the cells in my bone-marrow had mutated and started over-producing blood. My white blood count was over 300 when it should have been below 10, and I had hundreds too many platelets, which was why I kept getting bruises. There are many types of leukemia, some acute and some (like mine) chronic. With drug treatment it could be controlled and life would feel normal, but nobody knew for how long. If the disease became malignant – as one day it undoubtedly would – there was not a lot that medicine could do to prevent a speedy demise.

Life was never going to feel normal again – at least not the kind of normal I knew then. I began to live with an extraordinary conundrum: I had a life-threatening illness, but I was not exactly ill. The world calls these conditions 'terminal', yet they are no more terminal than life itself. Nevertheless there is always an awareness that terminal illness could be just around the corner; it focuses the mind wonderfully.

In the aftershock my preoccupation with life (how long?) and death (when and how?) begged the real question, which is *how shall I live?* I kept my sense of humour but part of me was screaming. How could I not have 'noticed' that my spleen had swollen down to my navel, and that I was very, very tired? I just hadn't allowed myself to notice. Like so many of us I was not educated in the art of well-being, only in the appearance of compulsory OK-ness. At the hospital there was no information about where to seek help with these existential questions. My terribly nice (and good-looking) registrar went red when I asked about counselling: 'Only when you're terminally ill... near the end,' he murmured. This is not true of every hospital department of course, but I reckon my experience is quite usual and support is random.

In a hospital setting even the strongest of us is liable to surrender our autonomy to the magic white coat. I admired what they knew about my chromosomes and to some extent I was relieved to be swept into this benevolent patriarchy. The system expected and offered nothing more than for me to turn up for blood tests, take the medicine and live as 'normally' as possible, which indeed is all that many patients wish to do.

But another way opened up for me. My librarian housemate rushed home with a pile of useful books. Among the devastating 'factual' tomes which charted the course of a hundred different cancers was a personal account of the Bristol Cancer Help Centre where it is acknowledged that cancer affects everything about us, not just bits of our bodies. We can be disempowered and bewildered as patients, but the book argued that if we took charge of our lives illness could even be an enriching experience. I booked a day at the Bristol Centre, and my eyes were opened to all sorts of things – to dietary therapy, relaxation and meditation, spiritual healing, and to the fact that I was allowed to make choices, to behave as if I mattered.

Emerging from this reorientation I proclaimed the virtues of what I had until then called self-indulgence. It was OK to relax, really stop, not just watch TV; OK to go for what felt right, even if others thought it bizarre; to spend time discovering who I really was deep inside, and where I wanted to go. Wow! Everyone should do this. Oh no, said a lot of my friends and colleagues. It's all right for you to do that because you're ill. You've got far harder things to deal with. It would just be selfish for us. How deeply ingrained this kind of self-denial seemed to be! It was OK to give, but not to yourself. From my new perspective this seemed potentially dangerous.

Nonetheless friendships grew deeper and more vital. I was lucky: nobody dropped me; nobody looked the other way as so often happens when a serious illness is diagnosed. But beyond my close circle I met the 'poor you' syndrome ('Poor you, but you *look* all right'; 'Oh, you *must* be feeling awful'). Mostly genuine concern, but underneath is all that horror about illness and death for which we have no honest language. As soon as you are life-threateningly ill you become a repository for others' death fears: as good as dead, except, of course, that you *must not die* because death is a sign of weakness, a failure for the medical science in which we place our faith, and a reminder that it's going to happen to all of us and we are in no way prepared. I still don't know how to respond to unsolicited sympathy.

Life began to feel like a quest. I negotiated the hospital world which was often kind, wise and humorous and occasionally patronizing and infuriatingly arrogant. I took drugs by mouth, and injected myself with Interferon which made me feel as if I had 'flu all the time. I even spent nine weeks in isolation having all my bone marrow (and most of the rest of me) temporarily wiped out in the name of 'slowing down the disease process'.

The hospital world is limited by the assumption that you will go through medical hell ('slash-and-burn medicine' as it was once described to me) just to survive, and that nothing else really counts. But this ignores what I see as the nature of healing. I was grateful for medicine, but I needed more. I needed to find meaning and adventure, to plumb the mysteries of life, to fill some of the gaping holes that hospitals do not even pretend to patch up. I would have loved to have had a massage while languishing in hospital, and couldn't the gentler natural therapies have helped? And yes, I have met doctors who are open to all this, and who have looked me in the eye and said: healing is a mystery, we know nothing and nobody can say with certainty how a person's life, or their illness, will progress.

My thirst for discovery took me into the 'mind-body-spirit' world. This can seem a confusing, new-age marketplace offering every kind of salve and inner journey if you can find your way through the over-bright smiles, bogus claims and rainbow colours – and if you have the cash. However, there is gold to be found if you are selective. Swollen like a balloon with excess fluid from drug side-effects which the hospital could do nothing about, I tried acupuncture and dietary therapy, which both helped. And now that I see a homeopath I feel better than I have for years.

I did relaxation and visualization exercises to try and reach a wisdom beyond my over-educated intellect. I joined support groups. My relationship life went crazy. I read books which identified a link between serious illness, spiritual malaise and neglect of our creativity and deeper needs. This took me into therapy – to find where I had lost that part of myself, and when I was ready I explored all sorts of creative avenues until I realized that I wanted to play and sing and be a clown. This has blossomed into a strange kind of vocation. Religious education had taught me little about spirituality, but healers and other inspiring teachers have helped me to reach a strong sense that there is a great deal beyond the world I know. I still have the illness and I still take the drugs, but in many ways I feel healed.

There are still huge challenges to negotiate. How, for instance, do you tell a new partner that you have a life-threatening illness? And a potential employer? Unexpectedly out of work, I've been poring over job descriptions, alarmed at the challenge of selling myself and offering guarantees about what I can achieve and when. Chronic leukemia rarely causes trouble in itself, except that years of drug treatment and stress do take their toll. Applying for a job confronts me again with the question; am I a 'normal', 'useful', 'paying-my-way' member of society, or a non-person, a patient forced into passivity, who cannot expect to contribute and who must wait for what is dished out financially, medically, socially?

And what if the truth lies somewhere in between? People like me, who can hack it most – but not enough – of the time tend to fall through cracks; not disabled or incapable, yet having to swim twice as hard to stay afloat, which doesn't make sense when we need to take care of ourselves more than most. That's why being a clown, a vulnerable clown with an open heart, is part of survival for me. Life is unpredictable and gives you knocks, but the clown's way is to transform that into treasure, be it glorious and funny or sad and painful, and to live as fully and richly as possible with all the cracks and contradictions. ■

Amanda Hazelton worked for a development agency for 14 years before becoming a free-lance writer, cook and clown. She died in 1997.

July 1996
Traitor!
Who would have thought what the consequences of uttering the word 'ambiance' might be? **Alan Hughes** *describes the anguish that comes with the class system in Britain.*

'The charm of Britain has always been the ease with which one can move into the middle class.' Margaret Thatcher.

'Come on you lot, I wanna gettoff 'ome tonight.'

My Uncle Ken, his sons Stephen and Andy and myself were lingering in the huge upper tier of the Holte End at Aston Villa Football Club, Birmingham. I'd travelled up that day from Oxford for the last home game of the season. It was strange going back to my working-class roots, to the world where I once worked in a Dudley factory as a sheetmetal worker.

In Oxford, where I've lived and worked for the past 11 years, things are very different. There I'm a graphic designer and purportedly middle class. Still, sitting here with my relatives in the warm late-May sunshine felt good. Like going home.

We were reluctant to leave the ground, choosing instead to soak up the end-of-season atmosphere. In mock despair a steward was imploring us to vacate the now almost-empty stadium, which only moments before had been awash in a sea of claret and blue, the club colours.

'It's okay,' I replied to the impatient, grey-haired man dressed in a violently luminous orange waistcoat, 'we're just taking in the *ambiance.*'

I couldn't believe it. I just said it. The word came out of my mouth, italicized for emphasis, as though I had no control over it. I groaned inwardly. He looked at me as if I was from another planet.

'Am you takin' the piss, mate?' he queried, now more menacingly.

'No, honest, I...' my voice trailed off as I looked round to see my relatives staring at me in disbelief.

'Listen to 'im, 'e talks posh, don't 'e?' Stephen said in his broad Black Country accent. Ken and Andy nodded in agreement, with expressions on their faces that suggested they'd lost me to some strange religious sect.

We left the stadium in a shroud of awkward silence that was only broken when news came through that one of Villa's rivals had lost. The mood lightened but the damage had been done. Somehow that single word had condemned me as a class traitor. But what did that mean? Who, or what, was I betraying?

We joined a jubilant throng of Villa supporters in a pub close to the ground.

The talk was of football. Shouting above the din I changed the subject.

'So you think I'm posh, do you Ste'?' I asked, apprehensively.

As I spoke I noticed his huge hands were splattered with dried paint of differing hues. Ken had been a painter and decorator all his working life and his sons had joined him when they left school.

'Well, you've lost your accent for a start, ain't yer?' returned Stephen.

We managed to grab an empty table while Ken and Andy headed for the bar and were soon swallowed up by the raucous crowd. I wondered if I'd ever see them again.

'Yes, I suppose I have,' I answered defensively, 'but I live in a different world now.'

'Ya mean, with the middle class.'

'Yes, and I have to be able to communicate with them. Having an almost unintelligible accent would make that impossible.'

'So they wouldn't understand me?'

'Well...'

'I'm as good as them.'

'I know, I'm just saying...'

Somebody, clutching a pint glass of amber-coloured beer, bumped into us and a portion of his drink ended up on my trouser leg. By now the pub resembled the inside of a claret-and-blue sardine can. The walls vibrated as a hundred voices smote the air with repeated choruses of inane chanting. I began again.

'I suppose, what I'm saying is, well, the two worlds are very different.'

'Per'aps they am, but they think they'm betta than us, don't they?'

'I suppose some of them do, yes.'

'An' what about you, what do you think?'

'I'm in the middle...'

'Ya mean, middle class?'

'No, er, yes. I mean, it's complicated. Oh, God knows.'

Ken and Andy returned from their expedition to the bar. Beer spilled everywhere as they plonked down a quartet of pints and several packets of crisps. I rubbed at the wet patch on my trouser leg. It felt uncomfortable.

'What yer talkin' about?' asked Ken as he sat down.

'Fuckin' clever types who think they'm betta than us,' answered Stephen as he picked up his pint. Leaning forward he took several huge gulps, emptying almost half the glass in an instant. I opened a packet of crisps, grabbed a handful and handed the packet round.

'They're not all like that...'

'Am you like them?'

'*They* say I am. I mean, I have a degree. I work in a profession. I go to dinner parties and drink Beaujolais. And I talk "posh". I suppose that makes me like them.'

'An' what am *we* like, then?'

'Well, you're supposed to be thick, inarticulate and pig out on a diet of junk food and tabloid TV.'

'Ya see, they think they'm superior to us.'

'Of course they're not, but they do have advantages.'

'Like what?'

'Education for a start. They'll go to any lengths to make sure their kids get a good one. And most of them are left money or property by parents or relatives so they're always one step ahead of the rest. To be honest, I reckon whatever happens to them, they always come up smelling of roses.'

'So what happens to us. Do we always get the worst of it?'

'Well, who's going to leave you, or me for that matter, pots of money? And besides, the education system is geared to cream off the smartest. There's never any time to let the others catch up and develop their talents. When I left school in 1963, at 15, most of us were herded into factories, diploma-less and almost fucking brainless.'

'It's like that today, ain't it?'

'Yes, except nowadays working-class kids queue up on the dole or end up in mind-numbing jobs you wouldn't give to a monkey. So nothing has really changed. The status quo remains intact.'

'That's a pop group,' observed Andy with a mischievous glint in his eye.

'Very funny.'

'But *you* managed to move out, eh?' continued Stephen, ignoring his brother's attempt at humour. 'You left the factory and left us behind.'

'I was lucky, I suppose. But does that make me a class traitor?'

'What do you think?'

'I don't know. That's the honest answer. I feel I'm stuck somewhere between the two classes and in some ways I hate it, you know, not feeling I belong anywhere. But it's what I wanted. And I wanted it so badly I burned bridges. In my rush to get away I wanted to deny my past, even the way I spoke. I still feel bad about that. Guilty, I suppose. And yet...'

Just then a muscular, lanky youth, sporting a haircut from a Nuremberg rally and a cavernous mouth that lacked several front teeth, slapped Stephen on his back with such force that my cousin and his chair were projected several centimetres forward. A bout of male banter ensued. I leaned back, supped at my beer and contemplated our conversation.

Those words kept coming back to me. Traitor. Betrayal. Guilt.

What did it all mean? What was so bad about my previous life? Why did I want my new one so badly?

Well, I wanted something else. Something better. Something worthwhile. Something that *meant* something. Back then, as a sheetmetal worker, I had no plan. No strategy. Only a burning desire to *get out*. To get out of the relentless grind and crushing tedium of the factory. The factory I languished in for nigh on 14 years, like a prison sentence – where the only thing that mattered was time. Where the huge clock on the wall was both your enemy and your friend. At eight o'clock it scowled, at five o'clock its face smiled and shone as though sunrise had appeared at the end of the day.

And what of my fellow workers? The comrades I shared this hell with?

I was certainly contemptuous of many of the people I worked with. I was appalled by their apathy and willingness to settle for the cheap dreams offered by consumerism. I hated the way anything regarded as intellectual was derided. And the renowned philistinism prevalent amongst the uglier sections of the working class is still being proclaimed a virtue. It isn't clever to boast about not being clever.

I wanted, and still want, them to see that knowledge is power. That failure does not have to be their fate, and waiting to win the lottery will never get them, or the rest of us, anywhere. As John Lennon said, they are living someone else's dream, it's not even their own.

Well, I certainly had no allegiance to all that. So when I say I'm proud to be working class, what am I proud of?

I'm proud to be descended from the millions of women, men and children who sweated blood in the world's factories, shipyards and mines, and from the workers who fought and died in the eternal struggle for a better world. I'm proud of the old working-class sense of community and decency that seems to have long since vanished.

But whatever the reason, I wanted out. I craved the world of the intellectual and the progressive. I read books, got myself politicized and eventually, through the auspices of what was left of the welfare state, went to college. I gained a degree and eventually moved to the city of dreaming spires. But when I got there I didn't fit in. There were new rules to learn, new games to play.

The midday meal changed from working-class dinner to middle-class lunch. Fishfingers metamorphosed into smoked salmon and people threw snippets of French into their conversation. *Dis donc!*

'Well, I'll tell yer...' said Stephen, his friend now creating havoc at the next table. Stephen motioned Andy for another pint. It was Andy's round. He gathered the now-empty glasses, turned, took a deep breath then headed in the general direction of the bar and vanished once more into the noisy mass of bodies. '...all I know is that we are still here and still being shat on from a great height. But no fuckin' smart arse is gonna tell me what to do.' He banged the table with his fist.

I looked at Ken. He winked. He adored his sons. They adored him.

Perhaps that's it. Perhaps I'm riddled with guilt at creating a sort of success and leaving behind family and friends to sink or swim in the free-market nightmare of Nineties Britain. And, for all my confusion, do I feel guilty because I actually *enjoy* quite a lot of my new life?

'Jesus, I've got middle-class angst!'

'What?' said Stephen looking surprised at my outburst.

'Oh, nothing. Just thinking out loud.'

Suddenly the conversation dried up. I chomped on a handful of crisps and listened to the communal singing that had continued unabated. I surveyed the scene. It was depressingly male-dominated; all tattooed arms, farting, belching and gross, lager-bloated stomachs. Somebody close to our table was re-acquainting himself with his breakfast. This didn't feel like home. I wasn't proud of this. But did Oxford really feel any better?

My position in the scheme of things – in the middle, as it were – might cause me some unease but it does allow me to straddle the two worlds, taking metaphorical temperature readings. I feel like a kind of cultural anthropologist; observing, taking notes. And as I flit from one to the other what I see is disturbing.

I see the gap widening between each group, both becoming more wary and distrustful of the other. The stereotypes remain stubbornly intact. I see scared people scrambling to compete for a slice of an ever-decreasing economic pie.

I see the working class: low-achieving, lacking confidence, willingly accepting their fate, destructively turning in on themselves; drug abuse, crime and violence. Or turning outwards, looking for scapegoats: black people, women, Jews, lesbians and gay men. Easy targets for the panic-stricken. And then, with money they don't have, embarking on an obscene orgy of spending, being conned into buying anything they see.

I see an increasingly nervous middle class with their traditional values of hard work and thrift under threat. The spectre of unemployment and insecurity now hangs over them and they are more than willing to pull up the ladder on the masses below. Still insisting there's no such thing as class, their acclaimed bonhomie has become an intolerant scowl.

As for me? I continue to live in my cultural limbo land – feeling guilt at betraying what remains of the struggle for working-class emancipation, then thanking God I'm not there any more; still reacting to middle-class cerebral intimidation and thanking God I'm here, reading my books, visiting the opera and drinking good wine.

'Perhaps you're *truly* classless?' said Stephen, as though he'd been reading my thoughts.

'My God, perhaps I am...'

He then winked at his dad, looked back at me and smiled warmly.

'But don't worry Al, whatever you are, we still love ya.' ■

Alan Hughes joined the New Internationalist *as a graphic designer in 1985. Since he wrote this piece he has added weekly therapy and writing a novel to his multiplying list of middle-class attributes – and a much-loved daughter, Esme, to his family.*

7

Guide to the ruins: whatever happened to 'development'?

FOR most of its life the *New Internationalist* magazine has carried on its front cover the banner line: 'The people, the ideas, the action in the fight for world development.' If you look at a copy now you will find it has changed to 'The people, the ideas, the action in the fight for global justice.' The change may only be two words but it is significant, and took at least a decade's worth of mounting unease to bring about.

At the outset the magazine was proud to nail its colours to the mast of the world-development project. It accepted that development was a broad church and that people on the opposite side of the nave had different priorities from those of the **NI**. But it assumed that the fundamentals – looking first and foremost after people's basic needs for nutrition and healthcare, sanitation and education – were shared.

During the 1980s the strains within the concept of development became ever more marked. This was known as development's 'lost decade' because of the way in which, particularly in Africa, the IMF and World Bank insisted on cuts in health and education that did disproportionate harm to the poorest. But by the 1990s it was becoming clearer that this agenda was actually fundamental to development itself rather than a distraction from it. As the lines of the globalization project became clearer we could no longer gloss over the fact that 'development' was the invention of an American President, based on the idea that poor countries would be helped along the track to the promised land of Western capitalism.

If there was a single turning-point it was the whole issue we dedicated to the ideas of Wolfgang Sachs in 1992. His remarkable opening essay, *Development: a guide to the ruins* is included here. But so too is his piece about the implications of the Gulf War, which he saw as marking the end of Western interest in development and the beginning of the 'security' era. Ten years on 'the war on terror' makes his words look prophetic. ∎

January 1980
The art of development

*The optimism of the early 1970s has given way to widespread gloom about world development as, one after the other, technological breakthroughs which promised to solve the problems of poverty, hunger and ill-health have failed to do so. **Peter Adamson** argues that such failures are the result of fumbling with the wrong key in the development lock.*

The popularity of crossword puzzles has something to do with the problems of world development. A crossword is a paradigm of a certain kind of problem. It can be solved. There is only one solution. And when you have arrived at that solution you know that it is the right one. The individual answers interlock and confirm each other, and the whole adds up to a solution which is self-evidently correct, complete, self-contained, unimpeachable and momentarily triumphant. And there is nowhere else to go.

The problem of how to make a relationship work or how best to bring up your children is a different kind of problem. There is no one answer. There may be many possible and partial solutions from which the best must be chosen. And when you think you have an answer it cannot be easily checked and may change with time and circumstance. Its component parts need not interlock and may even contradict. And the whole adds up to something which is messy, incomplete and elusive.

These two types of problem have been called by different names. But at the risk of inventing more jargon let us call them 'reducible' and 'irreducible'. The 'reducible' problem, the crossword puzzle, can in the end be solved. In theory it can be boiled down to A = B.

No matter how complicated the equation may be in practice, it is ultimately reducible to a formula which can be written down and passed on intact to solve the same problem for somebody else in a different place or time. I can be told that the square on the hypotenuse will equal the sum of the squares on the other two sides and it will work as well for me as for the person who told me. But I cannot be told, in the same way, how to make a relationship work or how to appreciate Michelangelo. The solution to this kind of problem will never be 'reduced' to a formula.

The distinction between these two kinds of problem may go some way towards explaining why there is still a food problem when we have discovered how to grow three or four times as much food from the same acre of land; or why there is still a population problem when we have discovered cheap, safe and effective methods of contraception; or why more than half the world is still suffering from ill-health when almost all of the major diseases have been 'conquered'; or why there is still so much poverty when our capacity for converting our environment into material wealth has never been greater.

Recent advances in human capacity have been confined almost entirely to increasing our capacity to solve 'reducible' problems. By contrast, our capacity to cope with 'irreducible' problems has barely grown and may even have shrunk. Imagine, for example, a Plato or a Buddha transported, without notice, into the 20th century. It is safe to say that they would be lost in a fourth-grade science class let alone a discussion of particle physics. But it is equally safe to say that they would not be out of their depth in a discussion of, say, how to balance personal and social freedoms or what constitutes a just relationship between two people. Or take all the sophisticated computerized world economic models published in recent years by organizations like the Club of Rome. Perhaps their most significant feature is that they feel the need to head each chapter with a quotation from Aristotle or JS Mill or Mahatma Gandhi. It is almost an unconscious confession of the fact that we have grown in knowledge but not in wisdom, that one leg has grown long whilst the other has remained stunted. And the result is a pronounced limp and a more than occasional stumble.

The main lesson of this last decade is that it has shown the limitations of 'reducible' solutions when applied to 'irreducible' problems.

How did it happen, for example, that the new high-yielding 'miracle seeds' which promised 'to banish the age-old spectre of famine from the pages of human history' made so big an impact on yields per acre and so little impact on the incidence and severity of malnutrition?

In practice, an agricultural extension worker brings the good news about the new seeds from the laboratory to the fields. First, he probably makes an appointment with the relatively prosperous farmer, say with 200 acres of land. The farmer is used to dealing with government officials, understands their language, and can read the literature they leave behind. Most important of all, he has 200 acres and can afford to risk 20 of them on the experimental seeds. He can also afford the irrigation, fertilizer and pesticides without which the new varieties are unproductive. The result is a bumper crop – perhaps three times his previous yield. The next year, he puts all 200 acres under the new seeds.

When the agricultural extension worker calls on the small farmer down the road, subsisting on perhaps one acre of land, his reception may be different. Unused to dealing with city officials, unable to read the literature, unable to afford the inputs, the small farmer may well feel that 'this is not for him'. Most important of all, he has only one acre of land and cannot take a risk on the new seeds because if anything goes wrong he and his family will go hungry. He politely listens, accepts the pamphlets, and carries on, with his wife and children, trying to maintain their precarious hold on the basic necessities of life.

Next year, his richer neighbour's higher yields have depressed the market price slightly and so the poor farmer has not earned enough cash from the sale of his small surplus crop to pay for the necessities he must buy. And perhaps he has gone into debt with a local moneylender. Meanwhile, the larger farmer is looking round to invest his new profits in more land and in machinery which more land will justify. He sees his neighbour struggling along in debt on his one acre and makes him an offer for his land, throwing in the chance of seasonal employment. A bargain is struck between unequals. The net result is that the large farmer grows larger and the small farmer joins the ranks of the landless labourers amongst whom poverty and hunger is at its worst. And all this may eventually turn up in regional and national statistics which show increased food production per head and hence 'development'.

This small dramatization, although obviously telescoped, is nonetheless not unrecognizable in countries like Mexico, birthplace of the Green Revolution, where the average farm size has increased from 400 to over 2,000 acres and the proportion of landless labourers has risen from 57 per cent to 75 per cent.

In this case, tackling the 'reducible' problem of increasing crop yields whilst ignoring the 'irreducible' problem of inequalities in landholding actually exacerbated the problem of hunger which it sought to alleviate. Indeed it is almost an unwritten law of the development effort in the 1970s that the injection of technical improvements into unequal situations tends to increase the inequality and so work against the interests of the poorest.

In Africa, where the unequal relationship between men and women is manifested in the far longer hours worked by women, the tractor has been introduced to enable larger acreages to be ploughed in less time. This has further shortened the working day of the men who do the ploughing and lengthened the working hours of the women who do the weeding.

A similar analysis of the inadequacy of 'reducible' solutions when applied to 'irreducible' problems could be made of contraceptive pills and population growth, of medicines and health, and of other development problems which seemed, ten years ago, to be chiefly problems of technique.

What these brief examples argue for is that man cannot live by the reducible alone. It is not that the pill, the miracle seed, and the medical breakthrough are in themselves failures. They are brilliant solutions to the 'reducible' part of the problem. But when treated as solutions to the problem as a whole they are, to borrow an image from Zen, like the sound of one hand clapping.

In each of the major problem areas to which we have failed to find satisfactory answers in the 1970s and which face us still in the 1980s, the 'reducible' approaches are nearing the limits of their potential. To move forward, and to make what has been achieved in the realm of technique more truly useful, we shall have to turn and wrestle again with the 'irreducible' problems which humanity has always had to struggle with.

By definition, there can be no formula for the solution of 'irreducible' problems. They are, in short, the business of living. And if there were an equivalent of $E = Mc^2$ to deal with them life would be as unchallenging as the Garden of Eden.

In this sense, the main lesson of the last decade and main challenge of the next is that development is quintessentially an 'irreducible' problem. Hard as it may be to accept, there is no formula. But it is perhaps possible to go as far as to say that the core of the problem lies not in our capacity to manipulate external circumstances but in our ability to create and be involved in just and sustainable relationship.

If that is indeed where the problem of development lies, then however messy and inconclusive the struggle may be, it at least signposts a new direction.

First of all, it implies that development is essentially a decentralized process. For one of the definitions of the 'irreducible' problem, whether it be making a relationship work or achieving social justice in a community, is that it is not susceptible to the imposition of centralized solutions worked out in one place by a few and applied in all places to the many. Such a technique may work for the application of 'reducible' solutions such as new seeds, but the solution of 'irreducible' problems depends on a diversity of approaches and experiments, on accumulated wisdoms and creative ideas in context.

Second, it implies that just relationships between countries, and between communities and individuals within countries, are the fundamental precondition for development.

In this way also, the 'irreducible' approach demands decentralization and genuine participation. For if the problem of development is ultimately a problem about relationships then it need not be the preserve of experts, the conventionally educated and conventionally intelligent, who are not noticeably better at forming and sustaining just and loving human relationships than are the poor and the illiterate. In the area of human relationships, in the heart of the matter, there are no experts to alienate.

For all these reasons, no amount of 'technological fix' can resolve the problems of poverty and development. And progress in the 1980s will depend not on 'more of the same', on the continued throwing of 'reducible' solutions at 'irreducible' problems, but on changes in the economic, social and political relationships which are and will remain the rockbed of the development problem.

There are some signs in both industrialized and developing countries that the honeymoon with technology is over and that fundamental questions will resume their pre-eminent place. There are also signposts in the opposite direction. One concerned and committed movement in the United States is now campaigning around the idea that 'we decided to put a man on the moon and we did it; now let's decide to get rid of malnutrition on the earth and we'll do that too'.

However well-meaning such a sentiment may be, it is dangerous. Ending hunger and putting a man on the moon are extreme examples of 'irreducible' and 'reducible' problems and as such require fundamentally different approaches.

The one demands an attitude of aggression and arrogance, the will to compete and dominate, and depends upon the centralization of effort and the input of more money, more scientists, and more technology. The other demands an approach of humility and respect, of co-operation and the sacrifice of cherished vested interests, and it depends upon participation and wisdom. Development, in short, is an art as well as a science. That is its real challenge. And from that perspective the walk on the moon was a very big step for a man but a very small step for mankind. ■

October 1989
Where has all the conscience gone?

India's young idealists of the early 1970s gave up bright futures to work with the poorest. **Mari Marcel Thekaekara** *was one of them – and she finds today's 'development professionals' with their five-star expense accounts decidedly difficult to take.*

I came of age in the early Seventies. A Calcuttan. Schoolgirl dreams evaporated as we witnessed the Bangladesh war. Genocide. Then millions of refugees flooding the city. Final examinations bombed by a Naxalite[1] raid. Gurudev and Gandhiji on the floor in smithereens.[2] Kennedy too. I was horrified at 15.

University was a diet of John Donne, Beowulf, Chaucer, cultural festivals, *Rabindra Sangeet,*[3] Ravi Shankar, Indian classical dance, ballet, Carole King,

Joan Baez, Pink Floyd, the Stones. Scripture – all of it, the Bible, Qu'ran and Gita.[4] Conversations screamed around cricket and politics. The Marxists had won. Student power, Tariq Ali, debates on the irrelevance of the education system.

Then Catholic Action geared its guns. Ask not what your country can do for you. Contemporary Christmas – Christ born in a five-foot diameter sewage pipe, birthplace of countless Calcutta babies. 'Know India' project at 18. New statistics hurled at us: 70 per cent of our fellow citizens live below the poverty line. Translated this means homelessness and hunger, deprivation and death. God didn't will this. Men did. Landlords and multinationals.

Christ, why ME, Father Beckers?! Study groups and analysis. Group dynamics and leadership training. Capitalism and colonialism and neo-colonialism. Camus and Kafka. *Jonathan Livingston Seagull, The Little Prince, Hope for the Flowers.*[5] If you don't devour all of them, you're illiterate. The Russian model, the Chinese Revolution, Paulo Freire[6] – none of them will do. Evolve the Indian alternative.

We were the Seventies people. And the network spread. All over the country there were activists, community organizers, doctors, health workers, journalists, lawyers. People in villages. People in the mines. People in trade unions. People who were infused with a fervour which drove them on. They were determined to change the world. And, unbelievably, they were convinced they could do it. Many were from middle-class city backgrounds. Scorning the establishment, they left homes and heartbroken parents. They shed jeans and cut hair to become part of the proletariat. They changed names and language to identify with the people. They lived in mud houses without electricity or water, revelling in the glory of the mission. Nothing was too difficult, no sacrifice too great. The cause was everything. They marched on, goaded by a fanaticism which made everything possible, a manic gleam in the eye.

They fought for land rights and minimum wages. They held legal-aid classes and conducted adult-education schools. They led processions and demonstrations, delivered babies, saved lives. Many died triumphantly. In jails, at the hands of landlords, vested interests, police, during the Emergency. They sang 'We Shall Overcome' with faith in the words, convinced that the kingdom was at hand.

Many of them got burnt out. The loneliness, the below-the-poverty-line lifestyles. Identification with the masses brought them the people's problems – tuberculosis, malnutrition, diarrhoea and dehydration. Emotional problems, breakdowns – the deprivation and hardship took their toll. Many were forced to opt out. These were the Seventies people. The establishment thought they were crazy, quixotic, unrealistic, even ridiculous.

Then came the Eighties. The Seventies people who survived were now thirtysomething. A decade and a half with its blend of idealism, fanaticism, commitment and fervour now churned out kids and families. A 20-year-old crusader who could live on rice, salt and chillies once a day had to decide whether she could foist that option on her kids. Can I opt for tuberculosis for my five-year-old daughter, even supposing my husband and I include the possibility in *our* life options?

Those who decided they couldn't afford children struggled on. The others reorganized their lives. They became part of the development game. Dedication remained, but tilting at windmills had to stop. So radicalism had to be watered down. Lifestyles remained simple but identification with the masses was impossible if kids had to get a decent education.

My own life is contorted with conflicting ideas, plans and decisions. My children's cousins are in the US or the UK with the best education facilities open to them. Ideology and all, can I cripple my five-year-old's creativity at the appalling government school because I opted to work in a backward area? Even if I fight to improve the school (the battle began two years ago but victory is nowhere on the horizon) my child is a child for 10 years more. Can I risk having her curse me 10 years hence because my ideology ruined her education? Therefore I compromise and send her to Calcutta with her grandmother and suffer pangs of guilt both for packing her off and for conforming to my elitist background.

Compromises and all, the Seventies network stands. But along the way most activists realized the futility of trying to struggle with no funds and impossible odds. They began to accept foreign funds – albeit condescendingly, as if they were doing the funding agency a favour. Who was a mere donor to evaluate a lifetime's struggle? At this point the agencies too were staffed by people with commitment and genuine concern for development problems. This was reflected in their relatively low salaries and simple lifestyles.

But in the Eighties the picture changed completely. Audited accounts were demanded by the Government and funding agencies demanded a more efficient accounting for development money. Thus was ushered in the era of management in the development game. Accusations began to be levelled at the Sixties and Seventies people. They were well-meaning and full of idealism, but inefficient and unprofessional. Therefore professional 'management' people began to appear in funding agencies.

It is true that planning, professionalism and efficiency were needed. After all, why should anyone balk at accounting for public money publicly? And setting targets and measuring sticks to evaluate projects would definitely increase efficiency if done properly. However an alarming argument which crept in, and seems here to stay, was that the 'cream' (so called) in terms of personnel was going to private industry. Since development is far more important, it was argued, we should attract the cream to ourselves by offering competitive and lucrative wages. And this is where the crunch comes. Development now offers proper 'management' salaries to its staff without the attendant rat-race problems. So scores of yuppies are being drawn into the development game. Corporate yuppie culture is oozing insidiously into the development world and the old order is inexorably crumbling.

But development is *not* industry. There are no profits. We're dealing with people, not commodities. And when management 'perks' include business as usual at five-star restaurants on expense accounts, who's paying? Does the little old lady, the widow, the pensioner, the schoolgirl know that her precious pound is going into a 'management' meal at a five-star restaurant, the inside of which she herself could never afford in her wildest dreams?

It doesn't just look bad. It STINKS! How does anyone justify such expenditure? Where has all the conscience gone?

The second terrifying thing about the Eighties is that it's the age of the professional. Right now the development game is 'in' and everyone's jumping on the bandwagon. Together with 'efficiency and good management principles has come the crying need for experts to take charge of every field. Doctors, lawyers, media people, architects, educators – in every field the experts are crucial if there is to be professionalism. Agreed. But at what price? Theirs? I was shocked to hear that 'professionals' called in as consultants were being paid 200 rupees ($12) a day plus travel and expenses. The average government teacher is paid 200 rupees a month, without expenses. Nobody thinks there's anything warped or convoluted about the arrangement. But I do.

The committed ones will continue to come. We've carried the game pretty well until now. But the development world has to stop trying to buy people. We don't need to compete with industry. Throughout the ages people have answered the call. Let the yuppies go. And make room for real people. ∎

*This was **Mari Marcel Thekaekara**'s debut piece in the **NI**, submitted out of the blue. She has been a regular contributor ever since. She lives and works in the Nilgiri hills of south India.*

1 Naxalites were the guerillas of the Communist Party of India (Marxist-Leninist). 2 Gurudev is a respectful name for Bengali poet Rabindranath Tagore. Gandhiji refers to Mohandas (Mahatma) Gandhi. Their reputations were in smithereens – assaulted by Naxalites and others. 3 *Rabindra Sangeet* is a collection of Tagore's poetry. 4 The Bhagavad Gita is the Hindu holy book. 5 A theology book by T Paulus. 6 Brazilian educationalist.

February 1992
Meditation on a bucket of lugworms

*Are relief workers puppets? An incident on an African beach triggers some troubling thoughts for **Tony Vaux**.*

I like the dawn – when the mind wanders freely between sleep and the creativity of action. I walked along the narrow line of sand between the lead-grey ocean and the towering white apartments of Maputo, capital of Mozambique.

It is a narrow path. A hard stone embankment juts out against the chaotic shore, where old shells lie scattered among the rubbish from ships, struggling sea-birds and wormcasts. On the other side, the asphalt road aprons the tower blocks as they crowd into the only really safe place in this huge country, huddled together like refugees from the unbearable terror of Renamo and its cruel ritualistic killing.

At that time of day I do not like to speak or be spoken to. I sorted out and reconciled the experience of yesterday, the plans for today. It was the third time I had visited Mozambique since Oxfam launched massive relief programmes in 1986. Up to that time international attention had been diverted elsewhere – mainly Ethiopia – and this ex-Portuguese strip of the Africa coastline had been abandoned to the sphere of Soviet influence.

But Renamo 'bandits', backed by South Africa, and fired by an incomprehensible blend of spiritual, ethnic and political grievances, had ravaged most of the country, and even threatened Maputo itself.

Oxfam lobbied governments and the UN to provide relief to the villagers displaced by the brutal killing. We urged support for the Mozambican Government's Disaster Department, and ourselves airlifted seeds, tools and clothes to remote districts that had seen nothing at all before.

It was a great success. International aid poured in. The UN included Mozambique in its appeals on a par with Ethiopia and Sudan. Only in retrospect did I see the wider political focus – above all the connection between Western relief and shifting Mozambique's Government away from communism and Soviet support. That massive aid in 1986 perhaps showed that the West wanted to win over Mozambique, which it had previously ignored. Then, an influential American report in 1987 finally labelled the Renamo 'guerrillas' as psychopathic killers, and placed them beyond the possibility of direct support from the US Government. Up to that time the US had apparently toyed with the idea of backing the killers, if their enemy was communism.

Perhaps no-one had predicted the speed of collapse of Soviet influence, but I wondered then, kicking the wet stones on the beach, if all that lobbying, campaigning and hard work had all been part of somebody else's wider plan? Did that make the achievement any less?

While in the middle of this thoughtful daze I suddenly realized that a little tragedy was being enacted in front of me. A street boy in tattered clothes and a cocky blue baseball hat had come to collect lugworms from the shore and had filled a bucket full of them. As he was walking back up to the road a youth came down, gave him a hard shove and seized the bucket. The younger boy reeled back in fear from the sudden attack but soon controlled his emotions. He stood still, a few steps from me, looking down at the sand. After a few more seconds he walked on along the way he had come – almost as if nothing had happened.

I did not feel sorry for him at all. I just admired his stoic resignation. But I began to wonder who was watching this little scene from the great white skyscrapers – and what they thought of me – standing by in my grand city clothes, doing nothing. The buildings seemed to loom up over me like child-comic ghosts, threatening me for my meanness. I stepped forward, and dropped some money into the boy's hand. He looked at me, amazed.

Confused now, my peace broken, I walked on quickly, head down, up the steps. At the top I collided with that same youth, coming down the other way, carrying the empty bucket. He thrust it into the boy's hands, who accepted it with the same dull resignation.

As soon as the youth had gone, he adjusted the blue cap and wandered down to the sea-edge, where he amused himself for a few minutes, throwing stones at the passing seabirds. Why had the youth given back the bucket?

Time had passed. I was late. I stamped along the street, angry at my endless Oxfam role – a sort of Paymaster of the Western World. Some other force seemed to drive on everything I did. It had been decided somewhere that scenes of abject suffering in Third World countries were not tolerable in the drawing room. Bob Geldof had made the issue really serious. Votes were at stake.

In Western countries, such scenes had been abolished (supposedly) by the welfare state, the social safety net. Now the system had to be expanded to the rest of the world. The difference being that instead of State benefit offices run by the Government, the job had been given out to the voluntary (or, if you like, private) sector.

In relief situations throughout the world Western governments now expect Oxfam, Save the Children and the like to make sure that no-one actually starves. I reminded myself again that there is nothing wrong with that. I have travelled to remote districts of Mozambique and seen broken families stumble out of the trees and collapse on the sand having reached 'safety' at last in some isolated village, guarded by a few fear-crazed soldiers. That is the best they can hope for, and the best that we can give is a set of clothes and a handful of food, to be shared in silence over the grey smoke of the fire.

They are twilight scenes, where consciousness is too painful and sleep elusive. That 'best' is at least something. We have to do what we can, but can never feel satisfied. The thought of great international machinations, of which we are often a part, is just salt in an existing wound.

But also my mind is uneasy about a kind of aid that shows so little attention to the cause. Who is really trying to stop the war? Is the West trying to help Mozambique or just to bring it within our own political sphere of influence? I suppose it is a mixture – a confusion of different purposes and pressures, and relief workers are tossed about like corks on the sea.

That boy – I gave him money to replace the lugworms that were supposed to be his income. In that way I salved my conscience. But it was lucky that the robber returned his bucket. Otherwise, tomorrow, he would have been no better off. Now at least he would collect more worms and have something to live on tomorrow.

I felt ill-prepared for my first meeting of the day. The calm of the dawn had been broken by pulsations of conscience that seemed to lead nowhere. I entered the great white edifice of the American organization that handled our emergency trucking. With money raised by Band Aid we had given 30 trucks to Mozambique to carry relief food to the needy. I wanted to know whether to send more.

The trucks had been given to the Government and the US charity was acting as 'Logistic Support'. In effect, they ran the trucks, but they were also supposed to train and support government staff so that in future there would be a permanent, efficient trucking fleet.

We shook hands. We established a small list of common acquaintances. We discussed computers and looked at the latest charts and diagrams. We got quite friendly: our particular agencies were not in competition. Their market for fundraising was the US. Ours was Britain.

'And what about new trucks?' I asked.

'I'd say the best thing just now is to back the private truckers. That's our philosophy. Government fleets never work. They are inefficient and don't achieve anything in the long run. The only way forward is by boosting the private sector.'

'But aren't you supposed to be backing the Government?'

'I can say what I really think, can't I?'

Our friendship began to dissolve. The day before I had heard exactly the same line from the American Embassy – and it was USAID that was paying the American that I had now come to meet. My gut reaction to 'stooges of American foreign policy' is still too strong.

We both agreed that private truckers would never reach the most needy, dangerous areas. They would only operate where it was safe and profitable. Yet I came away without any request for more relief trucks for the Government. The difference in attitude between two 'aid workers' was etched in the starkest relief.

Today it is often said that with the collapse of communism, the world has no further use for Africa. Its primary products are no longer important. Its military bases have been superseded by new technologies and the New World Order. It exists negatively as a source of humanitarian embarrassment, raked over by pop stars and the aid agencies – or, at best as a potential market of the future. US embassies throughout Africa make no secret of the fact that their main interest is to develop such markets through promoting 'free enterprise'.

Glum now, I walked back along the shoreline to my hotel. I felt surprised how blatant the American had been. But then aid agencies must inevitably reflect, consciously or unconsciously, the nature of the forces behind them. In the current climate aid agencies, especially in Africa, find themselves part of the sales literature of private enterprise.

Maybe private enterprise is a good form of development for those countries, but is it promoted for that reason or because it is a way to create exportable commercial wealth? The new system may leave many people just as poor as before, and could easily cause social division and conflict.

Politics continues its endless circle, revolving from individual freedom to state control as it must have done since the first wandering settlers discovered the Mozambican coast thousands of years ago and set up small communities on the shore. Society was always made up of those with power, those who are their victims, and a few people who tried to patch things up. It would be interesting to talk to the relief workers of earlier times...

Angry now at my own helplessness I watched the boy gathering lugworms on the beach. I admired his solid persistence.

His tormentor sat idly on the stone sea wall waiting for the bucket to be refilled. ■

Tony Vaux has worked in the Emergencies Unit of Oxfam UK since 1984.

June 1992
Development: a guide to the ruins

World development is like apple pie – nobody can be against it. Or can they? After three decades of development it is time to ask whether it has done much more than impose Westernization on the whole world. **Wolfgang Sachs** *begins his excavation of the development idea by explaining how, even at its birth, it was designed to remake the world in the image of the United States of America.*

Ruined buildings hide their secrets under piles of earth and rubble. Archaeologists, shovel in hand, work through layer upon layer to reveal underpinnings and thus discover the origins of a dilapidated monument. But ideas can also turn out to be ruins with their foundations covered by years or even centuries of sand.

I believe that the idea of development stands today like a ruin in the intellectual landscape, its shadows obscuring our vision. It is high time we tackled the archaeology of this towering conceit, that we uncovered its foundations to see it for what it is: the outdated monument to an immodest era.

Wind and snow stormed over Pennsylvania Avenue on 20 January 1949 when, in his inauguration speech before Congress, US President Harry Truman defined the largest part of the world as 'underdeveloped areas'. There it was, suddenly, a permanent feature of the landscape, a pivotal concept which crammed the immeasurable diversity of the globe's South into a single category – underdeveloped. For the first time, the new worldview was thus announced: all the peoples of the earth were to move along the same track and aspire to only one goal – development.

And the road to follow lay clearly before the President's eyes: 'Greater production is the key to prosperity and peace.' After all, was it not the US which had already come closest to this utopia? According to that yardstick, nations fall into place as stragglers or lead runners. And 'the United States is pre-eminent among nations in the development of industrial and scientific techniques'. Clothing self–interest in generosity, Truman outlined a program of technical assistance designed to 'relieve the suffering of these peoples' through 'industrial activities' and 'a higher standard of living'.

Looking back after 40 years, we recognize Truman's speech as the starting gun in the race for the South to catch up with the North. But we also see that the field of runners has been dispersed, as some competitors have fallen by the wayside and others have begun to suspect that they are running in the wrong direction.

The idea of defining the world as an economic arena originated in

Truman's time; it would have been completely alien to colonialism. True, colonial powers saw themselves as participating in an economic race, with their overseas territories as a source of raw materials. But it was only after the Second World War that they had to stand on their own and compete in a global economic arena.

For Britain and France during the colonial period, dominion over their colonies was first of all a cultural obligation which stemmed from their vocation to a civilizing mission. British imperial administrator Lord Lugard had formulated the doctrine of the 'double mandate': economic profit of course, but above all the responsibility to elevate the 'coloured races' to a higher level of civilization. The colonialists came as masters to rule over the natives; they did not come as planners to start the spiral of supply and demand.

According to Truman's vision, the two commandments of the double mandate converge under the imperative of 'economic development'. A change in worldview had thus taken place, allowing the concept of development to rise to a standard of universal rule. In the US's Development Act of 1929, still influenced by colonial frameworks, development applied only to the first duty of the double mandate – the economic exploitation of resources such as land, minerals and wood products; the second duty was defined as 'progress' or 'welfare'. At this time it was thought that only resources could be developed, not people or societies.

It was in the corridors of the State Department during World War Two that 'cultural progress' was absorbed by 'economic mobilization' and development was enthroned as the crowning concept. A new worldview had found its succinct definition: the degree of civilization in a country could be measured by the level of its production. There was no longer any reason to limit the domain of development to resources only. From now on, people and whole societies could, or even should, be seen as the object of development.

Truman's imperative to develop meant that societies of the Third World were no longer seen as diverse and incomparable possibilities of human living arrangements but were rather placed on a single 'progressive' track, judged more or less advanced according to the criteria of the Western industrial nations.

Such a reinterpretation of global history was not only politically flattering but also unavoidable, since underdevelopment can only be recognized in looking back from a state of maturity. Development without predominance is like a race without direction. So the pervasive power and influence of the West was logically included in the proclamation of development. It is no coincidence that the preamble of the UN Charter ('We, the peoples of the United Nations...') echoes the Constitution of the US ('We, the peoples of the United States...'). Development meant nothing more than projecting the American model of society onto the rest of the world.

Truman really needed such a reconceptualization of the world. The old colonial world had fallen apart. The United States, the strongest nation to emerge from the War, was obliged to act as the new world power. For this it needed a vision of a new global order.

The concept of development provided the answer because it presented the world as a collection of homogeneous entities, held together not through the political dominion of colonial times, but through economic interdependence. It meant the independence process of young countries could be allowed to proceed because they automatically fell under the wing of the US anyway when they proclaimed themselves to be subjects of economic development.

Development was the conceptual vehicle which allowed the US to behave as the herald of national self-determination while at the same time founding a new type of worldwide domination – an anti-colonial imperialism.

The leaders of the newly founded nations – from Nehru to Nkrumah, Nasser to Sukarno – accepted the image that the North had of the South, and internalized it as their self-image. Underdevelopment became the cognitive foundation for the establishment of nations throughout the Third World.

The Indian leader Nehru (incidentally, in opposition to Gandhi) made the point in 1949: 'It is not a question of theory; be it communism, socialism or capitalism, whatever method is most successful, brings the necessary changes and gives satisfaction to the masses, will establish itself on its own... Our problem today is to raise the standard of the masses...' Economic development as the primary aim of the state; the mobilization of the country to increase output: this beautifully suited the Western concept of the world as an economic arena.

As in all types of competition, this one rapidly produced its professional coaching staff. The World Bank sent off the first of its innumerable missions in July 1949. Upon their return from Colombia, the 14 experts wrote: 'Short-term and sporadic efforts can hardly improve the overall picture. The vicious circle... can only be broken seriously through a global relaunching of the whole economy, along with education, health and food sectors.'

To increase production at a constant level entire societies had to be overhauled. Had there ever existed a more zealous state objective? From then on, an unprecedented flowering of agencies and administrations came forth to address all aspects of life – to count, organize, mindlessly intervene and sacrifice, all in the name of 'development'. Today, the scene appears more like collective hallucination. Traditions, hierarchies, mental habits – the whole texture of societies – have all been dissolved in the planner's mechanistic models.

But in this way the experts were able to apply the same blueprint for institutional reform throughout the world, the outline of which was most often patterned on the American Way of Life. There was no longer any question of letting things mature for centuries', as in the colonial period. After the Second World War, engineers set out to develop whole societies – and to accomplish the job in a few years or, at the most, a couple of decades.

In the late 1960s, deep cracks began to appear in the building – the trumpeted promises of the development idea were built on sand! The international élite, which had been busy piling one development plan on another, knitted its collective brow. At the International Labour Office and the World Bank, experts suddenly realized that growth policies were not working. Poverty increased precisely in the shadow of wealth, unemployment proved resistant to growth, and the food situation could not be helped through building steel factories. It became clear that the identification of social progress with economic growth was pure fiction.

In 1973, Robert McNamara, the President of the World Bank, summed up the state of affairs: 'Despite a decade of unprecedented increase in the gross national product... the poorest segments of the population have received relatively little benefit... The upper 40 per cent of the population typically receive 75 per cent of all income.' No sooner had he admitted the failure of Truman's strategy, than he immediately proclaimed another development strategy with its new target group – *rural* development and small farmers. The logic of this conceptual operation is obvious enough: it meant the idea of development did not have to be abandoned; indeed, its field of application was enlarged. Similarly, in rapid succession during the 1970s and 1980s unemployment, injustice, the eradication of poverty, basic needs, women and the environment were turned into problems and became the object of special strategies.

The meaning of development exploded, increasingly covering a host of contradictory practices. The development business became self-propelling: whatever new crisis arose, a new strategy to resolve it could be devised. Furthermore, the background motive for development slowly shifted. A rising environmental chorus noted that development was not meant to promote growth, but to protect against it. Thus the semantic chaos was complete, and the concept torn to shreds.

So development has become a shapeless amoeba-like word. It cannot express anything because its outlines are blurred. But it remains ineradicable because it appears so benign. They who pronounce the word denote nothing but claim the best of intentions.

Development thus has no content but it does possess a function: it allows any intervention to be sanctified in the name of a higher, evolutionary goal. Watch out! Truman's assumptions travel like blind passengers under its cover. However applied, the development idea always implies that there are lead runners who show the way to latecomers; it suggests that advancement is the result of planned action. Even without having economic growth in mind, whoever talks of development evokes notions of universality, progress and feasibility, showing that they are unable to escape Truman's influence.

This heritage is like a weight which keeps one treading in the same spot. It prevents people in Michoacan, Gujarat or Zanzibar from recognizing their own right to refuse to classify themselves as 'underdeveloped'; it stops them rejoicing in their own diversity and wit. Development always entails looking at other worlds in terms of what they lack, and obstructs the wealth of indigenous alternatives.

Yet the contrary of development is not stagnation. From Gandhi's *swaraj* to Zapata's *ejidos*[1], we see that there are striking examples of change in every culture. Distinctions such as backward/ advanced or traditional/modern have in any case become ridiculous given the dead end of progress in the North, from poisoned soils to the greenhouse effect. Truman's vision will thus fall in the face of history, not because the race was fought unfairly, but because it leads to the abyss.

The idea of development was once a towering monument inspiring international enthusiasm. Today, the structure is falling apart and in danger of total collapse. But its imposing ruins still linger over everything and block the way out. The task, then, is to push the rubble aside to open up new ground. ■

Wolfgang Sachs *is senior research fellow at the Wuppertal Institute for Climate, Environment and Energy, Germany. Among his books are* Greening the North *(Zed 1998) and* Planet Dialectics *(Zed 1999).*

1 Mexican revolutionary Emiliano Zapata advocated a return to the ancient Indian tradition of community rather than individual land ownership. This *ejidos* idea was to some extent implemented in the Mexican land reform of the 1930s.

June 1992
Development ended in Kuwait

The Gulf War was development's final curtain, argues **Wolfgang Sachs**. *From now on the North will perceive the South as a sea of crises which must be managed – militarily.*

Even those who think that Heraclitus is the name of a rock formation know the two phrases that the philosopher of Ephesus bequeathed to the West's heritage of quotations. 'All things flow: nothing abides' was the formula he used to describe the continuous coming and going of existence. However, as history does not always flow slowly and quietly, but sometimes surges forward impetuously, Heraclitus coined the other phrase: 'War is the mother of all things'.

Heraclitus was referring to the clash between opposites in general, but there is considerable truth in the meaning that people generally give it: wars very often accelerate history, precipitate events and create new perspectives. My opinion is that the Gulf War marks the final curtain on the era in which the relationships between the North and South of the world could be considered in terms of 'development'. In its place, a new era is dawning in which relationships with the Third World will be dominated by the concept of 'security'.

The war made clear one essential fact: the terrifying technological divide that today, more than ever, separates the richer countries from all the others. This is a divide that expresses itself in macabre statistics: 115 American soldiers lost their lives as opposed to 100,000 Iraqis, a 1 to 1,000 ratio which must be unique in the history of war. In spite of the inhuman efforts which Iraq made to arm itself to the teeth, its army was wiped out because, technologically, it had remained at the level of the 1970s. The defeat of Saddam Hussein, however desirable it might have been, became the symbol of the speed of innovation in the First World and of the powerlessness of the Third.

It is no longer possible to deny it: the idea that all the countries in the world were marching along a common road was but a post-Second World War mirage. It is no longer possible to say that everyone is moving in an interdependent economic space. On the contrary, the international super-economy of the North and the poor economy of the South are separated by a wall.

Much time has passed since, as in the Brandt Report of 1980, the North was considered the South's engine of growth. It is still longer since the North was dependent on raw materials, agricultural commodities and cheap labour – all things that a highly technologized economy can substitute with increasing ease. The North no longer needs the South: it can prosper on the exclusion of the rest of the world. The world is no longer divided between capitalism and communism, but between fast economies and slow economies – to

quote Alvin Toffler. In the wake of the Gulf War it has become obvious that
the nations of the world are not at different points on the same road, as the
image of 'development' implies, but are rigidly separated in a situation of
planetary apartheid.

The way the peoples of the South are perceived is changing as a result.
For Truman, Third World societies were indeed poor, but also full of potential. They were 'young' nations and 'emerging', whose future was to shine
more splendidly than their present. Such optimism is implicit in the very
idea of development: where should the road of progress lead, if not to the
promised land?

In a situation of world apartheid, this concept collapses. No-one speaks any
more of a radiant tomorrow; the future appears grim and the South is seen
as the breeding ground of all crises. In a world divided, the countries of the
South are no longer looked at with hope but with suspicion. In the cynical eye
of the privileged, development aid is done for and the job at hand is to keep
a latent explosive force under control.

The Gulf War made it clear, once and for all, that Third World countries
are now risk zones. All kinds of dangers are to be found there, as the newspapers and television keep telling us: violence keeps exploding, the mafia is
in command, epidemics are spreading, deserts are advancing, ideologies are
rampant, and everywhere the demographic bomb is looming. And even the
stronghold of the North is not immune from the threat of immigration, the
greenhouse effect, drug traffic, terrorism and war: the 'one world' is discovering the boomerang effect of degradation. The more the threatening dangers strike fear into people's minds, the more the image of 'The Other' takes
on a different colouring. During the centuries it has been identified with the
pagan, then with the savage, then with the indigenous and finally with the
poor, which today embodies the 'risk factor'.

In these circumstances, the 'development' concept loses its reassuring connotations for the future: slowly it is being substituted by the concept of 'security' – from the North's viewpoint, naturally. There are already many development projects which have little to do with taking a country along the road
to progress and which simply content themselves with trying to prevent the
worst on a once-only basis. Once, the order of the day was to 'catch up' with
the North. Now the aim must be to avoid being engulfed by disaster and to
engage in 'security for survival'.

At the international level, too, the change of theme has been under way for
some time. Whereas, in the past, the discussion at conferences was about how
to give the South more opportunities to enter into the world's economic

growth, today conferences analyze how to keep the excesses of such growth under control. Governments are concerned about the signs of weakness in the biosphere – pollution of the seas, the ozone hole, global warming. Who should eliminate emissions, and how much, and in what time span? Who can claim what compensation? The focus of international negotiations has changed: the division of wealth has been replaced on the agenda by the division of risks.

Amidst all this, the way that the North perceives itself has had to change too. Truman was proud to consider US dominance not from a colonial viewpoint, as the trustee of peoples who are still under age, but rather in terms of the economic prosperity of the whole world. It was in line with this that institutions for 'aid' and co-operation' were set up.

Little has remained of all this under planetary apartheid: today, for reasons of self-defence, the North must stop itself being pulled down by the collapse of the South. From now on, the North will claim that it is obliged to dominate so as to protect the stability of the world system.

On 1 April 1991 *Time* magazine dedicated its front cover to fears about security, showing a uniformed body wearing a sheriff's badge marked 'Global Cop'. The new attitude has its military expression in the present planning of a multinational intervention force. Whether this belongs to the Western European Union, NATO or the UN is of secondary importance. What is under way is an epoch-making reorientation of the military apparatus towards war of low and medium intensity in the South of the world (and in the East, which is slowly slipping towards the South).

In a more charity-orientated variation, troops are being sent to relieve people who are struck by natural disasters, as Bangladesh and Kurdistan, while one is beginning to hear talk of 'green helmets' to intervene in the case of ecological disasters. And people are talking about the planetary environmental crisis in terms of 'ecological security'. Ecology, once the rallying cry for new public virtues, has become a problem of security policy. Satellites are launched that keep an eye on far-away countries – veritable environmental spies.

Global security is beginning to justify anything – just as it united the international community against the dictator of Baghdad. Rich countries are now increasing their diplomatic, charity and military instruments for risk prevention. But where there is no justice, there cannot be peace. Security has replaced development as the global guiding light – another tragic consequence of the continuing arrogance of power. ■

November 1996
Mea culpa run riot

Though aid may be a huge and complex 'industry' its function is to respond to moral imperatives. If we forget the humanitarian impulse, we quickly lose sight of the objective. **Maggie Black** *crosses swords with the 'developmenteers'.*

On the terrace of an old tea-planter's bungalow in Kampala, I had one of those conversations about aid which sticks in the mind, and in the gullet, for a long time after. This was a few years ago and I was looking at the impact of AIDS on family life in Africa – at that stage in the epidemic, a phenomenon barely yet noticed.

I had spent a day in the company of a remarkable Irish Sister, Ursula Sharpe, and her team of Ugandan nurses and social workers. We had visited a rural school, where children orphaned by AIDS and their carers had congregated from all over the neighbourhood for a get-together and counselling. We had sung and danced in traditional African style, eaten a meal they had prepared, shared experiences in small groups and given out long bars of soap, blankets and school uniforms to the children. It had been both a gladdening and an intensely moving day, and I recounted it to a representative of a Scandinavian children's aid organization.

I was outraged by her reaction. She didn't approve of handing out bars of soap and blankets to the children. She unfairly latched on to the fact that the head of the programme was an expatriate Irish nun, who had in practice stayed as much in the background as possible. Oh, my friend said in tones of politically correct superiority, we don't believe in hand-outs or charitable actions by white philanthropists. Outsiders with their old-fashioned ideas and irrelevant responses only succeed in disrupting local coping mechanisms.

In vain did I point out that Christian nuns were long part of the social landscape in Uganda and that not they but AIDS was the intruder. The traditional coping mechanism – the extended African family – was unable to cope with AIDS. That was the whole point.

Where, I asked in tones of fury in this delightful frangipani-scented setting, is the culture in which it is taboo to provide a gift to children who will otherwise shiver in the chill of night, who will otherwise have no clothes to wear to school?

Here, it seemed to me, was an example of the absurd extremes to which aid and development theorists can take the thesis that humanitarian assistance is highly deficient. It is damned every which way, even by those whose programme resources and professional careers depend on fundraising policies which deliberately capitalize on human compassion.

In this exercise, *mea culpa* runs riot. Humanitarian aid is motivationally suspect, ascribed to paternalism, surrogate power mania or middle-class guilt. Its impact is suspect: it creates a dependency culture and destroys coping mechanisms. Its unsustainability is suspect; resources spent this way are poured wastefully into a 'bottomless pit'. It is also attacked for maintaining inequities and postponing the glorious birth of the socialist state – although that song is less frequently sung these days. And in the contagion of conflict which at present characterizes the new world order, it is even fashionable to accuse humanitarian aid of prolonging wars. Soon someone will accuse it of starting one.

Where have such distortions come from and why do intelligent people believe them?

Leaving aside the Marxist critique and the mea culpaists, I put the blame squarely on the developmenteers. It is they, with their desire to be doing something more macho and important with their aid than mere philanthropy, who made the word 'humanitarian' into something soft, suspect and passé. They implied that aid provided under the humanitarian banner was an inferior affair, carried on by naïve do-gooders who cannot see past the brims of their solar topis or the cuffs of their sisterly habits.

By the developmenteers, I mean those campaigners who took up the cudgels some decades back on behalf of the ex-colonial world and declared war on its hunger and poverty. Before they came on the scene, overseas charity was directed at refugees, the disaster-stricken and the afflicted and indigent in places where there were no social safety nets. Its motivation was internationalist: an extension of the notion of assisting the helpless and needy to embrace the whole family of humankind.

But then came the era of 'development'. Resources and technology from the rich countries were to be transferred to the poor via 'aid' in a Marshall Plan-type effort to enable them to 'catch up'. This was not charity: it was something much grander. It was about economic growth, social justice, terms of trade, the welfare state writ large. It was not about helping leprosy sufferers, orphans, the halt, the blind and the lame.

The developmenteers were very keen on a Chinese proverb which encapsulated what they were about: 'Give a man a fish and you feed him for a day. Teach him to fish and you feed him for life.' How simplistic can you get? Why did anyone think he didn't know how to fish already? It was much more likely that fish stocks were exhausted or the river polluted; that other fishermen with larger boats were stealing the catch; that someone else had claimed the waterways, or the market for cod had collapsed. It might actually have been better to feed the man for a while until the river was cleaned up and restocked or alternative jobs in manufacturing or service industries were created. Meanwhile, often as not, he accepted the idiotic fishing instruction and then took off for town.

Oh dear. So many misconceived projects with inconclusive, even negative, outcomes. So what is lambasted? There can't be anything wrong with development itself other than it needs a bit of redefining. So it must be the mechanism – aid – which is at fault.

Having had a bad press from the developmenteers for a long time, humanitarian aid has recently enjoyed a renaissance. In 1984-85, the famine in Ethiopia – partly thanks to the television age – produced an outbreak of compassionate fever, stoked by Bob Geldof and Band-Aid. Almost all the major overseas aid charities, and a rash of new little ones, found their income soaring to unprecedented heights. Not for 'development', you notice, although this awkwardness was usually glossed over.

And although the emergencies of the late 1980s and 1990s tended to be murky affairs, their causes rooted in human rather than natural agents, their suffering caused by armed conflict rather than the weather, the flow of generosity was not impaired.

And it has been needed. Emergencies have recently multiplied and spread, becoming more brutal and sweeping whole populations into their maw. In Somalia, Angola, Liberia, Sierra Leone, Rwanda; in Afghanistan, Bosnia and Chechnya; among Mexican Indians, Marsh Arabs and Kurds; and now in Burundi.

The new world disorder has placed immense strains on the machinery of international compassion. Because today's wars are no longer skirmishes within the framework of superpower confrontation, other countries do not expend resources keeping them under control. Often, the only response the Western world is willing to offer is a humanitarian response. Troops go in under a UN flag, not to fight but to deliver aid. Suddenly, humanitarian activity is not soft and do-gooding; it is deeply difficult, fraught with danger and political complexity.

It is also expensive, and it is siphoning away resources for that much more important thing – development. The amount of official development assistance allocated to humanitarian aid by OECD countries rose from less than $500 million in 1980 to more than $3,500 million in 1993.[1] Agencies which normally focus on development see increasing proportions of their funds haemorrhaging into 'the bottomless pit'. UNICEF expenditure on emergencies, for example, has gone up from 10 per cent of its programme in the 1980s to more than 20 per cent in the 1990s.[2] This can't be helped, however much the developmenteers and efficiency wizards complain. Such organizations were invented to respond to humanity in distress. To ignore their worst hour of need would be a betrayal, and inexplicable to the donating public.

At the same time, in failed or limping economies of countries burdened by debt and structural adjustment, whatever fragile safety nets were put in place in the modern era have been abruptly stripped away. Health and social-services budgets are shrinking. Classrooms are falling down. And charges for drugs and treatments are being introduced to avoid that dreadful blight, the dependency culture. Everywhere in the world, caring services are being turned over to the private sector. In many places in all kinds of countries, it is people like Ursula Sharpe and the Ugandan sisters who are trying desperately to plug the gap.

There is nothing wrong with humanitarian aid. And it is certainly not a second-class affair. When so many people in so many countries are enduring emergencies, upheavals, calamities, premature death from aids, and an indigence forced upon them by bad 'development', all I can say is the more humanitarian aid the better. If some of it goes for longer-term and rehabilitation purposes, I am sure nobody will object. If it helps to call such purposes 'developmental', then that's fine too.

Hardened development tourist as I am, occasionally something touches me deeply. I recently visited Ho Chi Minh City. On the banks of the Saigon River are families living in excruciating poverty. Their shacks jut out over the mudbanks on stilts, with the poorest and flimsiest far out in the stream, liable to be washed away. At the end of a hair-raising catwalk I entered a one-room dwelling. The woman who lived there owned nothing except a bundle of rags. She had a daughter who had borne two children, one still a baby, from different men. This daughter had not been able to settle down. So she had gone, leaving her children with her mother, 'to try her fortune elsewhere'. Where this was, no-one knew.

Would it be OK, I asked the social workers I was with, if I gave the woman something? Yes it would. I turned my back to grope in my bag for a handful of dollars. When I turned round and gave them to her, the woman burst into tears. Upon which I also burst into tears. Across the gulf of culture, language and privilege, through the complexity of our several emotions, there was a momentary bond of complete human solidarity. When I left the community an hour later, she was waiting on the path dry-eyed, with the baby on her hip and a smile of mute farewell.

When I look back and think of that woman, I don't regret damaging her coping mechanism. What I regret is that I, and the world, didn't give her a great deal more. ∎

1 Aid under Fire: relief and development in an unstable world, UN Department of Humanitarian Affairs, UN, Geneva, 1995.
2 John Richardson, Review of UNICEF's Emergency Relief Operations, UNICEF, New York, 1995.

June 2000
Development as forced labour
C Douglas Lummis counsels against counting the votes people make with their feet.

Several years ago, in a book called *Radical Democracy*, I wrote that: 'Economic development... is anti-democratic in that it requires kinds, conditions and amounts of labour that people would never choose – and, historically have never chosen – in a state of freedom. Only by giving society one undemocratic structure can people be made to spend the greater part of their lives labouring "efficiently" in fields, factories or offices, and handing over the surplus value to capitalists, managers, Communist Party leaders, or technocrats.'

A book reviewer for the prestigious journal *Foreign Affairs* responded tersely that in fact 'the people have been voting with their feet in favour of capitalist prosperity pretty convincingly for some time now'.

This is the myth, stated with fine succinctness. Industrial capitalism was freely chosen. How can anyone call it anti-democratic?

Of course what most of the people in the world actually got, whatever they may have voted for, was capitalist poverty. But did this voting actually take place, and if so, when? 'For some time now' could mean recent decades or recent centuries. Are we supposed to believe that, at the beginning of the industrial revolution in England, the farmers who trudged into the cities to become the first generations of industrial wage workers were voting retroactively with their feet in favour of having been driven off their land by enclosure? Are we supposed to believe that the peoples of Asia, Africa and Latin America voted in favour of being colonized? Perhaps the reviewer is thinking of the era following World War Two, when colonialism and imperialism gave way to an allegedly more benign policy of 'the development of underdeveloped countries'.

For while few have claimed that colonialism had the consent of the colonized, part of the ideology of development implies such consent. Without it, how could development – which means the restructuring of societies such that they will sustain the industrial capitalist mode of production – support its claim to be different?

When Harry Truman in 1949 announced his 'bold new program' for 'the development of underdeveloped areas', he was launching the most massive sustained assault on both nature and culture that history has ever known. At the same time he was launching a massive paradigm shift in political economy. Before his announcement, 'modernization' did not exist as a technical term in the social sciences and the only thing that could be 'underdeveloped' was camera film. After his announcement the world was covered with underdeveloped countries in which development and modernization were either taking place or just about to.

The ideological power of the concepts of 'modernization' and 'development' comes from their use of retroactive teleology. Put bluntly, this means redefining something so that what you are about to do to it appears as its predetermined destiny. For example, we call a certain kind of stone 'iron ore', which means that if we crush it to powder and subject it to intense heat, it will yield iron. It wasn't 'ore' until this technology was discovered. But once we have the technology, we redefine the stone such that extracting iron from it is seen as the actualization of its latent potential, its fated end, its *telos*. Not only that: the dictionary defines 'ore' as 'native metal from which precious or useful metal may be *profitably* extracted' (Oxford English Dictionary; emphasis added). Even the market system is retroactively implanted into our definition of this natural object: when the market value drops, what was ore today may be stone tomorrow.

'Underdeveloped society' is a word like 'ore'. It is a redefinition made possible by the fact that the leaders in the industrial capitalist countries believe they have the power and the technology to smash such a society, melt it down and remold it on the industrial capitalist model. At the same time, the word gives the impression that to do this is to fulfil that society's predetermined destiny. This conceals the violently antidemocratic nature of development.

In the heady first years after Truman's speech, the new modernization/development ideologues propagated the myth that the chief motivating force behind development would be 'the revolution of rising expectations' brought about by the 'demonstration effect' of industrial capitalist life. Merely being exposed to this way of life – whether through pictures in magazines, or movies, or stories you got from your cousin who scrubs floors at the local Hilton – would cause the scales to fall from your eyes, after which you would drop everything (culture, tradition, values, whatever) to have it.

But at the very time the ideologues were popularizing this myth, they knew well that it wasn't really happening. In 1963, in his *Communications and Political Development,* Lucian Pye wrote: 'It is no longer possible to assume that people in traditional societies will readily experience a revolution of rising expectations simply by being exposed to the prospect of new standards of material life... Instead of having to cope with an agitated population carried away with exaggerated expectations, most governments in transitional societies are confronted with the problem of a disturbingly apathetic public which is inured to all appeals for action.'

Merely renaming the stones 'ore' did not, it seems, cause them to disintegrate into powder and leap into the furnace on their own. But this did not cause the developmentalists to abandon the revolution of rising expectations. The myth persists to this day. There is a doublethink here. What matters is not what people actually want but what they are theoretically bound to want. Underdevelopment is to development what the acorn is to the oak. Development is what the acorns want by their very nature, and if they aren't aware of that, well, they'll find out soon enough.

Developmentalists engage in a similar kind of doublethink with regard to the history of colonialism and imperialism. These unfortunate things happened, as Marion Levy argued in his *Modernization and the Structure of Societies,* but they weren't essential to the inevitable process of modernity overcoming tradition. To focus on imperialism can only be a distraction, since 'the morals of imperialists are essentially irrelevant to the problems faced by members of relatively non-modernized societies in contact with modernization'.

Of course, this won't do. What happened in colonial and imperial times is not peripheral to the story of economic development – it is the first chapter in that story. In the 1933 *International Encyclopedia of the Social Sciences,* written before the shift to the development paradigm, there is an entry which discusses forced labour in the modern world. In most tropical areas the 'white man' is unable or unwilling to perform manual labour and enterprise must rely either upon the local population or upon imported coolie labour. Since the material wants of primitive peoples are few and they are unfamiliar with a money economy and unaccustomed to arduous and continuous toil, they are usually unwilling to work for European entrepreneurs. Out of this conflict between native indifference and the desires of governments and industrialists, forced labour arose. Many of the chief tropical railways and roads have been constructed by forced labour. Indeed, it is doubtful whether the tropics could have been held and developed without it.

Forced labour, the author continues, is still – i.e. in the 1930s – practised in all of Central Africa, French Algeria and Indo-China, British India, Dutch

East Indies, Belgian Congo, British East Africa, Madagascar and French West Africa, Liberia, Portuguese West Africa, Dutch Java. The author goes on to describe some of the actual consequences. When the 'native' is suddenly and forcibly thrown into contact with industrial civilization their psychological resistance to diseases such as tuberculosis is lowered. Because of the compulsory methods used in the construction of the Congo-Ocean railway in French Equatorial Africa and a lack of adequate precautions, 17,000 native workers engaged on the enterprise died between 1925 and 1929.

The author then summarizes the justification colonialists offer for using forced labour, an argument in which we can see the postwar ideology of development in its embryonic form: 'Many businessmen and some colonial officials..: defended forced labour for private enterprises on the ground that primitive peoples will not progress until they learn to work and that the wealth of the tropics cannot be exploited for the outside world unless forced labour is employed.'

Still, in most colonies direct forced labour was used only for public works and not by private enterprise. In some colonies, however – for example, parts of British South and East Africa – indigenous people, having been deprived of land adequate enough for independent economic existence, were literally compelled to labour for European mine or plantation owners. They may also have been indirectly subjected to heavy cash taxes which they could not pay except out of wages.

Here we find the first generation of 'underdeveloped' people 'voting with their feet' for the life of the industrial wage earner. When you are driven off the land by new laws of private ownership, or when the forest from which you draw your livelihood is cut down and replaced by a plantation, there may be nothing for it but to trudge down the road to the owner's house and ask for a job. And remember, this process – the transformation of the natural, social and legal environment such that wage work becomes the only choice – is not something that disappeared when colonialism was replaced by development. This is development.

In the 1968 revised edition of *The International Encyclopedia of the Social Sciences* the entry 'Forced Labour' has disappeared. It is hardly ever mentioned in any work on economic development. Industrial capitalism is a system of rule; it rules people by gaining control over their means of subsistence. Economic development is the extension of this system of rule to every corner of the globe. In the age of colonialism this required direct forced labour. In the age of development it is done by means of indirect forced labour, supplemented by the political power of the Development Dictatorship. In the age of globalization the process seems to be nearing completion: industrial capitalism is now claiming to be The Only Game in Town. In this situation, to look at the long column of development refugees trudging down the road from the blasted countryside into the slums of the cities in search of jobs, and to say these people are 'voting with their feet for capitalist prosperity', is to make a bad joke. Isn't a plebiscite where there is just one candidate supposed to be a symbol of tyranny?

But of course this is not really the only game in town, nor the only set of rules. In recent decades people's movements all over the world have defied 'economic common sense' to block development projects that threaten their subsistence. The search for an alternative economic logic – or non-economic logic – is something that no longer takes place only in books. The Zapatista chant – 'the First World? Ha, ha, ha!' promises to echo deep into the 21st century. The real election of the feet – the long march to a democratized economy – is yet in the future. ■

C Douglas Lummis is an activist based in Japan and the author of Radical Democracy.

8

Adventures on the edge: travellers' tales

FOR the first half of its life, the *New Internationalist* could not afford to pay for its own editors and writers to travel to the countries with which it was preoccupied. Instead it had to rely on finding writers who were already there – or on editors exploiting contract work for UN agencies or the BBC to gather on-the-ground material for their own magazines. But some time in 1985 Peter Stalker had a bright idea. Why not use the money we set aside to pay contributing journalists to fund the research trip of an **NI** editor who would then write a whole issue based on their adventures and investigations in a single country?

Naturally, since it was Peter's idea, he was the first to give it a shot and travelled to Nicaragua – which then seemed like the world's front line as Ronald Reagan's US did its despicable utmost to destroy the Sandinista Revolution. The report he came up with – a mixture of serious investigation and random, often comic, encounters with ordinary people – established a template not just for his own later explorations of Chile and the Philippines but for other editors' travel writing as well, whether in Vietnam or Mexico, Kerala or Tibet.

The purpose of most of these journeys was to act as the reader's eyes and ears, asking the questions they would want answered – it was important that we were encountering these countries for the first time, seeing them afresh rather than imparting an expert knowledge. And our primary concern was to reflect the everyday drama of ordinary people's lives rather than to seek out screaming headlines of war or disaster.

In that sense most of the travel writing selected here is unrepresentative, since most of them show editors venturing into conflict zones. The magazine would never require a writer to seek out danger but occasionally we have ended up altogether more at risk than we'd anticipated. Though as we wrote our stories later in the safety of our homes and offices we could not but be painfully aware of the people we had left behind who could not escape the shadow of war or repression simply by boarding a plane. ∎

February 1986
Sandino sunrise
Is Nicaragua a shining symbol of liberation – or a dangerous outpost of communism? If you have doubts about our revolution, say the Sandinistas, come and see for yourselves. **Peter Stalker** *took up the invitation for the* New Internationalist.

I'm taking a photograph of a queue of women outside a supermarket – and I'm being watched by a shoeshine boy.

'Are you a journalist?' he asks. 'Do you work for the press?'

'Well, yes I do,' I say, a bit surprised he could guess. 'Why are all those women queuing?'

'I'm not sure,' he shrugs. 'But they've just reduced the prices of a lot of things. Maybe they just want to get there before everything runs out.'

'You can't shine my shoes I'm afraid,' I say apologetically (I'm wearing running shoes).

'I know,' he says, 'but can you do something for me? You see that snack bar over there?' He points to a rather smart fish restaurant, the *Pesca Fresca*. 'The owner won't let me in to shine shoes. You should put that in the paper – it's an injustice!'

I can see there's been a misunderstanding.

'Oh no,' I apologize, 'I don't actually work for *La Prensa.'* (*La Prensa* is one of Nicaragua's three daily papers – though in Spanish it just means 'the press'.)

'For *Barricada* then, or *El Nuevo Diario*?'

I explain that I work for a foreign magazine and that I don't think that the *New Internationalist* will cut much ice with the restaurant owner. But I will see what I can do.

This is my first day in Managua. I am hoping for a gentle start, just pottering around till the jetlag wears off. But I can see that my first interview has begun.

'It's very unfair,' he says. 'Everyone has the right to earn a living.'

'How much do you earn then, shining shoes?'

'Depends. About 500 cordobas a day.'

I haven't quite got a grip on the currency but as far as I know the basic daily wage is around 250 cordobas. So he (his name is Emilio Martinez and he's 14 years old) is not doing too badly – even if he can't get into the *Pesca Fresca*.

But I would have thought, in any case, that Nicaragua's popular democracy should have been able to solve his problem. There are Sandinista Defence Committees, 'CDS', one committee for each zone, where people can air their grievances. I ask him why he doesn't try this.

'That's no good,' he says. 'I live in a different zone. This is Bello Horizonte and I live in Waspan. Each zone has its own CDS.'

Emilio hasn't lived there very long. He and his family, he explains, are refugees from the north-east of the country, from territory where the Government and the *contras* are locked in combat – and from which many young boys have been forcibly recruited by the *contras*.

'It was getting too dangerous. A lot of people have been killed or kidnapped. We've decided to stay down here till the war is over.'

If he's 14 years old I wonder whether he should be at school. I ask him and his eyes start to look vacant and a bit evasive. His sister, he says, is teaching him how to read and write. Enough questions have been asked; his look implies it is time to get on with some work.

I think I can draw some conclusions now. Nicaragua is a country in which *contra* attacks have displaced of lot of the population. Local democracy may be fine in principle but can't always respond to people's needs. There is a strong faith in the critical power of the press. Independent entrepreneurs, on the streets, can earn twice as much as those on official salaries. And the schools have a serious absentee problem.

A bit premature, you might think – and based on a smallish sample. But this is journalism after all (though I must say, looking back on this later, and after talking to many more people, it does still seem to stand up).

This report is made up of such casual conversations and inquisitions, sometimes with people I meet in bars or at bus stops, sometimes conducted as formal interviews. Nicaraguans invite anyone and everyone to come and talk to them – to see precisely what is going on. And this magazine has been written in the form of a travelogue to give some impression of the things you *can* find out if you take up that invitation.

I was curious about Nicaragua – a country that shook off one of the world's most corrupt dictatorships only to find itself under attack from the most powerful nation on earth. I wanted to know what it had done to deserve such treatment. Is it, as radical supporters will tell you, a popular grassroots revolution? Or is it a marxist-leninist dictatorship? Or is it an open and pluralist democracy? Do any of these questions even make sense?

Managua is the obvious place to start. But it's a ruin of a city, one of the most bizarre capitals on earth. Almost the entire centre was flattened by an earthquake in 1972 and has languished vacant to this day. Just a few skeletons and shells of buildings rear up here and there through a forest of weeds. And there are even a few isolated structures which survived perfectly intact: the square tower of the earthquake-proof Bank of America, for example, pokes resolutely through the skyline – though its ex-owners probably wish it had crumbled with the rest, since it was subsequently nationalized by the Sandinista Government.

Rebuilding has taken place in parts but has largely been confined to the periphery. So Managua is a cluster of suburbs: the Los Angeles of Central America you might say. But the similarities (with LA, or anywhere else for that matter) don't stretch very far.

For one thing, there are no street addresses. Plenty of streets, but few signs and scarcely any numbers. So how do you find a particular building? In my case, you frequently don't. But the locals have developed a system which seems to serve. The headed notepaper of an institution will carry a set of directions like: 'Three and a half blocks up from where the Morales house used to be'. But where on earth *was* the Morales house? And which way is 'up' for that matter? This was a code I never managed to crack.

Then there is the transport system. The overcrowding of buses in Managua, indeed in Nicaragua in general, is something beyond my experience. There appears to be no limit to the number of humans (and sometimes livestock) that can be absorbed.

The analogy most frequently used by the suffering passengers is that of sardines in a tin. But fish, once tinned, are under no obligation to move. The experienced bus passenger knows, however, that if they are not within striking distance of the exit at the critical moment there is little chance of getting off. So the mass of bodies inside must always be moving through, a writhing fluid of arms and legs and trunks experiencing every position in which human bodies can be made to fit against each other.

Sorry to go on about this. But I do have to use the buses to get from A to B, so they figure largely in my recollection of the country. I have to use one, for example, to get to the satellite town of Ciudad Sandino.

I want to visit Ciudad Sandino to find out more about those Sandinista Defence Committees. They might offer little help to itinerant shoeshine boys but they are supposed to be Nicaragua's fount of popular democracy. And Ciudad Sandino had been a focus of insurrection at the time of the revolution, so I would expect to find the Committee particularly active here.

Ciudad Sandino is named after the stubborn 1930s nationalist leader Augusto Sandino, who led a guerrilla struggle against the US presence in Nicaragua but who was eventually murdered on the orders of the founder of the Somoza dynasty. Literally it means 'Sandino City' but it is nothing like as spectacular as it sounds. It's a poor dormitory district some 13 kilometres from the centre of Managua, with wide, muddy streets and ramshackle, improvised housing sprawling towards the horizon much like any other Latin American shanty town.

The 113 bus squeezes me out by the new concrete market building. Dripping with sweat (Managua is hot and very humid) I badly need a drink. No fruit juices available so it has to be a fizzy 'Rojita', the 'little red one', a drink which has been unkindly and accurately described as 'carbonated cough mixture'. A fellow Rojita drinker offers to take me off to meet a friend of his who is a *brigadista,* a member of the voluntary health 'brigade' who will be able to tell me about the local CDS.

I'm interrupting her washing when we arrive but she doesn't seem to mind and invites me in.

We can't have been talking for more than two minutes when two men materialize as from nowhere. They have been alerted that there is a journalist in town.

'Journalists tell so many lies,' says one, who introduces himself as Antonio Lopez. I can't argue with that. But I do try to convince them that I am at least open minded, and possibly even biased towards them. I am free to talk to anyone I like, he says quickly, but I gather that it would be best to talk to CDS officials first to get a 'fuller picture'. Antonio has introduced himself as a Secretary for Propaganda, a word used much more freely in Spanish than in English (it does not imply that what is being propagated is a lie).

The propaganda he treats me to, on the way to see the top man in the CDS, is straightforward enough, about the impact of the US support for the counter-revolutionaries, the suffering that it is causing, and about Nicaragua's determination to stick it out.

The Sandinista Defence Committees are branches of a quasi-independent organization set up to maintain the momentum and the enthusiasm that brought about the revolution – as well as to make sure that individuals have a voice in government: to express the will of the 'masses' (another word used much more cheerfully here).

But the CDS officials also have power of patronage; they allocate some of the local resources and are in charge of ration cards, for example, so they can be tempted to favour whose who are most loyal to Sandinistas. You might suspect, therefore that the same channels that can be used to expose the Government to the people could also be used in the other direction as a way for the Government to keep an eye on its citizens.

Jose Inosente, the 'Zonal Co-ordinator' for Ciudad Sandino, is at pains to point out that *his* CDS is nothing like so partisan. He is a charming, soft-spoken character, nothing like the sloganizing politician I was expecting. The

desk in his cluttered office is piled high with papers and he is constantly interrupted by people coming to ask his advice on this or that.

Recently the CDS have been accused of having lost touch with the people. They have shown that they can mobilize people for certain 'blitz' campaigns like the current onslaught against the mosquito that carries dengue
fever. But they run into the same kind of problems as community organizations everywhere – that people's enthusiasm wanes and that everything is
left to a few activists.

But when I talk to people randomly later it does seem that they are happy
with what the CDS are trying to do – and indeed with what the revolution
itself has achieved, Juan Pinoza, for example, is sunning himself in front of
his house reading the newspaper *El Nuevo Diario* when I arrive.

'I'm a baker,' he says. 'I've been running my own business for the past ten
years; there's a small oven in the house here. Things have improved a lot
since the Triumph. For one thing, since we do a lot of things in common, like
cleaning the street, we have got to know all the neighbours.'

His wife Heidi asks where I come from and then says: 'We've had quite a
few *internacionalistas* here. There was a Danish work brigade that spent six
months building those houses over there.'

All foreigners in Nicaragua seem to be called 'internationalists', which
makes a pleasant change from *gringo*. Many of these are working here as vol-
unteers. Indeed I'm starting to feel a bit guilty that this particular *interna-
cionalista* is doing nothing more positive than scribbling away in his notebook.
Heidi cheers me with a couple of cakes from the bakery.

Another woman brightens up my day still further just as I am about to leave
the district altogether. At the bus stop there is a fierce argument at the front
of the queue.

'You men are all the same,' a woman is saying. 'You machos!'

A portly grey-haired gent is arguing that men deserve their freedom
because it is they who bring home the wages.

'Really?,' she scoffs, 'what about all the jobs that women do?' Then she
starts to mime chalking up figures on the wall behind her. 'Let's say 4,000
cordobas for a month's worth of cleaning. Another 4,000 for the cooking and
the same again for washing and ironing. Think what would happen if we had
to be paid for all that.'

Her opponent is trying to maintain that when a couple splits up the man
should be allowed to keep all the property his earnings have paid for. She has
strong views about this too but now the bus appears and, with evident relief,
her 'macho' disappears into the crush. ∎

April 1991
The river, the forest and the people

The Amazon rainforest and its people are caught in a cycle of destruction. **David Ransom** *embarks on a journey to find out why.*

The *Chico Mendes* is a beautiful Amazon river boat, named in defiant memory of the rubber tappers' leader who was assassinated two years ago.

But it is also a bomb. Stored in the bow are six huge barrels of diesel oil. They fill the boat with fumes. Some of my companions are sitting on them smoking cigarettes. Overhead, lightning bolts flick from dark clouds like the tongue of a snake scenting its prey. I light my pipe, reasoning that this is the most pleasurable way to face an explosive end to an expedition that hasn't yet begun.

All too often I've heard the Amazon rainforest talked of as if it contained no people. That false belief has made much mischief in the past and seems in danger of doing so again now. People have lived in the forest for thousands of years. If it is finally being destroyed then it's not destroying itself. People are doing that. I want to find out why. To do that I need to know who they are and what they think of the forest they live with.

So here I am on the waterfront of Cruzeiro do Sul. This is the most westerly town in Brazil – dozing quietly away since the First World War and the end of the Great Brazilian Rubber Boom – in a part of the country that until 1903 belonged to Bolivia and Peru. It's slap in the middle of the forest and incredibly remote – 'off the map' was the expression they used in Rio de Janeiro.

We're headed for the Upper Juruá Valley Extractive Reserve. It is two and a half days away by boat – 45 minutes and $1,000 by one of the rare private planes or air taxis that fly there. 'Much prefer the romance of the boat', I think smugly to myself.

Until, that is, the motors start up. Imagine yourself locked in a coffin with two pneumatic drills and you will have just some idea of what it is like to travel on the *Chico Mendes*. It is impossible to talk. Of Amazonian wildlife I can expect to see nothing at all. Only the vultures circle undisturbed over Cruzeiro do Sul.

Darkness promptly falls. The idea is that we should travel through the night. Zé the skipper is an obliging man, a middle-aged *ribeirinho* (someone who lives by the river and makes a living from it) who knows what he's doing. His young *motorista* Evilásio must love the huge outboard motors dearly if he's prepared to stand anywhere near them. But we have only a small electric bulb to light our way ahead. Zé soon tires, takes us into the bank and repairs to his hammock.

For a few minutes we swing in our hammocks in silence; just the sound of river water lapping against the boat, frogs croaking, the occasional enigmatic grunt and rustle from the forest. It shines with a thousand fireflies, like a dark audience carrying candles.

But for Leonardo and Tonhão this is all too much. They are 'technicians' being sent up river by the National Council of Rubber Tappers in Cruzeiro. They have to sort out some small local difficulties in the Reserve without getting themselves shot – the odds are even, I'd say. Leonardo is large and powerful, with a menacing stare. I think he's taken against me. Tonhão is thin, with a crooked little finger. Silenced by the motors, ill at ease with the absence of noise and no doubt a bit on edge, they burst into farts, jokes and giggles that slowly spread through the boat. Macedo, the boss, remonstrates with them to no avail.

So he takes the helm. Moisés starts the outboard motors. He's the son of a Kampa Indian chief returning to his people after helping an anthropologist in São Paulo with her translations. Like me, he's just a little bit aloof. We blast off again into the night, effectively dispatching Leonardo and Tonhão back into silent submission.

Thus they remain, even when we run aground. No-one stirs from their hammocks. To my alarm, Moisés jumps overboard into what I take to be the piranha-infested waters of the river. But I am never to see a piranha in the Amazon, not even a dead one. Half an hour later Moisés has pushed us off the sandbank and climbed safely back on board. And so, I suppose, I drift into fitful sleep.

The first light of Amazonian dawn comes through a thick mist. The great forest slowly looms out of the darkness. Majestic giants, buttressed like the columns of a chaotic temple, spread at their summit into perfect vaults over a tangle of palms, vines and creepers. Every shade of green I know, and more I've never seen, flash around the coloured specks of flowering trees and orchids. Above them all the *samauma*, an awesome tree shaped like a mushroom cloud.

'Pull over!' calls Macedo.

On the bank is a black man hailing the *Chico Mendes*. As we lodge in the mud a dozen people descend the river bank to the boat. Blond children and dark adults alike are subdued perhaps by apprehension and, to judge by the terrible grey pall of malnutrition that hangs over them, hunger. In their midst, supported on their shoulders, is a man who moans distractedly. He has a deep, circular wound in his leg.

One of our number is Marinilza Poyanawa, a young Indian health worker funded by the London-based Health Unlimited. So far all I've noticed is her child-like laughter but now her calm competence takes over. She says he has gonorrhoea, untreated for two years. He is literally falling apart. As he does so his family loses the labour of an adult that it cannot do without. We head for the nearest medical post, several hours up river.

'It's only because that man had the nerve to call us across that we found out,' says Macedo. 'There's plenty more sickness we've been passing without even knowing it. They should have taken him down to Cruzeiro long ago and demanded treatment. How to overcome the attitudes that go with a century of exploitation – that's our biggest problem. Take my father. Fifty years a rubber tapper and he has nothing. The older he gets, the poorer he becomes. That's wrong.'

Captivated by the forest, I've ignored the wooden houses on stilts thatched with palms that line the banks at regular intervals, where the children, always blond, come out to watch us pass. Here the rubber tappers live, the people of this rubber-rich part of the forest. They were lured from the poverty of Brazil's Northeast by the rubber boom and the vision of a better life that haunts the imagination of Brazil – and of the Northeast in particular. Here they have lived for a century in bondage first to the rubber barons and now to almost complete neglect, with a life expectancy of less than 50 bitter years. Seventy per cent of them cannot read. They have no doctors, roads, electricity. They pay for their debts with their lives.

But this is no casual neglect. It is entirely constructed. People like Macedo – or his inspiration Chico Mendes – who talk of solidarity, who spin their own philosophy into a weapon and dare to hold out hope, are done away with. Two attempts on Macedo's life have been made already. No-one bothers to conceal who is behind it – the hated *patrões*, the 'barons', once of rubber, now of drugs and hardwood. These local agents of a mighty power flaunt their wealth not in secret but in the midst of terrible, debilitating poverty – their closest ally.

Macedo must have been designed for his job as co-ordinator, bolted together as he seems to be from the parts of different people: legs bowed and back bent as if by the weight of physical labour; sharp eyes peering out from metal-framed spectacles that give him a vaguely intellectual air; a restless, fluid mouth quick to smile or chuckle, the only punctuation in an endless flow of homespun philosophy. Shrewd. He describes himself as something akin to a vagabond, and I wonder if he is ever afraid.

'Yes. I am afraid that the people of the forest may one day just give up and leave for the towns. If they do that there will be no-one left to defend the forest, and no forest left for anyone to defend. The death of Chico Mendes came as a terrible blow to those of us who knew him, militants in the movement. But there's no denying it brought international attention to the forest and what is happening to its people. That has helped us.'

I ask him if there isn't a danger of his slipping into the role of a boss himself. 'That's the mentality we're fighting against. People put you on a pedestal. They think you're a *patrão*, only a better one. It's an easy trap to fall into. But everyone must be another Chico Mendes. Everyone must be a militant.'

'Want a go?' asks Leonardo from the helm.

Our mutual suspicion has begun to abate. I am to become almost fond of him. 'Don't worry, I'll take care of you', he says, 'otherwise...' and he makes a discouraging diving motion with his hand. We are travelling against a whirling current. It carries entire forest giants on its back. One argument with these and it won't be just Leonardo's hand that makes a diving motion.

The trick is to keep to the relative calm inside the bends, where the current is weaker and there are no logs, without running aground on the sandbanks that lurk there. But to get from one bend to the next you have to cross the turbulent main stream, picking your way between the logs. After a while, and still afloat, I turn for approval from Leonardo to find him fast asleep in his hammock. Looking back down the boat I realize with alarm that *everyone* is fast asleep.

Or so it seems. There are yells from overboard, to one side of the boat. It is Rena, Marinilza's sister. She is in the dugout canoe we are towing beside us that's the best place to take a bath. I've got too close into the bank and we've been invaded by the dreaded blackfly. This is an Amazonian refinement of the mosquito, more devious because you can't feel it bite, so voracious it leaves a mark larger than its own body. It stays with you, crying out to be scratched, for weeks.

Ahead of us stretches the great Juruá River, a major southern tributary of the Amazon; its water is called *branco*, or white, because it is thick with the silt-rich sediments of the Andes – part of the newest mountain system on earth. But white it is not. Nearer to the colour of blood, I'd say.

Here, more than 2,000 kilometres from its estuary as the parrot flies (reasonably straight I would hazard from my observations), 3,000 as the river bends, it is still an astonishing sight. Now at the height of the rainy season it runs quick, flat, silent and wide, sweeping through the jungle, scything down the forest as it goes, dropping silt where it slows to form new forest territory.

In this way all the myriad plant species of the forest are brought successively to the river bank to deposit their seeds, before themselves being consumed.

Anything further from an ageless, pristine paradise is hard to imagine. As if to emphasize the point, a huge explosion behind us, exactly where we had been a few minutes earlier, marks the collapse of another forest giant into the river.

What is actually going on around us is a violent, elemental struggle for life; rubber trees whose sap is designed to 'zap' predatory bugs, flowers that trap flies with the lure of a scent that resembles rotting protein, and so on and on in a ruthless round of mutual predations. The idea that people might some-how try to live in 'harmony' with such a place seems to me to have no real meaning. What they have most in common with the forest is their own violent struggle for life.

As the *Chico Mendes* blasts on it is as if I am being led blindfold towards some confusing secret. I have lost all sense of direction along the meander-ing course of the Juruá. My tired, hungry, bitten, sweating and aching body no longer looks for a spiritual El Dorado in the only place where it could pos-sibly still be hiding.

Evilásio, the gentle young *motorista*, tried living in the town and came back to the forest. Macedo grew up in it and can never seem to leave it for good. Marinilza and Moisés both have the look about them of people who are coming home; Leonardo and Tonhão of people arriving in enemy ter-ritory. For myself I cannot – do not wish to – abandon a culture that has so far proved unequal to the task of understanding the forest yet is unable to leave it alone.

As darkness falls at the end of our second day's travelling we pull up by wooden steps. The bank of the river conceals what lies beyond it. Leonardo insists that I climb the steps and take a look. The place is called Taumaturgo, and it sits astride a mound at the entrance to the Upper Juruá Valley Extractive Reserve. There is a single main street – a dozen or so houses along a brick path – and a monument to the battle in 1903 when this place passed from Peruvian to Brazilian control. Spent cartridges can reputedly still be found strewn about the town.

I'm a bit puzzled. Taumaturgo at night is not exactly a tourist attraction. Why is Leonardo so insistent that I see it? And where is Macedo? Sitting on chairs outside what looks like an empty café are two young men in smart shorts and trainers. Leonardo greets them, and as we return to the boat explains that these are the same police officers who arrested Macedo without charge a few months earlier. I get the feeling I've been paraded through the town, a sort of totem from the foreign press.

Perhaps I have my uses. As for the forest, having once felt its assault upon my senses I shall never again be able to look upon its destruction with indifference. ∎

September 1996
Field of dreams

Nikki van der Gaag sets out for Ikafe, a Sudanese refugee settlement in northern Uganda. The plan is to spend three weeks there and to write a whole issue of the NI about the lives of the refugees. But fate – in the form of Colonel Juma Oris's rebels – steps in and plans begin to go awry...

'Calling November Base. Come in November Base. This is Mobile 12. Over.'
'Hello. This is November Base. How are you? Over.'
'Fine. How is the road? Over.'
'Not good I'm afraid. A landmine has exploded on the Koboko-Ladonga Road. Find out what you can at your end and we will speak at three.'
'Copied. Three this afternoon. Standing by.'

The radio crackled and went dead. We looked at each other gloomily. More delays. Issa, the driver, swung the vehicle round and back onto the road.

We had been waiting for three days now to get to the Ikafe refugee settlement located a couple of hours' drive to the north near the Uganda-Sudan border. I had arrived at Entebbe airport on Thursday morning, expecting to head off to Ikafe the next day. But that was not to be. Instead I was immediately put on a ten-seater plane straight to Arua, the nearest large town to Ikafe.

As the plane came down I could make out houses and mud huts. People were walking or biking down the road carrying huge bundles on their heads. Goats grazed, tiny moving specks of brown and black. The colours were startling: from the blues, pinks, yellows and reds of women's clothes to the bright green of the trees and grass and the ochre-red of the road.

We flew over a football field and finally bumped down in Arua. I breathed a secret sigh of relief as the wheels hit the runway. A small crowd was waiting beside a tiny house and I was whisked off in a white Landrover whose enormous radio aerial could have graced any major communications centre.

It was presumably via that same radio that the first news of the hijacking had come earlier that day. Two trucks and two Landrovers had been taken by unknown rebels, the occupants forced to march for a hour and a half not knowing what was going to happen to them.

It turned out that the rebels were an anti-Government group known as the West Bank Nile Front. They were led by a Colonel Juma Oris, who had been in Idi Amin's army, but seemed to be backed by the Sudanese Government in Khartoum. They had come over the border from Sudan at Midigo the night before and had been planting landmines along their route. Rumour had it that they had also slit one man's throat.

We spent a lot of time in Issa's Landrover over the next few days, radioing Ikafe and back to the capital, Kampala, for news and for permission to move. We got to know the best radio reception spots – and so did all the little boys in the area, who lounged around listening to our strange conversations until they were shooed off, giggling.

On the Saturday morning we heard that an Italian aid worker had taken one of the roads that we had been planning to take. His Landrover hit a mine and he was now in Arua hospital. We drove frantically round trying to find out what had happened and finally found the watchman at the aid agency's office. 'Director in hospital,' he said grimly. 'He hurt his foot.' He made a dramatic slashing gesture at his own leg: 'Off.'

That night we listened in the small hours to radios buzzing and trucks revving away. The next morning an army Lieutenant-Colonel staying at our hotel (the White Rhino Hotel, though there was not a rhino in sight beyond the painted ones on the hotel wall) told us there had been a 'major offensive' against the rebels in the night. Eighteen had been killed and nine captured. I prayed that the noises we had heard hadn't been the nine being questioned.

We now had permission to go and soon set off down the road to Ikafe, promising to radio in to November Base every half hour. We met few other vehicles on the road, just curious children waving and neat grass huts in immaculately swept compounds.

The journey took just over two hours. En route we stopped at Yumbe, a town with a huge mosque – the Ugandans in the area are mainly Muslim – and many broken-down brick houses. 'They were destroyed during the war of 1979 when Amin was defeated and no-one can afford to rebuild them,' said Issa.

Idi Amin, under whose presidency hundreds of thousands of Ugandans were murdered, came from this area. The forces which came in after his regime fell wreaked a terrible revenge on the local people. The area has been neglected by central government ever since.

After Yumbe a truck passed us going the other way. It was full of young men, all standing up in the back. The driver waved and Issa waved back. 'That's Gideon, from Ikafe,' he said. 'And here,' he waved vaguely to the left, 'is where the settlement begins.'

I could see nothing that marked it off from the rest of the countryside. It didn't seem like a refugee camp – or at least not the images I had of a camp – at all. There were the same neatly thatched grass and mud huts (*tukuls*), the same children waving. Only here and there was an area of land which had been burned or deforested. Everywhere, people were hoeing or planting; spiky maize leaves grew among smaller clover-like plants which I later found out were groundnuts.

Then we pulled into Bidibidi 'base camp'; the 'November Base' that we had been communicating with so regularly. Built on a hill, the office block looms large above the bush, pale blue and incongruous. Two hours later, my things safely stacked in my tent, I heard that the truck we had met had been turned back five minutes down the road. The rebels had been right behind us. ∎

December 1997
State of fear

Chris Brazier journeys undercover into Moroccan-occupied Western Sahara.

My heart is in overdrive, an audible, thumping backdrop to the racing anxiety of my mind. The police are coming for me first thing in the morning.

As I lie there in the darkness, the bare box of my cheap hotel room, with its one small window high in the wall, seems like a prison cell. I am utterly alone. Here in Moroccan-occupied Western Sahara there are no embassies to turn to for protection, no phone I can use to let people know about my situation.

Escape is impossible, despite my foreknowledge that they are coming for me. The road to Western Sahara runs hundreds of kilometres through arid desert and at least ten Moroccan police checkpoints.

Rationally I know it is a good sign that they are not coming for me till the morning. Surely if they were going to inflict anything like my worst imaginings they would have swooped on me at whatever hour of the night? But reason does not loom large in the darkest hours of the night and as dogs howl and yelp incessantly in the streets of this desert city I stare wide-eyed at my nightmares.

I curse my own irresponsibility. Why had I not thought through the dangers beforehand? Why had I so blithely assumed that if the Moroccan police or military found out I was a journalist rather than a tourist I would simply be thrown out of the country? Two alternative ways of treating me suddenly seem all too possible. They could lock me up as a spy – after all, any serious search of my papers will pretty soon reveal that I am on my way to visit the head-quarters of Polisario, the Western Saharan liberation front with whom Morocco is still at war. And I have been taking pictures all day, including one or two of a military camp visible from the top of the hill.

Alternatively I might end up with drugs planted in my luggage so as to scupper my meeting with Polisario. There are already Western tourists locked up in Morocco on drugs charges and such is the official world's horror of drugs that almost anyone accused of trafficking them in a foreign place is automatically presumed guilty – I doubt that the British Foreign Office would be extremely energetic on my behalf.

And yet the most awful prospect of all is not that of a Moroccan prison, though I know full well from Amnesty International reports how brutal con-ditions in one of those can be. It is the idea that I might not see my family again for years, that I might not see my children grow up and that suddenly they might be deprived of their father. It is a long, long night.

The trip had started well. I flew into Casablanca, Morocco's economic (though not its political) capital. It was always my plan to start my investiga-tion of Western Sahara by travelling through Morocco, the country which invaded it in 1975 and now sees it as a frontier province – not least because I thought I was more likely to get in as a tourist travelling overland than if I arrived in the occupied Sahara by plane.

Reaching the desert involved two different kinds of journey. The first was a comfortable one by train to Marrakech, in the course of which the Mediterranean landscape of northern Morocco started to give way to more marginal country. The second was much less enjoyable – a gruelling 12-hour journey in two communal taxis (buses to the far south are pretty occasional) broken only by four further hours in the full heat of the sun wondering if the second of these jalopies was ever going to scrape up enough passengers.

South of Marrakech are the Atlas Mountains, which march across the country in three separate ranges. The Atlas are topped with snow in winter but in high summer they had none of that softening, mitigating cloak. No, this was bleak country – the hills were rugged and often raw-red, as if they were bleeding after savage treatment. The settlements were sparse and the only visible agriculture was the odd olive grove; the only glimpse of water, a deep-blue shock, was a reservoir hit in the course of the descent to

Taroudannt. This trip through the High Atlas is cracked up by some to be one of the great road journeys. On this evidence that's pushing it a bit.

South of Agadir – increasingly a Western tourist destination – the road cut through the Anti-Atlas, the last of the three ranges. Almost all the other vehicles on the road were trucks supplying the garrisons of the south. The most spectacular sight was that of whole herds of camel grazing gently. On one particular stretch of plain there were literally hundreds grazing amid the desert scrub as naturally as cows do in an English meadow.

Hour succeeded hour of country populated less often by villages than by police checkpoints, each of which took an inordinate interest in my new European passport, which I soon had reason to curse: it has no section for 'profession' and thus prompted everyone looking at it to ask me directly what I do. 'Company director' had a lot more authority when it was officially stamped on my old British passport.

Still, they let me through, and whereas at the early checkpoints I was on tenterhooks, by the fourth or fifth I was becoming blasé. At the last one, past midnight and on the outskirts of the Western Saharan capital, L'ayoun, I was summoned for a more formal interview with a uniformed captain who also let me pass. I crawled into bed in the cheapest of hotels, guided there by a local youth who spoke some English. I was beyond caring about the niceties. I'd made it to Western Sahara.

My first day in L'ayoun goes well too – at first. I wander around getting my bearings, all too conscious that it is going to be difficult to make meaningful contact with local Saharawis who will be courting trouble with the Moroccan authorities if they talk to me.

L'ayoun was the capital in the days when this was the Spanish Sahara, Spain's one colonial foothold in Africa. But few traces of Spanish rule remain – when Morocco invaded, denying local people their right to self-determination, the colonial buildings were dismantled and a new, functional city sprang up in its place. It is as if the Moroccans wish to expunge all signs of difference – and a different colonizer is as much evidence of that as the Saharawis' own traditions. Peculiarly, I witness this impulse made flesh: as I walk past the main post office, the old postbox on the side of the building is being repainted in Moroccan colours and the Spanish word Correos is in the process of being obliterated.

Morocco has invested a great deal of money in L'ayoun – in new buildings and infrastructure that it hopes will attract migrants from the north and persuade Saharawis that opting to be part of Morocco is in their best economic interests. There are many new apartment blocks and also a show-piece new city square, centred on intriguing sail-like structures which offer respite from the Saharan sun.

As I wander around I take eccentric routes across building sites and keep looking behind me, having been told that I will be watched by the secret police every step of the way. But I never detect anyone following – either they're very good at concealing themselves or else they're not as all-seeing as they claim. I reconnoitre the hotels where UN personnel stay but do not enter them, knowing that the Moroccans (outrageously) do not allow anyone, locals or visitors, to make contact with UN staff. I intend to try this later, but only at the end of my stay since it will alert the police to what I am doing.

Back in my hotel after lunch the youth who'd guided me the night before turns up and asks if I will come for a coffee so he can practise his English. I go along with him, thinking there can surely be no harm in this provided I avoid politics. Ahmed looks to be in his early twenties. I soon establish that he is a Saharawi rather than a Moroccan settler. I tell him that I would like to see the desert, which is hard to get a sense of within L'ayoun town. He suggests I take a bus to the port, some 15 kilometres away, and offers to go with me.

At this point I am in a quandary. If I am to have any more contact with this guy than a casual coffee I feel I need to let him know that I am a journalist and that it might be dangerous to be seen with me. Yet he might well be a 'plant', an informer for the Moroccan secret police, of whom I have been warned there are plenty. I decide that I have to take the risk of telling him. He does not seem fazed and still wants to accompany me.

The bus ride to the port is extraordinary: almost immediately you are in amongst Saharan sand dunes worthy of *Beau Geste*. They are fantastically beau-tiful: played on by a stiff sea breeze, they are constantly in motion, millions of particles of sand ever falling, falling. At one point the bus has to stop while a bulldozer clears the road of the latest invading dune.

The port is a scungy, dismal settlement that feels like it is at the end of the earth. I tell Ahmed to leave me and I wander through the chartered streets tor-mented by the swathes of grit in my eyes (contact lenses and the Sahara do not suit each other). The harbour itself, an important economic area for Morocco, is invisible. I play the naive tourist and wander up to its guarded gates saying I want to see the sea but am turned away brusquely by soldiers. After more dis-consolate wandering I catch the bus back and take my leave of Ahmed.

That evening, as I head to my room after dinner, Ahmed reappears. He seems agitated. He says he has overheard the hotel owner on the phone being told that the security police will be coming for me early in the morning. Ahmed says he is worried about me. I tell him to look out for himself and have no further contact with me.

His warning is a mixed blessing: it would have been infinitely easier had I been arrested out of the blue the next day. It is only later that it occurs to me that this might have been an intentional warning designed to consign me to a night of fear. As it is, apart from my feverish anticipation of what might happen, I am propelled into desperate attempts to prepare for the next morning. I write up an innocuous, touristic version of the day's events to go with my similarly bland account of my time in Morocco. I open the back of my camera to the light, worried that my photos will be taken as evidence of espionage. Then I sink back into the darkness, hoping I have done all I can.

It is the middle of the night before I realize that I have overlooked something vital. Back in Casablanca I met a Saharawi by chance who, over coffee, offered me the name and address of his cousin in L'ayoun. I hid the piece of paper somewhere deep in my luggage and now I can't remember where it is. It takes me an hour of increasingly panic-stricken searching to find it. But even then I have a problem. I tear it into tiny pieces but cannot think how to dispose of them. I can't chance putting them in a rubbish bin. The only alternatives seem to be to flush them down the toilet or to eat them. I am in no mood to appreciate the John le Carré quality of the second option and so investigate the first. But the toilet, of course, is little more than a hole in the ground and I am all too aware of the possibility that the paper will not disappear at the bidding of my bucket of water. The second bucket does the business without waking anyone, however, and I breathe again.

Dawn comes as a great relief. I can feel my spirits rising slightly as its fingers claw their way through the window and the wretched dogs cease their howling. I've made up my mind that if the police come for me en masse and bundle me away I will tell them I'm a journalist straight away and hope to minimize the risk of being charged with spying. But if they come in less threatening mode I will at least start off by continuing to try to bluff my way out of it.

When they come it is in the shape of a tall, balding man with glasses who introduces himself as the 'Controller of Foreigners' and is exaggeratedly courteous. He dismisses my cover story with polite impatience and takes me and my bag to the police station. There he homes in immediately on my camera – he takes my diary as proof that I am a journalist but shows no interest in deciphering the English in which it is written. But the photos are another thing; so often it is the case that photographic evidence is seen as infinitely more threatening than words, as if one has objective truth and the other is just opinion. He does not believe I have only taken one roll of film and examines the unused film suspiciously.

For about an hour of questioning by The Controller, with another official as a witness, I keep up my pretence that I am not a journalist. But eventually I conclude that I am never going to get out of there until I have told them who I am working for – and that if I take my refusal to admit what I am doing too far I might be courting more danger. He says as much at one point: 'I'd be perfectly within my rights to come down on you like a ton of bricks. But provided you don't play fast and loose with us again we're going to let you go. You have, however, to give us something in return.'

So I do: I tell him the name of my magazine and that I have been sent to report on both sides of the Western Sahara dispute. I confirm that I will be meeting Polisario in Algeria. Having got what he wants, at this point he chooses to raise for the first time the possibility that they might treat me as a spy. My heart naturally starts racing again but he is only playing with me, as well as emphasizing how generous he is being in letting me go.

There is no plane leaving before the evening of the next day so I have no alternative but to wait until then. The Controller is free with his dire imprecations as to what will happen to me if I so much as try to get hold of another camera or talk to anyone from the UN. I tell him that I will change to another hotel immediately and then will not set foot outside it again until I have to report to him again and leave for the airport. And despite the absence of any food but breakfast in the hotel, this is what I do; three goons are posted down in the lobby just to make sure.

I still fear that they will discover my film has been sabotaged, that they will contact London and find the *New Internationalist* is a magazine unlikely to be sympathetic to the Moroccan cause. When the phone goes in my hotel room I think it must be my summons to another round of questioning. Who else could it be?

It is Ahmed. I can barely believe it. He introduces himself by name (though I have used a pseudonym), says he found my new hotel via the old one. I tell him he is mad to phone me, that the police are bound to be listening in and that he should put the phone down. He ignores this and asks where he can meet me. I put the phone down myself.

My first reaction is that this is a crazy innocent who has put himself at grave risk out of concern for me – and my agitation is heightened by the idea that he might end up being tortured as a result of his contact with me. Later I realize how much more likely it is that he was a plant from the first. Any Saharawi knows far better than I do how dangerous it is to cross the local secret police and knows young people who have been detained and tortured for showing a Polisario flag or for a word out of turn. To ring up a foreign journalist and give your name when you can be sure the secret police are listening would be foolhardy beyond belief. I still can't know for sure, though – and this kind of uncertainty about people and their motives is entirely characteristic of life in a police state. If he was on the level I hope the story I have told shows the Moroccans how innocent was his contact with me – though they are likely to have acted on the assumption of his 'guilt'.

In my second interview with The Controller he makes a point of asking with a meaningful smile if anyone has been 'bothering' me. I know he is referring to the phone call but simply say 'no'. He stresses how foolish I have been and says that they have nothing to hide, that if only I had gone through official channels they would of course have run out the red carpet for me.

He says he feels sure that I will prove to be a journalist of 'integrity' who will write only about the truth of what I have seen in L'ayoun, which is, he says, that people are happy and economically thriving. He is sure I will not be like all the other journalists who are 'paid' by Polisario to slander Morocco and its King. In the event that I do 'slander' Morocco I will of course have to accept the consequences. What the consequences will be, he does not say.

At the airport I am a marked man, pointed out and stared at by every official. It is with great relief that I feel the plane's wheels lift off the ground and look down for the last time on L'ayoun. I feel very fortunate – but not entirely unscathed, as if my life can never be quite the same again. I think of the individuals locked up below suffering what I only feared. I will not return to L'ayoun unless and until it is the capital of a free and independent Western Sahara. ■

March 2000
Return to Ayacucho
Vanessa Baird revisits the birthplace of Peru's bloodiest civil conflict in search of people she met there more than a decade ago.

Like a lover, the golden orange glow steals across mountains, kissing them in their shadowy sleep. Once touched by the light the Andes rise out of the darkness, looking like an oddly soft, rumpled blanket of clay.

Part of my brain marvels at this strange intimacy of dawn. Another part is telling me something quite different: I'm feeling sick as a dog. The overnight bus from Lima to Ayacucho takes a brand-new road, rich in hairpin bends, that rises steeply up into the Andes and keeps you there at 4,000 metres (13,000 feet) for an oxygen-depleted age.

As we come down a little and enter a gentler terrain of plots and trees, I see something that shocks but does not surprise me: a group of men with guns, faces hidden by black balaclavas. They are peasants, ending their nocturnal *ronda* or patrol to defend themselves against the Maoist guerrillas of Sendero Luminoso (Shining Path) who launched one of South America's bloodiest armed struggles in 1980. In the ensuing civil war – which is still not quite over yet – 25,000 to 30,000 people died and 600,000 became internal refugees.

It's 15 years since I was last in Ayacucho, birthplace of this conflict. At that time the violence was heading for its bloody crescendo, with the peasants caught in the crossfire between the guerrillas and government forces that were then even more abusive. Now I'm back to try to find out what happened to the various women, men and children – people from all walks of life – that I met and interviewed then.

The bus finally pulls up in Ayacucho City – also known as Huamanga – the capital of the department of Ayacucho. I recall my previous arrival here on a grey March day in 1985, the military presence heavy as soldiers fired into the air and raised the flag in the main square. Local people stood under the colonial arches looking on, silent, unsmiling, giving away absolutely nothing.

Today the atmosphere could not be more different. In the bright Andean sunshine a group of kids whiz by on mountain bikes. Chicha – a twangy tropical Andean music that's far too cheesy for panpipe purists – blasts out of open doorways. Shop-shutters are rattling upwards to display windows crammed with all manner of consumer imports: mobile phones, video cameras, Sony Walkmans. There's even an Internet café, packed with computers and students. It looks for a moment as if Ayacucho has really taken off. Later I learn that this wealth exists mainly in deep little drug-lined pockets – the jungle coca-growing regions are not that far to the east. The surrounding economic reality in Ayacucho is little changed.

But the public places are spruce, clean and well kept. That's new. On one wall I see an official notice that warns me: 'Urinating is forbidden, on pain of arrest.' A troubling thought, after a long bus journey. There is a pervasive atmosphere of control under the rule of Alberto Fujimori, President of Peru since 1990. Now even the shoeshiners are regulated, and have to wear yellow jerkins showing official approval.

But my first stop is a hotel bed and plenty of coca tea to ease altitude sickness. Then the search begins for the people on my list. My main worry is the obvious one. Are they still alive? Are they still here? Or did they, like so many thousands, flee this place called Ayacucho – an inauspicious name that in Quechua means 'corner of the dead'? If they are still around, how will they feel about someone coming back to stir up old memories?

What is it that makes some people leave an indelible impression in the sand of memory, while others are washed away on the next tide?

Whatever it is has left me with a vivid image of Leonor Zamora: fine features, long straight hair, etched smile lines. But most striking of all are her eyes: alight with passionate, focused energy.

As mayor of the city of Ayacucho, Zamora was cutting a controversial figure when I interviewed her in 1985. A few months earlier she had used a visit by Pope John Paul II to protest against army abuse of human rights, waving a banner saying 'stop the killing'. The army managed to bar her from meeting the Pope, in spite of her position. But she was not going to be prevented from speaking to journalists. I was ushered up the great stone stairs of the 17th-century council building on the main square of Ayacucho and into her draughty office. Leonor had just returned from a trip to Lima to find the pictures of two children on her desk – one aged 12, one 14. They had bright, intelligent faces. The youngsters had gone missing. 'They take them in for questioning and torture them until they get five names out of them,' she had told me, speaking softly.

'Under torture children will give names of whoever is suggested to them. Mother, father, brothers, sisters, friends, neighbours, anyone. Then those will disappear too.' She paused to let the horror sink in.

Over 150 children disappeared in Ayacucho during these years.

'I don't know where it will end; where we are heading,' Zamora commented as we were parting. 'There's a limit to how much people can believe in, a limit to how much suffering they can take.'

I want to speak to Zamora now. She's top of my list.

She was also top of someone else's quite different kind of list, alas.

'They gunned her down in the street, in broad daylight, not far from her office,' says Oxfam's Ayacucho chief Elizabeth Leon. 'They did it in front of her children, if I remember rightly.'

'Who did it?'

'Army intelligence, we presume,' she says, with the caution that has for so many Peruvians become a custom of survival.

It happened in 1985, a few months after I had interviewed Zamora and, as with so many events that took place during those most fearful years, lots of people were present when it happened – but nobody saw a thing. Police opened an investigation but it was a mere formality, soon to be closed for 'lack of evidence'.

It's too easy – not to say morbid – to imagine in retrospect that one saw the shadow of death hanging over a person. But Zamora was an uncommonly valiant woman who operated so close to the edge that you could not help but be concerned for her safety. 'No-one confronted the Army so directly. No-one was so outspoken,' says human-rights activist Pablo Rojas.

None of her family remained in Ayacucho after her murder. They too received threats and fled.

I come away with a heavy heart, pondering the ease with which jackbooted brutality can crush a person's passion for justice, obliterate someone who cared not only about the present, but the future too. And I think of Leonor's concern for the children of Ayacucho, the children of violence. ■